The Playboy Advisor on Love & Sex

The Playboy Advisor on Love & Sex

James R. Petersen

Illustrated by Patrick Nagle

A PERIGEE BOOK

Printed in the United States of America

Contents

Introduction

All reasonable questions—from fashion, food and drink, stereo and sports cars to dating dilemmas, taste and etiquette—will be personally answered if the writer includes a stamped, self-addressed envelope. Send all letters to The Playboy Advisor, Playboy Building, 919 N. Michigan Avenue, Chicago, Illinois 60611. The most provocative, pertinent queries will be presented on these pages each month.

The first Playboy Advisor column ran in the September 1960 issue of *Playboy* magazine. There are different stories about its conception, but the official version is this: someone submitted to Ray Russell, the executive editor at the time, a parody of an Ann Landers column. Russell took the column to Hugh Hefner, who looked at the manuscript, took a draw on his pipe and said, "I *like* Ann Landers. We shouldn't do a parody. We should run our own advice column, for men, every month."

As so often happens in the magazine business, the first few attempts at the column were created within the walls of the office. Editors were asked to go out and find "provocative pertinent queries" and the answers to same. The first column was one page long. There were questions about fashion (what tie to wear with a tweed), a question about sports cars (to go all out for a Corvette or settle for an MGA), a question about tipping, a question about dating dilemmas, a question about whether the salad should be served before or after the entrée, a question about the eternal question: should one answer the telephone in the middle of sex? The final question was quite brief. "What do you think of those martinis and manhattans that come in those little plastic bags?" The answer: "We think they should remain in those little plastic bags."

The first column generated an enormous—at least for the time—reader response. Sixty-three readers wrote in, asking questions near and dear to their hearts. Hefner had created a dialogue. This was the first time in American history that anyone admitted that men had problems, that men needed advice. Long before the women's movement began its consciousness-raising sessions, men were talking to men in the pages of

Playboy. Four years later, the column was drawing three hundred letters a month. By the end of the sixties, between seven hundred and a thousand. It is estimated that a quarter million people have written to the column since its inception. For every person who encloses a self-addressed stamped envelope, we have returned a personal answer.

The column is the thing that people turn to second when they pick up a copy of the magazine. It is estimated that the column reaches some thirty million readers a month. Maybe 20 percent of those readers are women. The truth is not sexist. The column is and always has been the one place a person can turn to for the truth, the straight line, the state-of-the-art information. Over the years, the column has become a listening post. When something happens out there, we hear about it. Consequently this anthology of almost a decade of Advisor answers offers an interesting insight into American culture. It is not sociology. We did not take a random sample. We merely answered questions. These letters are from real-life people, in real-life situations. They are not statistics; they are only the voices of women and men in love. The people who write to the Advisor do so because they have no one else to talk to. They cannot ask their doctor, priest, coach, best friend, analyst or partner. They choose to write to an anonymous magazine column. The Advisor column has been a court of last resort for the curious, the iconoclasts, the people who refuse to settle for the status quo.

And now for a personal note: I was twelve years old when the first Playboy Advisor column appeared. I was twenty-four when I was hired to write the column in 1973. A lot of people have asked what my credentials are—who am I to give sex advice to the teeming millions. My answer: I went to Boy Scout camp. The Boy Scout motto is Be prepared. Since I was twelve, I have read everything I could lay my hands on about sex, in case it ever happened to me. When I took this job, I thought I knew nine things for sure about sex. It turns out that I had read eight of those nine in the pages of *Playboy*, in the Advisor column. The ninth was wrong.

I took the job because my favorite novel was Nathanael West's *Miss Lonelyhearts*, and I had a mad desire to read other people's mail. Someone from Reader Service dropped a folder filled with a thousand questions from readers. They were articulate, curious, stranger than I'd ever thought they would be. I didn't claim to know anything, but I was willing to find out.

My first job was to read the twelve years of Advisor Columns that preceded me. It was an education. The history of the Advisor is a history of America. Former Managing Editor Sheldon Wax was the first Advisor. It was his job to wander the halls of the *Playboy* offices, soliciting one or two answers from each of the other editors: "What do you know about this?" In the early sixties, the column was a James Bond guide to etiquette. It was snobbish, cultured, elitist. *(Should I wear an ascot? No, only assholes wear ascots.)* The ratio of service questions to sex questions was roughly 8 to 1. No one knew any better. The letters that passed for sex questions had more to do with dating etiquette and deflowering virgins than anything else. (I guess there were more virgins back then.) Michael Laurence, formerly an assistant editor, now assistant publisher, inherited the column, did it for a few years, quit and moved to Australia. Nat Lehrman (then an assistant editor, now associate publisher of *Playboy*) inherited the column. He was from Brooklyn; he couldn't care less about stereos and dating etiquette. He farmed out the service questions and began to use the column to answer the sensitive stuff—sex. The year was 1966. The culture was changing rapidly. There was no standard. Etiquette questions were absurd. Taste was turned over in favor of eccentricity: Do your own thing. Everything was allowed, as long as you did it well and with style. The column went from being opinionated to being open. The language changed from hyper (sartorial splendor) to real life, just like that. The voice of the Advisor and its companion, the Forum, changed. The Forum began to run letters about the war in Vietnam, drugs. The Advisor began to run letters about sex as we really know it. The questions changed from "Should I call her?" to "I'm already doing it. How do I do it better?" Lehrman changed the ratio of the column—sex questions ran head to head with service questions. Letters to the Advisor jumped from three hundred a month to a thousand. He had touched a nerve.

Lehrman built a network of experts, a cadre of friends of the magazine—sociologists, clinicians, researchers—who were happy to provide state-of-the-art information. The list is impressive: Albert Ellis, Alex Comfort, Masters and Johnson. The tone of the answers was clinical, in accordance with the times. It was safe to use medical language, to quote Masters and Johnson. The facts were astonishing in and of themselves. Pubic hair first appeared in *Playboy* in 1970. The word *clitoris* was first used in 1968. Prior to that, everyone thought the clitoris was a monument in Greece.

Lest you take these things for granted, *Playboy* has always fought the hard fight, pushed the limits of knowledge against the resistance of censors. Lehrman tells this story: "In 1968 I ran a letter about the caloric content of sperm. The printer complained, refused to print the rest of the issue. Hefner pulled the question. It appeared in the overseas editions and in Canada, but not in America. Two years later we ran the same question, with even more information. The point of this anecdote is simple: we aren't the prudes. *Playboy* has always existed in an atmosphere of repression. What you take for granted, we had to fight for.

It seems silly now, pulling that question, but believe me, the life of the magazine depended on it. Change occurs slowly. We will always walk that line where curiosity meets conservatism head on. We will always answer those questions."

Lehrman advanced to senior editor in charge of the Forum, the Advisor and all the sex and behavior articles in *Playboy*. Frank Robinson assumed the duties of Advisor. For six months, he answered questions on sex and service. One day he looked out the window and saw a fire on the eighty-first floor of the John Hancock Building. He asked himself: *Dear Playboy Advisor, What do you do in the event of a fire in a high rise? What is the proper wine to serve? Do the ladders reach that high?* He did some research, wrote a proposal and a week later was a millionaire. His book eventually became the movie *The Towering Inferno*. Later he wrote a book about nuclear meltdowns. Dear Playboy Advisor . . . something about the job prepares one for the problematic, if not the apocalyptic.

I took over the column in May, 1973, shortly after Alex Comfort published *The Joy of Sex*. Masters and Johnson had given us a new vocabulary to describe sex. They had given us basics. What used to be considered deep psychological problems—premature ejaculation, impotence, frigidity—were skin-deep, the result of ignorance. Learn a few basics and you were ready to play the game. There were no tragedies. Comfort gave us a new attitude, writing the first sex manual that was not medical or sexist (you have to lead the woman into her sexuality). He presented the whole cornucopia of erotic techniques. Everything was permitted. Enjoy. Normal was not enough. You didn't need to consult an expert, you had only to consult your partner, your playmate, your equal in bed. It was the year of the peak experience, the human-potential movement. What exactly are we capable of here? What will this sucker do? Comfort brought a sense of humor to the topic of sex.

When I took over the column I was not your basic sexual expert. I didn't know anything more than the rest of us, but I was willing to find out. The secret to running the column is this: only print the letters you have answers to. I sought advice from everyone—Masters and Johnson, my friends, Casey the doorman. I refused to send a writer to a shrink: if you couldn't work it out among friends, there wasn't an answer. I tried to maintain a sense of humor. When I took over the column, the letters seemed to fall into four categories: *Help, I suffer premature ejaculation. How do I increase the size of my penis? My girlfriend doesn't experience orgasm except through masturbation or carnal knowledge with a Black and Decker sander. What am I doing wrong? What do the stars in the letter P mean?* The questions about premature ejaculation and size diminished as the information gleaned from Masters and Johnson made its way into the culture. What used to be traumatic became a stage. These problems weren't permanent. They weren't psychological, the symptom of a deep underlying neurosis. There were a lot of questions about sexual preference: *Is this normal? Is this harmful?* Our readers quickly moved beyond Alex Comfort. I instituted the Playboy Test Bedrooms, and the column became a "consumer reports" of the erotic.

Over the years, the letters to the column have changed. Long before the medical profession discovered herpes or the media began to publicize the epidemic, we were receiving letters from victims. We sought out the researchers and published the latest forecasts. We wrestled with the etiquette questions of the seventies, the conflicts posed by women's lib. When Richard Gere strapped on gravity boots in *American Gigolo*, our readers wrote to us. When Bette Midler mentioned a taco joke that wouldn't play in Cleveland, our readers asked us for the punch line. This is serious business. I learned very early that the column could not play fast and loose with the facts. For years we had received letters asking if it was true that John Dillinger's penis was on display in the Smithsonian, in the medical oddities exhibit. Folk legend had it that Dillinger was particularly well endowed. That myth seems to have been recorded in our DNA or on the wall of every locker room in America. As near as I can tell, the Advisor was the only column in America to have brought this topic to light, in 1968. I decided to fight fire with fire, to counter one myth with another. When a reader asked what was the world's largest clitoris, I replied, tongue in cheek, that it was 19 inches long and belonged to John Dillinger—actually Joanna Dillinger. *She* had been labeled a *he* by J. Edgar Hoover, who was loath to have a woman on his Ten Most Wanted list. The said organ was on display, ecetera. For the next six months, I received letters that went, "The other day, someone told me that *Playboy* had said John Dillinger was actually a woman . . ." In a nation starved for information, one cannot play with the facts.

After ten years of reading letters, one gets acutely aware of the tragedy of misinformation. Most letters to the Advisor would never get written if we told the truth about sex or felt comfortable talking to our partners about sex. As long as there are born-again Puritans out there saying we already know too much, as long as there are the likes of the Moral Majority who believe that ignorance is bliss, there will be a place for this column.

I was asked to appear on the Phil Donahue show a few years ago. He asked, "Don't we know too much about sex? What about the mystery? What about romance?"

I replied: "I probably know as much as there is to know about sex as anyone in America. And yet, when I go home, I am still astonished. I have found that information only improves the sex act. The more you know, the better it is, the more closely it means exactly what you want it to mean. I have seen the effects of misinformation, what you refer to as mystery. There is no comparison."

People ask if we still make up the letters. No. Occasionally we receive an obvious put-on. Some frat brothers get together at Dartmouth and try to make it into the Playboy Advisor Hall of Fame with a letter that runs: "I came home and found my wife feeding our neighbor to the Waring blender. I'd like to share this erotic experience with you." You can tell the difference. So can our readers. Which is not to say we don't publish the put-ons. You can learn as much from something that's entertaining—that's pure fantasy—as you can from something that's factual. The column is not restricted to letters, mind you. Quite often I find myself at lunch with a friend. We will discuss a problem, work out an answer, and then I will realize that it is something we are all going through. I will ask if I can use the situation in a column. I appear on radio and TV shows. Quite often the questions that are asked appear in the column. The methodology (that's a word from sociologists and pollsters) is unique. The column is not an objective questionnaire. It is a conversation. This is how sex actually happens to people. The column gives you war stories, true confessions. It also gives answers. I inherited the cadre of sex experts developed by Nat Lehrman. When necessary, I turn to them for advice. I also read everything that has anything to do with sex. It's a dirty job, but someone has to do it. I consult the footnotes in *Medical Aspects of Human Sexuality*, track down the random unpublished essay quoted in the *New England Journal of Medicine*. Whatever out there that is new I work into the column. If I wait long enough, a reader will ask the right question.

The letters collected in this volume represent the combined expertise of over three hundred experts. Also the commonsense wisdom of two or three friends—John Rezek, Barbara Nellis, Arthur Kretchmer. When it comes to sex, there is no real difference between the credentialed pro and the curious amateur. We are all in this together. A lot of people read the Advisor for entertainment; occasionally someone comments on my "sense of humor." I have to thank my friends for that. The message of the seventies was this: lighten up. A lot of people with sexual problems suffer in isolation. If I can find something humorous in the situation, I will comment on it. A good chuckle can break the hammerlock, the craziness, in seconds, and the thirty million people reading the exchange are not as likely to go through a private hell when they encounter something like it. If it weren't for a sense of humor, I would not have survived ten years of writing this column.

One week into the job, I met a woman at a bar. She asked what I did for a living. I said that I wrote the Playboy Advisor. She responded: "That's neat. I have a friend who writes the Playboy Advisor all the time. What was your problem?" So much for authority, the presumption of prestige. In reality, I don't know any more or any less than the person who writes to the Advisor seeking advice. I prepare the column three months in advance. I do not hoard information. What I know or can find out, the reader finds out. Sex is my beat. I am a sportswriter for America's favorite sport. Thank God I didn't end up covering baseball, especially in Chicago.

Why this book, now? *Playboy* has not published a sex book in ten years. That is unfortunate. Someone has said that history belongs to the person who writes it. If so, the history of the sexual revolution has fallen into the wrong hands. There has not been a single piece of significant research since Masters and Johnson; there has not been an ecstatic, coherent sex manual since Alex Comfort. In the meantime, we have had feminist diatribes (the *Hite* reports); popular but not profound chronicles of fantasy (the Nancy Friday books); and a complete revisionist backlash on pornography (the feminist manifesto on women and pornography, *Take Back the Night*). These authors ignore the advances, the true breakthroughs, and try to foster a theory of sex based on rage, anger and violence. They have (almost) succeeded in giving sex a bad name. The men—and the women—who write to the Advisor are not represented in these accounts. They are the true pioneers of the sexual revolution. They don't need credentials, or computers, or statistics; they are in it up to their ears. The one thing they have in common is courage. They like sex. They like being in love. They are trying to work things out—without the dogma of sexual politics. They refuse to settle for second best. They do not whine or complain. They question. They go for it.

This book is divided into three sections, roughly about the body, pleasure techniques and the culture. The first deals with the physiology of sex—body awareness, drugs and sex, birth control, venereal disease. The second covers the basics and beyond: techniques, toys, positions and general weirdness that our readers discovered in the postsexual revolution area. In one chapter, we asked our readers to define the difference between good oral sex and great oral sex. We got incredible answers. The same sense of awareness, of self-discovery, is found in the last section: relationship hassles, the mixed signals that go with the new etiquette, ménages à trois, orgies, video sex and feminist politics. The book ends with a speculation on the roots of desire, the new frontier of research.

The selection of letters, with introductory essays, shows the evolution of sex over the past decade and brings us to the breaking edge of sex in the eighties. If some topics are omitted, that is because they were of no concern to our readers. This book may not be comprehensive, but it is compassionate. I hope you find it useful.

—James R. Petersen
Senior Staff Writer
The Playboy Advisor

The Body: An Owner's Manual

Let's get physical. In the past decade, there have been bestsellers called *Our Bodies, Ourselves* and *An Owner's Manual*, male and female. As repression—the organized ignorance of our elders—ended, we became curious about our bodies. The advent of birth control and antibiotics made us aware that most of the fears of the past were based on basic ignorance of the body. Masters and Johnson introduced a medical model of sex—described the responses of a healthy sexual human being. As people absorbed that information and began to examine themselves in the light of day—or at least outside the darkened bedroom—they began to ask questions. *Is this normal? Is this harmful?* I love these questions. The more I learn, the more I am amazed by the body's potential. We are, each and every one of us, a miracle.

And so we continue to pursue the facts of life. What passes for sex education in schools is laughable. It is not sex but breeding. If you cross a lima bean with a fruit fly you get a frightened member of the Moral Majority. What passes for sex education in medical schools is not laughable but tragic. Morton Hunt, in a *Playboy* article called "Where Sex Is Concerned the Doctor Is Out," pointed out that as recently as 1960, only three of the hundred-odd American medical schools offered any instruction in sexuality; at all the other schools, medical students were taught nothing about it. "Oh, to be sure they learned about infections, tumors and the like affecting the sexual organs, but about the human meanings of sex, the many problems people have with it and the techniques of dealing with those problems, they heard nothing."

Dr. William Masters claims that most physicians "know no more and no less about the subject than other college graduates. They share most of the common misconceptions, taboos and fallacies of their nonmedical conferees."

The people who write to the Advisor are curious. I've had as much fun researching these letters as I've had trying out the techniques mentioned in the next section. Some of the answers sound like they belong in *Ripley's Believe It or Not;* others are deadly serious. Take, for instance, the questions about birth control. During the seventies, we discovered that the Pill was not God's gift to pleasure seekers. The medical profession had, in effect, been experimenting on a whole generation of women. As various side effects came to light, couples began to look for alternate forms of birth control. They had to deal with the anger, frustration and sloppiness of this new responsibility. The Advisor fielded their questions and reported on new developments and new studies. The seventies also saw a rebirth of fear and anxiety over venereal disease. The specter of diseases that you could have without knowing it, of strains of bacteria that were resistant to popular antibiotics and, finally, of a totally incurable virus called herpes—all these were challenges that demanded straight information. The nature of "consenting adults" took on a new meaning. Consent meant "informed consent." The only safe sex life was one based on straight information.

After ten years of writing this column, I have seen the tragedy of misinformation. Ignorance is a prison. Many of the people who write to the Advisor have been suffering in solitary confinement, simply because they did not know the one thing that would alleviate a problem. It is interesting to note how the concerns of the populace have changed over the years. When I first took over the column, it seemed as though every other letter was about premature ejaculation. Masters and Johnson had given the condition a name, and suddenly everyone was aware of it. Fortunately, Masters also provided a cure. Premature ejaculation was not symptomatic of some deeper Freudian conflict; it was a matter of body awareness, technique, control. It was just a phase, not a terminal condition. At the same time, women were beginning to grow into their sexual rights, seeking their orgasmic potential.

By the eighties, the male's concern with premature ejaculation had diminished. He and his partner knew how to improve the situation. In contrast, the questions about female potential have increased. Concern over how frequently and in what manner a woman achieves orgasm has grown. With studies showing that only 50 percent of women achieve orgasm during intercourse, there was cause for skepticism.

In almost every instance, I have found that the more you know about sex, the greater the enjoyment. Anxiety does not belong in the bedroom. Sex belongs in the body as well as in the mind.

CHAPTER ONE

The Curious Male

Sleepy Penis

Does anyone else's penis fall asleep out there? When I sit or lie a certain way at times, I have found that my penis becomes numb with a very delightful tingling sensation, just like a foot or arm would but much nicer. I'm not into S/M, but let me assure you, if yours doesn't, you're missing something great. I wouldn't want to cure it if I could, so come on and tell me exactly where the pressure point is. You guys in research are going to love this one. —R. M., San Antonio, Texas.

Your problem is not uncommon. Men who ride ten-speed bikes have described similar feelings after long rides. Doctors call the phenomenon the penile-anesthesia syndrome or, simply, the celibacy of the saddle. It's caused by unrelieved pressure on the area under the scrotum. Unconfirmed reports suggest that listening to disco music, watching "The Gong Show" or prolonged reading of *The Hite Report* can cause the same condition.

How Much Blood in an Erection

I often feel sluggish and dull-witted after a large meal. A classmate explained that this happens because the blood being used for digestion does not reach the brain, and temporary anoxemia, or oxygen deprivation, occurs. He went on to suggest that the same thing happens when you masturbate or make love, since an erection is essentially trapped blood. What's more, he claimed that the larger and more prolonged the erection, the greater the chance of brain damage. I asked him why no one had ever noticed the phenomenon. He said that this oversight only proved his point, because it showed that no one was able to think during or immediately after intercourse. Is there any truth in my friend's theory? —A. B., San Diego, California.

Your friend's crank theory is one of the best we've heard, but there is almost no truth in it. For one thing, we can't accept the implication that superstuds suffer brain damage and geniuses are underendowed premature ejaculators. Digestion does call upon circulatory reserves, but the relaxed air of a dinner table contributes equally to post-prandial restfulness. An erection also taps the circulatory reserves, but even at maximum distention, the average penis holds no more than 100 c.c. of blood. The average adult male has a total blood volume of almost 5 liters (5000 c.c.); obviously, the volume of blood necessary for an erection is an insignificant fraction. If even a brief loss of the amount of blood in question caused temporary mental sluggishness, we doubt whether most people would be able or willing to donate blood. Finally, both men and women (remember that the clitoris, labia and pelvic viscera also become engorged with blood during intercourse) think and fantasize at an intense rate during sexual activity. Your friend will have to look elsewhere for the cause of his feeble-mindedness.

Does Speed-Reading Pornography Contribute to Premature Ejaculation

I recently completed a speed-reading course. The techniques I learned have been a great help on homework and such, but I'm worried about pleasure reading. If a person speed-reads pornographic novels, will he develop a tendency toward premature ejaculation? —J. R., Chicago, Illinois.

No. If anything, the technique has certain beneficial effects. Now instead of spending six hours in the bathroom with *Jungle Fever* or *Teenage Stepmother*, you breeze through the collected works of the Marquis de Sade in a few minutes, with 80 percent appreciation. Your parents will no longer suspect that you are a depraved child, and thus, freed of this source of guilt and anxiety, you should grow up to be a depraved adult.

First-Time Frenzy

I'm a lonely college student and the only sex I've had is with myself. Last Christmas, a friend invited me to stay for a week at his house. His girlfriend's friend and I had been sending letters back and forth. She sent me a picture and I immediately fell in love. When we met at his house, the four of us went to the movies and everything was fine. But afterward, when my friend dropped us off at her house, the trouble began. Actually, I had been hard from the minute I first saw her that evening. We went inside to watch television. After a while, she put her hand on my thigh. I instantly blew my load. Is this quick ejaculation curable? It is quite embarrassing trying to explain the come stains on my pants to a girl who hasn't even kissed me. Should I see a doctor? —B. S., Corydon, Indiana.

You don't say how the evening turned out, but we can guess. Why be embarrassed? We're not sure this even qualifies as premature ejaculation. After all, you had been thinking about this girl since last Christmas, right? You were simply overexcited. Most women, if you told them, would take that as a compliment. You don't need to see a doctor. Just see the same girl again and again.

Can a Virgin Come Too Quickly

Because I have a problem with premature ejaculation, at the age of twenty-three, I am still a virgin. Is there a solution? —R. B., Philadelphia, Pennsylvania.

First, define your terms. In one sense, every ejaculation that a virgin has is premature, but that is not the same as a shortcoming. If you discovered your problem while masturbating, then you do not have a problem. If you discovered your problem during an intimate encounter, then you do have a problem but probably not the one you think you have. It's called end-point release. For some men, sex is a test and ejaculation becomes the bell that signals the end of the exam period. You have to hand in your answer whether you think you've passed or not. Relax. One orgasm is no reason to end the evening. It's not hard to recover and there are plenty of things to do in the interim. Don't feel embarrassed or anxious; we heard of one guy who, having ejaculated, tried to change the subject and started lecturing his date on the political implications of Watergate. She lost interest, as you can imagine. Don't digress and don't expect your hair-trigger sensitivity to disappear overnight. Novelty creates a friction that can come as a surprise to the most experienced lover. Masters and Johnson say that before you can condition yourself, you must first learn to sense the level of sexual stimulation that precedes the stage of orgasmic inevitability (just prior to ejaculation). When you've learned to identify this (masturbation is one way to learn, intercourse another), ask your partner's help in remaining relatively inactive at that point. The urge will die down; then you can start coital activity again. You may have to start and stop many times, but eventually you should develop a sure sense of control. Don't be afraid to talk to your companion; more and more women realize that duration of intercourse involves both partners' response ability and are willing to improve the state of the union.

Is There a Cure?

My sexual experiences to date have been of the wham-bam-thank-you-ma'am variety. In short, not very satisfying for myself or my partner. I believe that my problem of premature ejaculation stems from my younger years, when I was prone to excessively quick masturbation. I've read various theories that claim my problem is the result of an unconscious sadistic impulse toward women or that it's the result of an especially sensitive penis. Needless to say, I'm confused. Recently I've noticed ads for desensitizing creams that promise to increase endurance. Do they work? —R. F., Seattle, Washington.

Not really. For one thing, the snake oil also desensitizes your partner. According to Masters and Johnson, the creams may actually increase the problem. Premature ejaculation is nature's way of telling you to slow down: Most doctors feel that it is the result of anxiety and that it reflects a lack of voluntary control of the ejaculatory response. The prevailing forms of therapy try to decrease anxiety (learn to love the one you're with) and increase the man's perception of the internal sensations that signal the approach of orgasm. Master those signals and eventually you will learn voluntary control. (The procedure has been described as erotic toilet training, but don't let that throw you. It's part of growing up.) Find a cooperative partner and try either the tease method (letting yourself almost reach the point of no return and then doing absolutely nothing) or the squeeze method (reaching the point of no return and having an arm-wrestling match with your girlfriend). The two simple mechanical cures have about a 95 percent effectiveness rating—so hold off on a session with a shrink until you've given these methods a fair shake. Practice, and next time your ladyfriends ask you to make love, your response won't be "No sooner said than done."

How to Go It Alone

All of the sex books I've read recommend Masters and Johnson's squeeze technique for curing premature ejaculation. However, there is one flaw in that technique. You need a regular partner, one who is willing to play therapist for the night. What about the guy who is single and, what's more, who is so embarrassed by the condition that he's not actively dating? I have suffered this for several years. If I can't find help, I'm going to become a monk. Any suggestions? —K. L., Miami, Florida.

Help is on the way. We recommend that you find a copy of *Sexual Solutions*, by Michael Castleman. The book is the best common-sense guide to sexual problems we've encountered. If it were required reading in high school, this column would be out of business. There is a whole chapter devoted to do-it-yourself techniques for curing involuntary ejaculation. Castleman writes: "There are two keys to lasting longer: Reduce tensions and become more comfortable with your body's sensual responsiveness. A body under stress for any reason looks for ways to relieve the pressure. If a man bottles up his emotions and denies himself other means of stress reduction, his body may decide that the only way out is to release the stress through ejaculation. Learning to last longer involves transferring stress reduction away from the penis to other parts of the body. In other words, expand sexuality to include sensuality." Among the techniques discussed by Castleman are deep breathing (people under stress hold their breath), vocalizing to release tension (forget being the strong, silent type) and various muscle-relaxation techniques (some men find that they can exert more control if they keep their buttock, anal and stomach muscles relaxed through loveplay). Castleman provides exercises that you can practice during masturbation or intercourse. You can order *Sexual Solutions* from Self-Care Associates, P.O. Box 161, Boulder Creek, California 95006, for $14.45.

Age Before Beauty

Is premature ejaculation related to age? I've read sex manuals that claim that young men suffer from the condition but that they outgrow it in time. Or at least most of them do. I've heard that many middle-aged men also come too quickly to satisfy their partners. As a teenager who unfortunately belongs to the ranks of the minute men, I'm more than curious. What's the outlook for my future? —D. J., Minneapolis, Minnesota.

At least one study supports the theory that young men are more responsive than older men, and therefore more prone to sudden, acute overexcitement. In 1977, R. L. Solnick and J. E. Birren found that men aged 19 to 30 achieved erections 5.8 times faster than men aged 48 to 65. What the subjects did with the erections after they had them was a matter of personal control. Premature ejaculation is in the mind, not in the mouth or any other part of the body. Young men are not experienced, and they have not learned to identify the odd twitches and hair-pulling pulsations that signal an impending orgasm. Also, they can't believe their good luck and this astonishment often takes the form of a premature release—sort of like applauding before the end of a performance. It's a small embarrassment you will eventually avoid as you learn the score. Some young men master themselves quickly, some older men never do. Keep at it.

The Woman's Point of View

*Please reconsider your advice to the man who was worried about his so-called premature ejaculations. The idea of premature ejaculation is a myth perpetuated to keep men feeling guilty about sex and about enjoying themselves with abandon. An ejaculation is not premature as long as it accompanies orgasm. On a more personal note, I thoroughly enjoy turning a man on so totally that he loses control of himself and spurts forth here, there, anywhere. I feel more at ease telling the gentleman what he can do for me once he has had a turn of his own, anyway. And I am quite pleased when all his activities are directed at gratifying me. I need not fear that he will lose sight of me in his last throes and ruin my up-and-coming orgasm by thrashing around arhythmically or, worse yet, violently. I can assure you that a soft warm penis is quite as efficient at stimulating me as an erect penis, a tongue, a shower-massage spray or my own hand, as long as it is moved around consistently in the appropriate area. Indeed, the only drawback I associate with men who have quicker-than-average orgasms is that I hate to deal with a crestfallen guy who won't stop apologizing long enough to let me tell him that he's okay and that I actually like it that way. Please tell the guilt-ridden sufferers that they can all be perfectly fantastic one way or the other as long as they don't immediately assume they've failed. Please point out (again) that it's the whole show that counts, not the performance of one member of the cast.
—Miss S. D., Santa Clara, California.*

We've been telling our readers that for years. If there were more women like you around, we'd be out of a job. Thanks.

Once Is Not Enough

The first time I make love with my girlfriend, everything is fantastic. But when we want a second round, I'm a dud. I can get it up, but I've pumped for at least ten minutes sometimes with no orgasm. She, meanwhile, gets off a couple of times, begging me to do the same. The second attempt is usually within five to ten minutes of the first one. What the hell is wrong with me? Should I leave more time between attempts. Or am I expecting too much from my system? Any enlightenment would be very helpful. —S. H., Raleigh, North Carolina.

Since when is ten minutes *too* long? As a man approaches an orgasm, he becomes aware of various physical signals. One of these is a feeling of fullness that develops as the seminal fluid collects in the prostatic urethra. With each succeeding orgasm, the amount of ejaculate diminishes, and so, to a certain extent, does the feeling of fullness. The signal of impending ecstasy is faint, and you're liable to miss it altogether if you're looking for the same thing you experienced the first time. If you don't feel yourself coming, you may think you're not going to come, and this can become a self-fulfilling prophecy. To compound the problem, the penis is usually less sensitive the second time around and the lubrication left over from openers cuts down on the friction. It might help to give your body time to recharge, but there are other solutions. When you've satisfied your taste for apples, switch to oranges. Instead of repeating the same-old-same-old, try a radically different position or approach, be it oral, anal or manual. Finally: What are you worried about? There is no law that says you have to have an orgasm. Indeed, such an obsession can lead to more serious problems. See the following letter.

Retarded Ejaculation

Help! I have sex almost every day, in one form or another. I try to limit my affairs to one person, but it is getting very hard. You see, unlike most males, I cannot ejaculate until I have had an incredible amount of sexual stimulation. This usually translates into balling sessions that last for several hours. My girlfriend just doesn't have my endurance. I bring her to an average of four or five orgasms, until she says that she can't take any more. I am then left unsatisfied, while she quickly dozes off. My passion being worked up to where it is, many times I am forced to masturbate in bed until relief comes. My girlfriend discovered this practice recently and said that unless I stopped, she would leave me. I don't want to lose her—I love her and want her to be my wife. I would like some advice on how to bring myself to orgasm during sex so that we can both enjoy our relationship. —S. D., Boston, Massachusetts.

Endurance can be the enemy of sexual satisfaction, especially when it is not appreciated by the recipient. It sounds like you may suffer from *ejaculatio retardata*—which is not one of the more famous Gregorian chants but, rather, an inability to achieve orgasmic release even after sufficient stimulation. The symptoms vary from one individual to the next, and even from one partner to the next. Some men equate staying power with the permanence of a relationship—they do not let themselves go, for fear of losing their partner. Others hold back as a sign of their lack of commitment. Sometimes the condition is the result of an early sexual trauma—a parent walking into the bathroom while you were masturbating, a policeman investigating the fogged windows of a parked car or bushwhackers tossing a cherry bomb into your room on a big college weekend. Forgive them, for they knew not what they did. In your case, the almost daily indulgence in sex may be taxing your natural urge—lay off for a week and see what happens. Explain your problem to your girlfriend. Perhaps you can adopt a style of lovemaking that combines coitus with manual stimulation (for example, the girl reaches down to grasp and stroke the testicles). Or she might learn to masturbate you to orgasm. Otherwise, if you keep it up as you've been doing, you may succeed in limiting your affairs to one person—yourself.

Contributory Negligence

A question in the Advisor gave me the idea that I might be an exceptional case. If so, I'd like to know what I can do about it. I am eighteen and it takes me a long time to come. I'm always extremely involved with my girl and what we're doing, and I'm extremely excited both physically and mentally; but sometimes after, say, ten minutes of steady, full thrusts (the expression is not for effect; I think it's essential to good sex that one applies full thrusts), I still feel no indication of impending ejaculation. After ten minutes, my girlfriend is complaining that I'm rubbing her raw, she's tired and why don't we go to a movie? Such sessions are, to say the least, extremely embarrassing and ego deflating. Occasionally, after a week of abstinence, I get it off after a minute or so. She apparently enjoys those encounters more than my other, more time-consuming efforts. I thought girls went for staying power! She says she likes to go to bed with me, but I don't know. I also don't know how to make it more exciting; we use different positions, but I reserve the proverbial whips and spiked heels for when I get bored with straight screwing, if and when that happens. What'll I do? I'm thinking of leaving her for greener pastures, but she's kind of special, so I'd appreciate advice? —L. B., Nashville, Tennessee.

Your friend sounds terminally bored. Anyone who punches a time clock or takes time out to read movie reviews in bed is in serious trouble. Her "less is more" attitude might be okay for poetry, but when it comes to sex, the opposite is true: If you like it, you want it to last forever. Our guess is that she hasn't yet learned to achieve orgasm during intercourse—therefore, the longer it goes on, the greater her sense of failure. Talk it over. Don't assume that you know what turns her on (i.e., the full thrusts). You might suggest that she set the pace: If she wants you to reach your destination quickly, let her move her tail for you. A final note: Lubrication diminishes with time or as the woman's interest declines. Try some K-Y jelly, scented oils or plain old 40 weight. If that fails, it may be time for the whips and spiked heels.

How to Become Impotent

Can you perhaps explain the mechanics of impotence? Several times in the past year, I have failed to get it up. The sessions have left me embarrassed and anxious. Can you tell me what I did wrong? —N. I., New Orleans, Louisiana.

Well, for one thing, it's not a mechanical problem. In most cases, impotence is the result of a psychological pattern. Dr. Leo Jacobs of the Forest Hospital Sexual Dysfunction Clinic has formulated the following ten rules that, if strictly adhered to, will guarantee impotence:

(1) Reduce sex to genital activities, stimulation of genitals and copulation. Carefully exclude from your relationship with your partner the following: Discussion and expression of feelings of tenderness, joy in holding and being held, unhurried mutual total body caresses. Be sure to carry out sexual activity in complete silence. (2) Assume that the erect penis is the only important thing you can give to your partner, and assume that her upset following an occasional sexual failure is due to her concern about not being able to copulate and not to her anger about your withdrawal into a sullen sulk. (3) Include sex in your work ethic as a test, which you flunk if you don't ejaculate at least 20 minutes following penetration—at exactly the moment your partner has an orgasm. (4) Pick a partner who believes that all men have instant erections and that a woman should not have to give you an erection by touching you on the genitals. (5) Have exclusively good feelings about your partner and deny the possibility that you could be angry at her. (6) Believe that a woman's sexual arousal is the direct and sole result of your touching her on the breasts or genitals. Believe that her arousal is completely under control and is in no way related to how she feels about you and herself. (7) Always assume that when you find your partner unhappy or sad, it must relate to something you did wrong in the relationship or in bed. Do not ever think that she could be unhappy for her own reasons. Everything she feels must involve you. (8) Believe that your erections will continue to be steel-hard and will in no way change as you get older. (9) When you fail sexually, assume that your partner is not interested in being pleased by your hands or mouth. (10) Be demanding, aggressive and self-assertive in your business enterprises and passive and dependent with your sexual partner.

There you have it: Break even one of those commandments and you may be on your way to healthy sex.

The Last Resort

For the past few years, I have been impotent. The reason appears to be psychological. Recently, I've heard of a device that can be surgically implanted in the penis of a man who is unable to effect or maintain an erection for physical reasons; it is said to get it up and keep it up for as long as it is needed. My urologist said that he knew of the research but that he didn't know a doctor in the state who would perform the surgery for a case of psychological impotence. He directed me to a shrink to determine why I can't get it up. Still, I'd like to know more about the device. —T. M., Minneapolis, Minnesota.

We assume that you refer to a technique developed by Dr. Brantley Scott of the Baylor College of Medicine in Houston, Texas, and Drs. William Bradley and Gerald Timm of the University of Minnesota Hospital. The doctors implant two collapsible silicone-rubber cylinders in the corpus cavernosum of the penis; these are connected by tubes to a pump tucked away in the scrotum and to a reservoir of fluid implanted behind the stomach muscles. By squeezing the pump, the patient transfers the fluid from the reservoir to the cylinders in the penis, which then becomes erect. Pressing on a tiny valve returns the fluid to the reservoir. Patients armed with the device can experience orgasm and ejaculation. (The brain centers that normally control erection are different from those that control pleasure. It is possible for a man to have an orgasm without an erection. Try it sometime.) Now for the drawbacks. The operation is expensive (not quite on the scale of those of the "Six Million Dollar Man" but, what with inflation, close). The closed hydraulic system can become damaged or worn out (as yet, there are no 5000-inch warranties); the replacement costs are equally expensive. And where are you going to find a plumber in the middle of the night? The device is an invaluable aid in cases of physically causd impotence, but, essentially, we agree with your doctor—why rely on a mechanical aid if you don't have to? (It's like saying to a friend on his way to the barbershop: "Get one for me.") See a psychiatrist or a sex counselor to get at the root of the problem.

Is That All There Is?

I hope my problem isn't unique. I just need to hear some calm words from an expert. I'm nineteen years old. I've noticed that when I ejaculate, my semen doesn't spurt out in forceful gusts but, instead, lazily spills over and onto my beaten cock. This problem has plagued me for years, and now I'm convinced that I'm not going to outgrow it. What can I do to change my situation? —B. P., Boston, Massachusetts.

Relax. Since most lovemaking takes place at point-blank range, you don't need a forceful ejaculation, unless you're planning to become a sniper. Dr. Alfred Kinsey found that men experience a wide variety of orgasmic responses. For about 20 percent of men, the climax is a relatively mild event. The penis does pulsate, but barely, and the semen dribbles instead of spurts. At the other end of the spectrum, about 5 percent become frenzied, hysterical and stark-raving bonkers. The rest of this sample fell somewhere in between. It's different strokes for different folks—the pleasure's the same in the end.

Wet Dreams

During periods of abstinence, my husband has wet dreams. I assure him that it's normal, but he thinks he's some sort of weirdo. Is he? What causes wet dreams? Do men experience them throughout their adult lives? —Mrs. C. M., San Diego, California.

Involuntary orgasms (or nocturnal emissions) are natural and normal and in no way are cause for alarm. The phenomenon begins in youth and tends to diminish with age: Kinsey and his associates found that 71 percent of all single males between the ages of 21 and 25 experienced nocturnal emissions. By the age of 50, only about a third of the men surveyed reported having wet dreams. By the age of 60, the figure was down to 14 percent. Although no one has yet proved it, the generally accepted theory is that wet dreams are caused by inadequate or unsatisfactory sexual outlets. Abstinence will lead to more frequent emissions as nature seeks to regulate sexual tension. (If you want to cure your husband, end his abstinence.) Oddly, a man can experience a nocturnal emission without having an erotic dream. Joseph J. Kaufman and Griffith Borgeson, in *Man and Sex*, suggest that the erotic dreams that usually accompany a nocturnal emission are not the cause but one of the results—the mind's attempt to produce an appropriate dream to accompany the sensations that might actually be caused by irritation, congestion or, as in one case, the rhythmic vibrations of a passing train. Do you live near the tracks?

Willpower

Is it possible to will an erection? —M. S., Des Moines, Iowa.

Yes, but the inheritance taxes are incredible. Actually, it depends on how you define *will*. (Philosophers have been at it for centuries; we'll settle for a meaning that includes some degree of self-control; i.e., the ability to take your life in your own hands.) Sexologist Wardell Pomeroy tells of a subject who claimed he could go from complete flaccidity to erection to ejaculation in less than ten seconds, then proceeded with a demonstration. Judging from some of the letters we've received on premature ejaculation, that is no record. But it still makes us wonder what the subject had on his mind. Talk about erotic fantasies!

Unwanted Erections

I get turned on with ridiculous ease. Climbing a rope in gym class gives me an erection. Riding in an airplane gives me an erection. Lifting weights gives me an erection. Watching "Charlie's Angels" gives me an erection. It's downright embarrassing. What do you do with an unwanted erection? —G. S., Phoenix, Arizona.

Put it up for adoption. If there are no takers, hold a gun to its head until it beats a hasty retreat. Or don't do anything. Better to have an erection when you don't want one than not have one when you do. There's nothing to be ashamed of; an erection is not a lightning rod to attract divine wrath. It is simply a pooling of blood in one part of your body. Strain (such as that experienced during exercise) can precipitate an erection. So can television. (There's nothing to worry about, as long as you don't get turned on by the Six Million Dollar Man.)

Force of Ejaculation

What can you tell me about the so-called basketball player—the guy who dribbles before he shoots? Long before I ejaculate, drops of semen appear at the tip of my penis. Is there any way to correct this condition? —J. A., Pittsburgh, Pennsylvania.

What you describe is completely normal. There is nothing you can do to correct the situation. The penis secretes a small amount of fluid during early stages of excitement—presumably to ease the way for a full-court press. (Or is it a fast break?) The amount varies from individual to individual and from time to time. By the way, the secretion can contain sperm. If you've been counting on coitus interruptus as a form of birth control, you may fake yourself out—right into fatherhood.

The Male Orgasm

It seems to me to be fashionable these days to downplay the male orgasm while glorifying the female's. Hasn't this service to women's lib gone far enough? Okay, specifically: just how many contractions or spasms do most men seem to have during ejaculation? A recent magazine (women's) article stated a man "usually" has between three and eight contractions, with the second half of them being weak and irregular. Three to eight? Listen, I've counted, and during what I'd call an average orgasm, I never have as few as three and nearly always more than eight. And my first six or seven contractions are all strong and intense. My orgasms are always longer and more intense than those described in most articles. The contractions do not really weaken until after seven or so, and then they still continue through as many as fourteen. So what's the story out there, you guys? —S.A.W., Rochester, New York.

The male orgasm has two phases—emission and ejaculation, or perhaps more simply, load and fire. In phase one, the internal organs (the prostate, the seminal vesicles, the internal part of the urethra, etc.) pump seminal fluid into a staging area (the prostate urethrae). In stage two, the urethral sphincter contracts at .8 second intervals, expelling the seminal fluid. (Interestingly, this is the same frequency with which the female experiences her orgasmic contractions.) These are probably the contractions you notice. For most men, the first two or three contractions are pleasurable, but the most sensation comes from the feeling of the *volume* of the ejaculate. According to Masters and Johnson, the force of the first contractions seems to develop a slight anesthesia— many men do not notice subsequent contractions. Obviously you do. Your orgasm is your own responsibility. Don't try to measure it or compare it with others'. There are two things that writers can't describe. One of them is a sunset.

The Ever-Popular Prostate Gland

I have been hearing a lot about the prostate gland—that anal sex can cause infections of the little bugger, that too much sex can cause inflammation, that too little or a break in one's sexual pattern can cause inflammation, et cetera. It seems as if the prostate were nature's way of telling you to slow down, to stop enjoying yourself, et cetera. Just what is the prostate and why is it such trouble? —T. G., San Diego, California.

The prostate is the weak link in man's chain of pleasure. The gland lies behind the base of the penis, just below the bladder, right in center court for both sex and urination. It produces the seminal fluid needed for ejaculation and can become congested if not emptied at regular intervals. Preventive medicine—a healthy diet of good solid lovemaking—should help you avoid trouble (orgasm flushes out the prostate), but don't go way beyond what you're normally used to. When the prostate becomes inflamed or congested, the victim may feel a lower-back pain, pain on urination, a general tenderness of the tubes, chills, fever and exhaustion. He may discover that it is painful to have an erection or to ejaculate. That's not as bad as terminal cancer but, for some men, close. Doctors usually treat prostate troubles with hot baths and anti-inflammatory drugs. They may tell the patient to abstain from alcohol, hot foods or marijuana, all of which seem to cause irritation of the prostate upon urination. To relieve the congestion of the gland, doctors massage it (the greased-glove-up-the-rectum technique sounds more gruesome than it feels). The prostate is susceptible to V.D. infection and, more critically, to bacterial infection. Perhaps the one and only danger involved in anal sex is the transmission of the usually harmless *E. coli* bacteria from the anus to the urethral canal and prostate. The two just do not get along and infection can result. (One solution: wear a condom during anal sex. If you engage in manual stimulation, do not move from the anus to yourself without first hitting the washbasin.) Later in life, the prostate tends to enlarge, putting pressure on the urethra and causing some discomfort with urination. In a few cases the prostate must be removed. Prostatitis has been called the priest's disease—perhaps because it requires you to give up wine, women and weed. Check with your doctor for the complete information on the care and feeding of the prostate. Treated properly, it can last a lifetime.

A Cure for Cancer?

I thought I had heard everything, but a guy I was out with the other night told me that sex is a cure for cancer. He couldn't remember the details of the article he'd read but suggested that if I valued his life, I would go to bed with him immediately. I admired his sense of humor and enjoyed saving his life. Now I want to check his facts. What do you say? —Miss W. S., Chicago, Illinois.

We are glad to see science being put to such good use. Sex may not be a cure for cancer, but it does seem to prevent a certain type—prostate cancer. Dr. I. D. Rokin compared 430 patients with prostate cancer with 430 healthy men. He discovered that sexual repression seemed to contribute to poor health. The cancer victims had a greater-than-normal sex urge but actually engaged in less sexual activity than did the men who did not have cancer. The theory is that sex hormones build up during abstinence and subsequently reduce the immunity of prostate cells by 16 to 80 percent. What can we say? Get it on if you want your friend to remain in good health.

Who Sleeps on the Wet Spot?

Something has been bothering me for a very long time. I'm ashamed to ask anyone about my problem, which is this: each and every time I disengage from my woman, my semen gushes out and soaks our love bed. We find it very uncomfortable to sleep in such pools. Is it normal that most of my sperm ends up in our laundry? —J. S., Montreal, Quebec.

The phenomenon you describe is completely natural and not uncommon. One of our researchers recently discovered a graffito in a ladies' rest room that indicates others share your predicament: "If he's so liberated, how come he doesn't sleep on the wet spot?" Beneath that, someone else had written, "If he was really liberated, there wouldn't be a wet spot. He would lick the plate clean." It is an unfortunate aspect of American upbringing that what was glorious during intercourse is viewed as a mess a few moments later. Once you accept your bodily functions, the problem disappears. There's nothing to be ashamed of. A towel at the bedside or underneath your partner might be appreciated, if she does not want to get out of bed after making love. (Some folks suggest a warm washcloth.) Condoms would contain the source of the discomfort. Other alternatives: do it somewhere else—on the floor, in the road, wherever—or do it several times before you retire. The quantity of ejaculate diminishes with each encore.

The Spare Penis

While drinking at our favorite bar, a friend and I traded stories about our days in the Navy. My friend recalled that the bell-bottoms worn by sailors in the old days had an unusual feature. Instead of a centered fly, the front of the pants had a flap that was secured by a row of buttons on each side. He proceeded to tell the story of a sailor's visit to a whorehouse in a foreign port. The sailor unbuttoned the row of buttons on the left side of his pants, pulled out his organ, had at the wench, tucked himself in and buttoned up. Then he unfastened the buttons on the right side of the pants and announced, "Now for the other one." Amusing, but we were left wondering: has there ever been a case of a man born with two penises? —W. E., San Diego, California.

Believe it or not, yes. Approximately one out of every 5,500,000 males is born with an extra penis. Some eighty cases have been reported in the past four centuries: for various reasons, few have reached adulthood. (The joke about the sailor may be more than shipboard bravado.) In most cases, both penises were capable of erection. A survey of medical literature uncovered one fifty-year-old patient who confessed to making it from both sides of the plate. No doubt the double-jointed fellow kept his spare tucked in the trunk.

The Love Muscle

For years, I've heard the term love muscle used to describe the penis. Is there really a muscle involved in sex? If so, can it be exercised? —W. S., Cleveland, Ohio.

Sex researchers have theorized that there is a love muscle—the pubococcygeus—and that it plays an important part in the pleasure of both male and female partners. Arnold Kegel first noted that since an orgasm is a release from muscle tension, the tone of the muscles involved would affect the quality of the orgasm. He focused on women who were experiencing difficulty having orgasms and taught them a series of exercises (now known as Kegel exercises). The women learned to tighten and relax the pubococcygeus (the muscle clenched to control urination) and practiced daily. During intercourse, they tensed their abdominal and perineal muscles to facilitate climax. Now, doctors are looking at the role played by the pubococcygeus muscle in the male orgasm. In an article in *Medical Aspects of Human Sexuality*, Daniel S. Weiss and Dr. David B. Marcotte suggest that by learning to *relax* the pubococcygeus muscle, a man can avoid premature ejaculation. The authors believe that the method is superior to the squeeze technique invented by Masters and Johnson, since it does not require partner cooperation or interruption of the lovemaking. We don't know of any gyms devoted to the relaxation response, but two experiments by Raymond Rosen suggest the shape of things to come. Rosen hooked up forty male students to a red light and had them listen to a recording of pornography. The light would go on whenever the student got an erection. Students soon learned to go from full erection to half-mast at will and were better at doing so than those who had not been hooked up to the light. In a related experiment Rosen told students to try to increase the size of their erections—an orange light would change intensity according to size. By the end of the study, the students who were guided by the light were able to turn on at will. Rig up something yourself and work out.

Does Penis Size Count?

What gives? For years you've been telling your readers that penis size doesn't count. Then, in the "Sex Poll" in the October issue, you come out with the findings that it matters to some people. What's the true story? —S. V., Chicago Illinois.

Are you suggesting that we've been caught with our pants down? Okay, we confess. It's all been a conspiracy to delude the masses. The fiends responsible for the misinformation have been fired. Size counts. Now what? The most recent research, reported by J. Scott Verinis in *Medical Aspects of Human Sexuality*, suggests that initially the size of a man's penis matters to both the male and the female. "However," he says, "as the relationship progresses, the size of the penis becomes less important to most women and factors such as the quality of sexual performance and the nature of the interpersonal relationship receive higher priority." The men, however, continue to value the size of the penis at all stages of the relationship. (That makes sense—it's their burden to bear.) So probably the real truth is this: Size matters to some of the people all of the time and to all of the people some of the time, but not to all of the people all of the time. By the time you figure that one out, you'll be an old man and it won't matter anymore.

Can You Increase the Size of the Penis?

The other day, I was reading a book that promised to tell me everything I wanted to know about sex, when I discovered something that I didn't want to know; i.e., that the average length of the erect penis is six inches. My own erection checks in at a mere five and a half inches. I've considered several solutions, including trimming my pubic hair to reveal a half-inch that most men don't show. I've even considered replying to ads for devices that promise to increase the size of the penis. Do any of them work? —B. G., New York, New York.

No one ever went broke underestimating the insecurities of the American public. The penis-enlarging techniques for which you shell out hard-earned cash have been around for centuries and according to Dr. William Masters, provide "little or no return to the anxious male." In short, either they don't work or the small increase in size that does occur is meaningless. The techniques fall into three categories: First, some claim that increasing the blood flow to the penis via a vacuum pump causes the penis to grow. The vacuum pump can be dangerous; imagine going through life with a permanent hickey. There are safer ways to get the same effect. P.T. Barnum pointed out there's a sucker born every minute. Find one and let her do the work. Second, the ads claim that by stretching the erectile tissue, one permanently increases the penis' capacity for blood. It's not Turkish taffy you're playing with and the results can be harmful. Third, some of the ads promise secret stimulation techniques that will increase the size of the penis. Sure. It's called an erection and it happens every time a woman slips her hands into your jeans. Actually, there is some truth to these claims. The penis does swell and subside according to the level of stimulation. It's up to your girlfriend to decide just what model she wants.

Can a Penis Be Too Large?

Having an 11-inch penis can be a problem. Whenever I get to the point where sex is possible with a girl, she usually takes one look at my club and refuses to join. The other night, I met a girl at a bar and we hit it off great. Back at my apartment everything went well until I took off my clothes. She freaked and said something like: "You could cripple someone with that!" She balked at intercourse and, instead, performed fellatio, which was less satisfying. I haven't had coitus in three months and things are getting bad. Any suggestions? —T. K., Des Moines, Iowa.

Wear dark, solid-color suits. Never mix stripes with plaids. Make sure your socks match your trousers and keep your shoes shined. Turn out the light before you take off your clothes, then go gently into that good night. By the time she notices anything different (if she notices anything beyond her own pleasure), you will have hidden or disposed of most of the evidence.

Reader Response

After reading the letter in the August Playboy Advisor about the gentleman with the 11-inch penis, I took out a ruler and, well, I discovered that 11 inches is quite long. According to one book I read, the average penis is only six inches long. Curious, I took out my own penis and found that there was a difference of several inches in total length, depending on where I placed the ruler. Do the statistics stem from top to tip, or along the bottom to include the part under the testicles? What is the correct way to take the measurement? —L. K., Culver City, California.

Sex researchers Masters and Johnson know the correct way but won't tell anyone, for reasons of national insecurity. So feel free to invent. Our guess is that anyone who feels compelled to pull out a ruler will discover the two points that yield the largest figure; that's the way it should be. Then he'll convert the measurement to the metric system (one inch equals 2.54 centimeters). If anyone asks, he can say that he's a healthy 15.24 or whatever. It might interest you to know that size does make a difference—at least to some folks. We received eight letters requesting the address of the 11-inch penis. Two were from girls.

The Hard Facts

For years Playboy *has been telling its readers that penis size doesn't matter. I'm willing to buy that, except for one thing. You never publish statistics to go along with your advice. What is the average size? —F. C., Detroit, Michigan.*

Averages are for the simple-minded. Here's a list of measurements of erect penises of white college men, in quarter-inch lengths. The Alfred C. Kinsey Institute for Sex Research reviewed the data and found that of the college males it measured, .2 percent checked in at 3.75 inches, .3 percent at 4 inches, .2 percent at 4.25 inches, 1.7 percent at 4.5 inches, .8 percent at 4.75 inches, 4.2 percent at 5 inches, 4.4 percent at 5.25 inches, 10.7 percent at 5.5 inches, 8 percent at 5.75 inches, 23.9 percent at 6 inches, 8.8 percent at 6.25 inches, 14.3 percent at 6.5 inches, 5.7 percent at 6.75 inches, 9.5 percent at 7 inches, 1.8 percent at 7.25 inches, 2.9 percent at 7.5 inches, 1 percent at 7.75 inches, 1 percent at 8 inches, .3 percent at 8.25 inches, .3 percent at 8.5 inches, .1 percent at 8.75 inches, .1 percent at 9 inches. A veritable locker room of figures. Convert everything to metrics if you aren't satisfied with your size in inches.

Cold Water and Nude Beaches

Shortly, I will be leaving for a vacation in the Caribbean. I plan to visit a "suits optional" beach: I hope to repeat the nice experiences I had last summer at California's liberated shores. (I was very impressed by the friendly nature of everyone I saw. There was no peeking or gawking—just eye contact.) I do have one question, though: are the women who utilize nude beaches enlightened enough to know that many males retract a great deal from the stimulation of cold water and air, not to mention anxiety? I wouldn't want to be judged as inadequate in the flaccid state because someone wasn't aware of a basic biological response. —W. C., Santa Ana, California.

The women who frequent nude beaches are probably more enlightened than the men who frequent the same beaches. They aren't hung up on locker-room definitions of adequacy: They know from firsthand experience that while flaccid penises vary greatly in size, there is only about a 20 percent difference in size of fully erect members (cf. the Masters and Johnson finding that the smaller they come, the larger they grow, and vice versa). So stop worrying: We heard of one fellow who was driven to absurd lengths to make certain that women knew what he had to offer: A tattoo high on the inside of his thigh proclaimed, THIS IMAGE ONE QUARTER LIFE SIZE. Beneath that, in fine print, was the statement "If you are close enough to read this, the above is no longer true."

Exercise and Sex

A friend of mine who works out a lot claims that exercise increases sexual desire. Especially if you work out at a coed health club. Sounds like a lot of hype to me, but I'm curious. Has anyone done a study relating exercise to sex? —F. A., Dallas, Texas.

A study done at Indiana University suggests that there is a relationship between exercise and sex—if you are willing to believe the person you're talking with, that is. Researchers interviewed students in classrooms and students walking into a field house. Not surprisingly, the people on their way into the field house reported that they had a median of 39 minutes of exercise a day (vs. 21 minutes for classroom subjects). They also reported having more sex (7.58 times per month vs. 4.18 times per month for the classroom crowd) and a greater desire for sex (they wanted to do it 13.98 times per month vs. 7.60 times per month for the eggheads). It makes sense to us: The more you get in touch with your body, the more you want to see what the sucker is capable of. And then you're trapped in a vicious circle (see next letter for the effect of sex on exercise).

Abstinence Before the Big Game

I've always heard that if an athlete engages in sex the night before a big game, he may perform poorly the next day. Coaches always seem to equate celibacy with increased drive and concentration. My wife and I have entered a mixed-doubles tournament at the local tennis club and we're wondering if we should abstain from sex for a few days before the competition? —R. H., Lansing, Michigan.

For some athletes, celibacy is superstitiously linked to victory; it's like never washing a pair of socks that once brought good luck. (We can see how the latter might lead involuntarily to the former, but neither is a guarantee of high performance.) There is no biological reason to remain chaste before a big game. A West German professor named Manfred Steinback questioned four thousand Olympic athletes and found that they make love an average of four to five times a week. He concluded that if an athlete does feel substandard after a night on the town "it is not sex that has sapped his strength. It is the attendant frivolities such as drinking, dancing and dashing around until the early hours of the morning." Knowing the psychology of most mixed-doubles teams, it's our guess that if you abstain and one of you performs poorly anyway, you won't talk to each other for weeks, let alone make love. Enjoy yourselves while you can.

Blue Balls

My boyfriend thinks that all kissing, cuddling and fondling in bed must culminate in intercourse. He says it's bad for his body to get aroused without achieving release. I say bullshit. I think cuddling and touching can be fun and satisfying in themselves. It's not necessary for a man to have intercourse every time he gets an erection from seeing a good-looking chick or from thinking about last night's bedroom activities. So what do you think about my boyfriend's attitude that sex means copulation only? —Miss K. G., Portland, Oregon.

We don't feel that every form of kissing, cuddling and fondling must culminate in intercourse—only the kissing, fondling and cuddling that occurs between members of the opposite sex who qualify as consenting adults and who know each other on a first-name basis. Actually, sex counselors have discovered that the level of affection between two partners increases in direct proportion to the amount of nonsexual touching that goes on between them—the occasional hug, the unexpected kiss, the copped feel. Of course, as affection increases, so does the frequency of sexual intercourse. It's a vicious circle. Unfortunately, from the sound of your letter, the circle has been broken. Your boyfriend's attitude is a bit one-sided. It is a sign of insensitivity when one person assumes that his or her partner will be ready for sex at the same moment he or she is. You can't light a fire without kindling. An unrelieved erection can cause a temporary physical condition known as blueballs. The blood congests in the genitals and causes discomfort. It is rarely fatal. Women who have been aroused but not satisfied can suffer a similar condition. Next time your partner asks you to relieve his symptoms, tell him that you would have more sympathy if the disease were contagious.

Telltale Testicles

Please settle an argument that is going on in our office. One of the girls has come up with the theory that she can tell whether or not her spouse has had sex within the past week. This is done by examining his testicles for tightness, with any limpness obviously showing recent sexual activity. The males contend that is no indicator, because other variables, such as underwear and weather, affect the way they're hanging. Is that a dead giveaway, or does this girl just have an unusual husband? —Miss D. M., Raleigh, North Carolina.

No. The husband has an unusual wife. Her theory implies that she hasn't had sex for a week, unless you call her copping a feel as sex, which we don't. The testes rise and fall according to temperature, short-term excitement, fear and danger. They rise just prior to orgasm. The left testicle, incidentally, usually hangs lower and roves more. In this case, it may rove out of the house.

This Letter Saved Three Men's Lives

My girlfriend visits her gynecologist every six months. Part of the examination involves checking her breasts for early signs of cancer. Recently, she returned home and said that her doctor told her about a test—similar to a breast examination—for testicular cancer and that I should do myself a favor and find out about it. Is there such an exam? —M. C., San Francisco, California.

You've got a great girlfriend. Keep her. She cares. Apparently, there has been a surge in testicular cancer. In most cases, by the time victims go to the medical profession, it is too late. That's the bad news. The good news is that if the cancer is detected early, it is almost 100 percent curable. The telltale symptom is a lump, thickening or swelling of the testicles. Not all lumps are cancerous, but they should be checked out. To examine yourself, start with a warm shower or bath. When the skin of the scrotum is relaxed, explore each testicle, rolling it between thumb and forefinger. You are looking for a small lump that may be the size of a pea, located (in most cases) at the front of the testicle. If you find one, don't freak. Consult a doctor. Better to sound a false alarm than to find yourself in serious trouble.

Bedroom Eyes

What are bedroom eyes? A number of girls have mentioned this anatomical turn-on, but none has been able to describe them except to say that I don't have them. What do they look like? —S. C., Montreal, Quebec.

The exact definition depends on the taste of the beholder, but generally, bedroom eyes are considered to be sleepy, seductive, come-hither peepers made popular by Giancarlo Giannini and King Kong. (Scientists have found that pupils dilate involuntarily when someone is interested in another person.) To develop the look, try staying up for several days in a row. That, plus a case of acute horniness, should convey the proper image to the intended victim. If the girl persists in telling you that you lack her favorite turn-on, don't take it personally. Explain that you left your bedroom eyes on the night table, next to the glass that contains your false teeth, and move on.

CHAPTER TWO

The Curious Female

Cooper's Droop

Most of the medical reports I've read warn that going braless may lead to pendulous breasts, a condition known as Cooper's droop. I have not worn a bra for six years, yet my breasts do not sag. I seem to be defying the law of gravity. Is there a local ordinance I don't know about, or were those reports simply exaggerating the problem? —Miss J. N., La Grange, Illinois.

There's nothing like a woman's breast to make a doctor put his foot in his mouth. As near as we can tell, there has never been a controlled study of the effects of going braless. (Uncontrolled studies are another story.) One doctor who wrote to Ann Landers at the peak of the braless fad stated, "Almost everyone has seen films of tribal African women, which are conclusive evidence. The females have never worn bras and they all have Cooper's droop." Other doctors, who cut their visual teeth on pictures in *National Geographic*, make the same claim, using still photographs of Polynesians. Never mind that the first doctor didn't look at comparable films of tribal American women or that there is no accounting for the editorial tastes of certain magazines—the fact is that you don't need Columbo to tell you that this is not conclusive evidence. We are less amused by the scare tactics of bra companies. One ad reads: "And everybody said that nothing is going to happen to your breasts if you go braless. But the truth is, something can happen. . . . So please put your bra back on." They fail to specify that the something that can happen is probably going to happen anyway, whether or not you wear a bra. It's nature's way. The shape of a woman's breast is largely the result of an internal net of fibrous tissue called Cooper's ligaments, which connect the fatty tissue around the mammary glands to the pectoral muscles. Cooper's ligaments tend to grow lax as one grows older (cf. Buck Brown's dirty old lady). Also, if ligaments are stretched, they cannot contract to their original length (cf. a football player who has wobbly knees after a clipping injury). Cooper's ligaments may stretch when the breasts swell during pregnancy or when a woman gains, then loses weight. Factors such as individual tissue tone, heredity and general health all determine the degree of change. It is impossible to predict whether or not one woman's breasts will sag: A large-breasted woman may have strong ligaments and a small-breasted woman may have weak ligaments. In the face of confusion, go with what's comfortable and/or pleasing to the eye. Love has no foundation.

Pubic Hair

This may sound kinky, but the hair on my mons is as straight and as silky as the hair on my head. The only time it has any curl at all is after a bath, and then for only about a half hour. My boyfriend says he's never seen or felt anything like it. No one in my family has an unbush, either. Have you ever come across anything similar? —Miss D. D., Columbia, Missouri.

Yes, we've come across it occasionally. Straight pubic hair is unusual, but that doesn't make it kinky. Don't worry.

Second and Seventh

Currently, I am attending medical school and have come up with a problem that may stump even The Playboy Advisor. One of the upperclassmen always gives his address as "between second and seventh." When asked what he means, he says to check Gray's Anatomy. I decided to ask you. What does he mean by that cryptic phrase? —G. D., Boston, Massachusetts.

He lives in our neighborhood. Medical students, art students and, indeed, anyone with a pair of eyes learns that the female breast is usually situated between the second and the seventh rib, with the nipple located on the fifth rib. The address is the same, but the Zip Code (the Unzip Code?) varies from girl to girl.

Erect Nipples

My girlfriend and I saw a flick called Night Moves, in which Gene Hackman plays a private detective who falls in with a blonde beachcomber. The latter gives a long, very sexy rap on how whenever someone kisses her, her nipples get erect. She is always walking around with erect nipples. Hackman eventually gets pissed at her and yells something like "You and your goddamn erect nipples." A great scene, but it left me wondering. I recall reading that erect nipples are a sign of sexual excitement, but, for the life of me, I can't tell when my girlfriend's turned on. Is there something wrong with her? —T. S., Los Angeles, California.

Probably not. You should stop trying to make mountains out of molehills. Nipple erection is an involuntary response—the smooth muscle fiber within the nipple contracts whenever it is excited. The reaction is most noticeable on women with average-sized breasts and normal-sized nipples. It is less apparent on larger protruding nipples. Also, Masters and Johnson have noted that small nipples do not have the physiological potential to increase in size. If you want to see what your girlfriend's nipples look like when erect, apply an ice cube. Gold sometimes produces the same response. Now for the next mouth-watering question.

Breast Size

My girlfriend and I have been having an argument about her breast size. She says that when I fondle or otherwise munch out on her tits, it keeps them from growing naturally. Her argument is that while I was away for a week, her breasts grew in size. But when I started back to my old habit, they stopped growing. Is there any evidence to support her argument? —J. B., San Antonio, Texas.

None. Breasts *increase* in size slightly when stimulated; they also wax and wane with the menstrual cycle. Tell your girlfriend she'll have to come up with a better story than that.

Clitoris Spoiled by Vibrator?

During our school years, my girlfriend and I enjoyed sex frequently, but most of our encounters were hurried or on the sneak—in a motel or a friend's vacant apartment. This was not annoying to me, but it did make my companion somewhat nervous. The only way I could make her reach orgasm was by placing a vibrator directly on her clitoris. Despite limited time and unfamiliar surroundings, she usually reached a fantastic climax. We used to joke about doing a commercial for a battery company—emerging from the motel room holding the vibrator, saying it saved us by working all night. Now that we share an apartment and have all the time in the world, we find that she cannot reach orgasm without the damned vibrator. I'm afraid that I spoiled her clitoris through harsh treatment. How can we start to enjoy sex in the traditional way? —C. M., Portland, Oregon.

You did not spoil your partner's clitoris, but you may have conditioned her sexual response. Psychologists believe that behavior is affected by its consequences: If a bit of food falls into a cage after a pigeon pushes a button, then the pigeon is likely to peck again. A woman is more complex than a pigeon, but the principle is the same. Your lover associates the vibrator with her climax, which is certainly a more persuasive reward than a pellet of food. She will have to work at recognizing and cultivating other forms of stimulation. We suggest that you start by not making orgasm the goal of your lovemaking. Instead, relax and enjoy each sensation for its own intrinsic value. Explore as many techniques as you can (i.e., push different buttons). Soon your friend should come to her senses—all of them.

Clitoral Adhesions

I have heard that some women have tissues covering their clitorises that prevent them from becoming aroused when their clitorises are stimulated. I really can't tell if my girlfriend has these, but I can seldom even get her to blink during intercourse. Is there a way to tell, and can some sort of clitoral stimulation help? Help! —J. F., Cleveland, Ohio.

We've heard of toe curling as a response to sexual stimulation, but the eye blinking you're apparently looking for is a new one on us. Clitoral adhesions, as these tissues are called, are rare and are seldom the cause of sexual dysfunction. Even when surgical correction has been done, there is little scientific documentation that it improves sexual responsiveness. Your friend's gynecologist can tell her if she has adhesions, but we suspect that you should look elsewhere for an answer to her lethargy. Instead of checking out her fluttering lids, why not ask her what turns her on? It could be *your* problem and the remedy a simple one. On the other hand, it could be her problem. In which case the remedy is equally simple: Find a partner more to your liking.

Lubrication Equals Arousal

Perhaps you can help me. I've led what I consider to be a normal, happy sex life for many years now and have engaged in sex with a number of women. I've found that regardless of the great diversity in sexual performance, one thing has remained constant—the women with whom I've been involved have always been adequately lubricated. Unfortunately, my present girlfriend is an exception to the rule. We've been having active sex for about eight months and during this time, we've never had intercourse. Our sexually oriented interludes consist basically of oral sex. She says that she is not ready for intercourse and, since I do love her very much, I am content not to force the issue. I do think it's rather strange that in this entire time she has rarely been lubricated enough to allow insertion of one finger. She does not object to tongue lashing, though. (It seems to drive her to ecstasy.) I'm getting desperate. Is the problem psychological or physical? Or, worse, is this some new kind of contraceptive method I haven't heard about? —B. W., Wichita, Kansas.

Yes, it's called abstinence. When your girlfriend says that she is not ready for intercourse, she means it—mentally and physically. The two are related. Most women begin to lubricate within ten to thirty seconds of sexual stimulation—the amount may vary from individual to individual and with the same person from episode to episode. Several factors affect the flow. If a woman is inhibited about sex, it is likely that the amount of lubrication will be limited. Although you don't mention how old your girlfriend is, we might add that diminished lubrication is also a by-product of menopause. Experience is a good teacher, though, and most older women simply switch to commercially available lubricants, such as K-Y jelly or Albolene. Don't let the friction slow down your sex life. If God had not intended the well to run dry, He wouldn't have given us petroleum jelly. Discuss with your girlfriend exactly what it is she's not ready for—it may be that she is worried about birth control, or perhaps she's saving herself for marriage. In any case, the physical evidence needs the support of personal testimony. Put your witness on the stand or bed and proceed.

Loose Women

On occasion, I've heard men claim that they can tell a woman's sexual morality by the condition of her vagina. A loose woman is loose inside. This bit of information came up in a rather embarrassing situation: Noting how relaxed I was during a lovemaking session, one of my boyfriends accused me of having been as busy as a beaver—he said the more a woman makes love, the more worn out the muscles. Frequency equals flaccidity. Personally, I think he was trying to shift the anxiety about his own size to me. Is there any truth to that speculation? —Miss S. K., St. Louis, Missouri.

Nope. Intercourse will not permanently increase the size of the vagina, nor will it wear out the muscles. If anything, an increase in the frequency of lovemaking will tend to tone those muscles, which contract involuntarily at the moment of orgasm. (Every workout should be so nice.) The only statistics we have on frequency relate the number of times a woman makes love to her satisfaction with lovemaking: A recent study found that the more a woman tends to get it on, the more she likes sex; and vice versa. If the loose lips of tactless and misinformed lovers are causing your relationships to sink, you might want to take control of the situation. It is possible to tone the muscles through a set of calisthenics known as Kegel exercises: Essentially, they involve contractions of the muscles used to urinate. For more details, contact your gynecologist.

Kegel Calisthenics

I have trouble reaching orgasm with my boyfriend when we make love. He is very understanding and suggested that I try performing Kegel exercises. (He remembers reading about them in a previous Playboy Advisor column.) What are they and why do they work? —Miss S. F., Savannah, Georgia.

Sex researchers over the past few years have begun to explore the relationship between sexual responsiveness and muscle tone, particularly that of the pubococcygeus muscle. In one experiment, doctors measured the "clenching power" of the pubococcygeus muscle and compared it with orgasmic ability. Totally nonorgasmic women registered an average of 7.42 mmHg on a Kegel Perineometer, while clitorally but not coitally orgasmic women measured 12.31 mmHg. Women who were both clitorally and coitally orgasmic rang the chimes at 17 mmHg. The Kegel exercises are simple: The woman contracts the pubococcygeus muscle, as though she were trying to refrain from urinating, in sets of ten, several times a day. Unfortunately, as simple as the exercises sound, a lot of women have had difficulty working out at the Y. According to a report in the March issue of *Medical Aspects of Human Sexuality*, there is new hope. An electronic device known as the Vagitone stimulates muscles through electrotherapy. Used twice a day, it rapidly and involuntarily tones, strengthens and conditions the pelvic muscles. The device is available from Techni-Med, 8135 California Avenue, Whittier, California 90602. Ask your doctor for details.

The Misplaced Vagina

Anatomy has always fascinated me, and after numerous encounters, I can say that curiosity has skilled the cat. However, last weekend I had intercourse with a young lady whose vagina was quite far underneath her. I found it so uncomfortable to enter from the conventional position that I had to put her on her hands and knees for a better shot at the prize. This is only the second time in my twenty-six years that I have found a misplaced vagina. What is the medical term for this condition? —J. E., Scarsdale, New York.

There is no medical term for a misplaced vagina, because the condition doesn't exist. There are distinct anatomical differences among women, but it is unlikely that a woman's vagina would be so placed as to prohibit face-to-face intercourse—in fact, ordinarily, face-to-face anal intercourse is possible. It's our guess that you and your partner simply were not cooperating.

The Hide-and-Seek Clitoris

I have always considered myself to be well informed about sex. I enjoy all forms of lovemaking, and I am a careful, considerate lover. Having read most of the sex books written in the past few years, I am well aware of the importance of the clitoris. Here's my problem. When I begin to make love or perform oral sex, the clitoris is usually easy to find. However, when I look up to catch my breath, I always try to see if it's still in view or if my grip has changed. Inevitably, it is no longer in sight, and it takes me a minute or two to find it again. Is it just me, or have other guys experienced that kind of hide-and-seek? —J. R., Memphis, Tennessee.

Relax. As a woman approaches orgasm, the clitoris retracts under a hood of skin. Why it chooses that moment to play coy and hard to get is beyond us. However, the best advice is to keep on doing what you've been doing. The woman is close to orgasm, and if you interrupt the motion or the rhythm to find your place, she will lose *her* place. According to Masters and Johnson, "it is important to re-emphasize the fact that the retracted clitoral body continues to be stimulated by traction or pressure on the protective clitoral hood. Once plateau-phase clitoral retraction has been established, manipulation of the general mons area is all that is necessary for effective clitoral-body stimulation." Our guess is that the clitoris hides itself in self-defense. There is a narrow line between stimulation and irritation. You might want to ask your partner to masturbate in front of you. See how she treats her clitoris; is the stimulation direct or indirect? Every woman is different. Put yourself in her hands.

When Is a Woman Horniest

One of my girlfriends claims that she is horniest just before ovulation. I can see that this might be true from nature's point of view—it would increase her chances of making love at a time when she is most fertile. But I have also heard that women are horniest just before or after menstruation. Is my girlfriend just being contrary? —E. S., Dallas, Texas.

We recall reading a report that asked 580 women if they experienced their greatest desire for sex at ovulation—and if such a surge were a source of frustration for those practicing the rhythm method. Seventy-three percent of the women said that they peaked during prime time (on or about the thirteenth day of the cycle); and 57 percent said that the poorly timed lust was a source of frustration. Other studies have shown that there are peaks of desire shortly before and after menstruation. Our advice: Take your partner's word for it—whatever it is—and act accordingly.

Female Ejaculation

Can you settle a debate that I've been having with several of the girls at work? They insist that when a woman has an orgasm, she ejaculates a small amount of colorless, odorless fluid. As proof of the phenomenon, they point to ancient pornographic texts. All of the racy Victorian novels that I've read contain mention of women "spending" at the moment of orgasm. It's my impression from reading Kinsey and Masters that female ejaculation is a myth. What's the true story? —Miss D. S., San Diego, California.

Welcome to the debate; it's been going on for centuries. When a woman becomes excited, the walls of the vagina secrete a fluid—it is the first sign of coital readiness. Kinsey, confronting the female-ejaculation question, concluded that "muscular contractions of the vagina following orgasm may squeeze out some of the genital secretions and in a few cases eject them with some force. This is frequently referred to, particularly in the deliberately erotic literature, as an ejaculation in the female, but the term cannot be strictly used in that connection." Havelock Ellis, years earlier, found that some women become so excited during gynecological examinations that they produced an ejaculation of fluid "sometimes described as being emitted in a jet which is thrown to a distance." (Next thing you know, they'll be able to write their names in the snow.) E. Grafenberg noted that cases of involuntary expulsion of urine sometimes accompanied orgasm, but in the cases he observed, the fluid was examined and "it had no urinary character." Now a new chapter to the debate has been written. In the February 1978 issue of the *Journal of Sex Research*, J.L. Sevely and J.W. Bennett review all of the literature on female ejaculation from Aristotle to Masters and Johnson. They conclude that the female possesses glands similar to the male prostate (the male prostate secretes the fluid that consitutes much of the male ejaculate). The female prostate glands are located near the opening of the urethra and apparently produce a fluid during intercourse. In most cases, this fluid mingles with normal lubricating fluids, but apparently in some women, it is more pronounced. The authors conclude that the topic needs more research. We agree. Dr. Watson, fetch our flashlight and magnifying glass.

Honeymoon Cystitis

I just met and went nuts over a terrific girl. Our relationship progressed and everything was going Gang Busters until we started to make love. On our first session, we hit it off so perfectly we didn't want to stop. But the next day, my girlfriend couldn't go through with another tryst, let alone a decathlon. She analyzed the problem as "honeymoon cystitis" and made an appointment with her doctor. What's honeymoon cystitis and how do you get rid of it? —M. R., Chicago, Illinois.

Honeymoon cystitis is a latent bladder infection stirred up by frequent and vigorous intercourse. The woman's symptoms include frequent and painful urination and sometimes the presence of blood in the urine. It is easily managed by antibiotics and other chemotherapy and usually goes away after a few days. The only known preventive technique is a dull sex life. You pays your money, you takes your chances.

Loss of Lubrication

My husband and I used to have a very good sex life. About six months ago, I started having problems with lubrication. I thought it was only temporary. I've gotten to the point where I'm totally uninterested in sex. I don't think there is anything physically wrong with me. I'm taking birth-control pills, and I wonder if that is the problem. I started taking them after our daughter was born, about a year ago. I'm only twenty years old, and this is terribly frustrating for me. Every time my husband touches me, I'm afraid he's going to want to make love—and he usually does. I don't know what to do. Any advice you might give me would truly be appreciated. —Mrs. A. C., Kansas City, Kansas.

Lubrication is the female equivalent of the male erection. When something goes wrong with anyone's sexual responsiveness, the result is frustration and an avoidance of sex. It's a vicious circle that has to be broken, but the more pressure you feel, the harder it will be to break. One thought to bear in mind is that although there may not be anything physically wrong with you, there may be physical reasons for your lack of response. The pill has been cited by some doctors for reducing lubrication and sex drive—most likely because it affects your body's delicate hormonal balance. Also, scientists are learning new facts about how childbearing and child rearing affect the body's sex chemicals. New mothers display anxieties and fears that are traceable to hormone changes. That may help explain why many marriages undergo enormous stress during the first two years after the birth of the first child and a significant number of divorces occur then. You may be experiencing stresses that are normal for this period in your marriage, and nothing ruins sex as much as anxiety. Your lack of sexual interest is probably temporary and reversible; you'd be in worse shape if you were interested in sex but not in your husband. Talk with a gynecologist about the physical basis of your problem. After that, a little patience while your body returns to its normal biochemical state ought to make you as horny as ever.

The Mystery of the Female Orgasm

Is it possible for a woman to have an orgasm and not know it? When I make love to my girlfriend, I can feel her vaginal muscles go into contractions (a sign of climax, according to Masters and Johnson), but she claims that she feels only brief twinges of pleasure, not the cosmic, all-encompassing, oceanic, mystical garbanzo orgasm that women's libbers are always talking about. Needless to say, I feel somewhat frustrated. What do you suggest? —L. O., New Orleans, Louisiana.

The word orgasm is like the word love: Maybe someday there will be a ten-ton stainless-steel ORGASM sculpture erected in Central Park and jewelry and stationery embossed with the word. After they've seen it in print ten million times, some women no longer know what it means and are always suspicious that what they experience isn't the real thing. The cure is fairly simple: First, a woman must acquaint herself with the various stages of an orgasm. As the clitoris is stimulated, blood gathers in the pelvic region and the vagina lubricates and expands. The build-up of blood produces a tension in the muscles of the pelvis, particularly in those that surround the vaginal opening and the rectum. Eventually, a reflex is triggered in the responding muscles and the vagina begins to contract, expelling the blood from the pelvic region. (If a woman does not experience this reflex, she may feel discomfort from the accumulated blood.) That's all there is to an orgasm, folks: The contraction, followed by the expulsion of blood. It can be strong or weak, cosmic or suburban, depending on the woman's attitude toward herself. If she doesn't put her mind to it, she may not feel anything or, worse, she may experience excitement as discomfort. The current idea is that a woman can learn the stages through masturbation or cunnilingus, and then, when she has intercourse (a distinctly inferior method of directly stimulating the clitoris), she will locate them more quickly and surrender to the flow of her own sexuality without fear or hesitation. Then watch out.

The Miracle of the Female Orgasm

Some of my friends and I have been discussing human sexual response. One of them suggested that, contrary to women's lib, there was no reason to expect a lady to have an orgasm, since, as a rule, the females of other species don't. Can this be true? Do female animals have orgasms? —O. R., Los Angeles, California.

We never asked. Actually, Dr. David A. Goldfoot brought up this topic in a recent issue of *Medical Aspects of Human Sexuality*. If you define orgasm in physiological terms—i.e., the body changes that Masters and Johnson divided into four phases: excitement, plateau, orgasmic and resolution—the answer is probably no. A female rhesus monkey that was mechanically stimulated went through three of the phases but did not actually experience the orgasmic phase. (Nevertheless, her social calendar is filled for the year.) According to Dr. Goldfoot, "Certain behaviors of females . . . occasionally look like orgasmic responses to observers, but obviously this is hardly acceptable evidence for orgasm. For example, the rhesus female sometimes repeatedly clutches her leg, the leg of her partner or even his scrotum . . . in a vigorous manner during copulation. . . . The female stump-tailed macaque occasionally displays muscular body spasms, rhythmic expiration vocalizations and an openmouthed expression during coitus which resembles facial expressions described for humans during orgasm. These behaviors, including the characteristic facial expression, are very similar to the responses shown by male stump-tailed monkeys during ejaculations." (They probably knew they were being filmed.) Most other species don't even come close. Also, several studies have shown that rodents will behave the same way during intercourse even when their genitals are anesthetized. So, although it appears that females of other species do not have orgasms, this in no way suggests that the same applies to human females. In fact, one of the things that differentiates man from other animals is his ability to use a tool, and woman, her ability to appreciate it when he does.

Our Sex Life Is Great, Except for One Thing . . .

Early this year, I met a lovely divorcee. Our relationship appears to be flowering in every way save one: She is unable to experience orgasm. This condition developed during the last years of a stormy, violent marriage. As she put it to me: "I just turned off sex." A psychiatrist told her that our relationship was too new yet to conclude that her problem was a problem. He anticipated that as we got to know each other better, she would be able to enjoy normal sex with me. I am not so sure. What is the best course to follow for the present: often to bed, on the theory that it will ultimately break down the resistance, or deferred as much as possible because of the possible adverse psychological impact on her of each frustrating experience? —M. N., Oakland, California.

Beds that convert to couches are seldom as comfortable as regular beds; since she already has a competent psychiatrist, we'd settle for being a considerate lover. Her condition is a common response to the breakup of a bad marriage and is probably temporary. Don't make an issue out of her lack of orgasms. If you put her in a position where she feels that all her reactions are going to be carefully observed and judged, she may never be able to relax enough to fully enjoy lovemaking. And if you invest your self-image in an attempt to "cure" her, the frustration and failure might undermine your own confidence. The pressure to produce, perform and achieve is the enemy of sexual satisfaction; one way to avoid anxiety would be to engage in nonorgasm-oriented activities such as storytelling, kissing or nongenital body massage. Learn to exchange simple pleasures. Masters and Johnson pioneered the view that sexual dysfunction is never a problem of the individual; they treat the relationship between partners as the patient. Take care of your relationship and orgasms should take care of themselves.

My fiancée and I enjoy a terrific sex life, except for one thing. She has never been able to experience an orgasm. She is perfectly normal in every other way. We enjoy fellatio, cunnilingus, all forms of intercourse and a lot of manual stimulation. She gets turned on, sweats, pants and shows all signs of excitement—but no orgasm. She complains that on the day after a heavy lovemaking session, her pelvic region aches. What causes this? Is it psychological? When I massage her clitoris, using either finger or tongue, she squirms and gets excited, then pushes me away, claiming that she finds touch unbearable. We really love each other and enjoy each other in every way, but things would be even better if she could begin having orgasms. I questioned her as to whether she could be having an orgasm and not know it, but she says no. Can you suggest some techniques we might employ to bring her to orgasm? —T. T., Bridgeport, Connecticut.

We suspect that she is not having an orgasm and knows it when she doesn't. The aching sensation the next day is the female equivalent of "blue balls." Blood gathers in the pelvic region during sexual excitement. An orgasm flushes out the accumulated blood, returning the body to normal. If the orgasm does not occur, the woman may experience that congestion as pain. Her other responses are sensitive during foreplay. The pleasure will turn to pain. That in itself is no reason to stop—just switch your attention elsewhere. The recommended cure for lack of orgasm is simple: self-help. Your girlfriend should teach herself to orgasm—via vibrators, or Water Pics, or shower massage units, or her own hand. Then she should take that knowledge to bed with her. Dr. Mary Jane Gray, writing in *Medical Aspects of Human Sexuality*, reports that, "apart from matters of technique, orgasm requires the trust which allows a complete loss of control. It may be that such loss of control is too much [for a woman] and that she pulls back from impending orgasm. She needs to recognize that the genital sensations of pleasure and pain can be very close together and to learn to relax into them rather than to analyze them."

What's Good for the Goose. . . .

My girlfriend suffers from a strange sexual reaction that—if I didn't know better—I would call premature ejaculation. She has a short, sharp orgasm as soon as I enter her. Thereafter, she ceases to lubricate and further stimulation is painful. My partner does not like to be left high and dry, so to speak. We're curious. Have you ever heard of this phenomenon and, if so, what is the cure? —W. U., Kansas City, Kansas.

Sex therapists have made a million-dollar industry out of the so-called problem of premature ejaculation. Now, it seems, they are expanding their business into new areas. A recent issue of *Medical Aspects of Human Sexuality* describes something called the female premature orgasm. Apparently, there are women who climax so rapidly that they are unable to fully savor the orgasmic experience. "If you shut your eyes, dear, you'll miss it completely." Two therapists gave the following solution to the problem: "Women with this complaint, like their male counterparts, need to learn to control voluntarily the timing of their orgasm. This can be done by having them practice getting to and maintaining the plateau stage of arousal. This is mastered with relative ease, simply by having a woman use a stop-and-go technique, first during masturbation and then with her partner, so that she learns to anticipate and then control her climax. The resulting orgasm is more pleasurable for her and, as it is integrated into lovemaking, for her partner as well." It seems to us that this overlooks certain factors. Too much emphasis can be placed on the state of a woman's lubrication—her dryness or wetness becomes an indicator of arousal. Dry is equated with impotence and/or failure. Many factors can affect lubrication; for example, if a woman is taking antihistamines, she will dry out all of the mucous membranes in her body, including those in the vagina. Also, most women tend to lubricate less after their first orgasm. If God had intended women to have only one orgasm, He wouldn't have invented K-Y jelly. Our prescription: Keep right on going after the quickie, using one of the commercial lubricants. A little dab will do you and her.

Pain on Intercourse

This spring, I met a beautiful young lady at a country-club dance. We started to date and gradually grew quite close. She confided in me that she was a virgin. One night, after an intimate dinner, I asked if we could make love and she agreed. I tried to be very gentle. I took off her blouse, kissing her neck, breasts and belly. (We had petted once or twice before, and I gave each area the attention it deserved and was used to.) I lay her on her back and lifted her by the buttocks to slip off her pants and underwear—then on impulse lifted her to my lips to perform cunnilingus. She responded completely and quickly reached orgasm. I was very excited, and so, without further delay, moved to enter her. She was a little tense and flinched when I tried to penetrate. There was no apparent obstacle, but she continued to experience pain. I am fairly well endowed and she didn't seem to be relaxing. I didn't know whether to slow down or speed up. My first orgasm settled the question for me. After resting, I tried to initiate a second round, but she refused, saying that once had been more than enough, that it had been total agony for her. Since then, she has refused to give it another try, for fear the same thing would happen. What should I do? —T. C., San Rafael, California.

An old sporting adage claims that if a girl hurts something while riding a horse, she should immediately get back in the saddle. The same advice holds true when it comes to sex. Fear and the anticipation of pain will often result in pain. In extreme cases, a woman can develop vaginismus—a condition in which the muscles at the entrance to the vagina tighten involuntarily at the thought of penetration. She may be totally responsive to other forms of stimulation but clench at the ultimate moment. Intercourse can be agonizing, if not impossible. Treatment for the problem usually consists of a gradual desensitization of the area, using a series of different-sized phallic objects. (Yes, there is a similarity to a set of upside-down Chinese boxes, but we refrained from mentioning it.) Find out from your girlfriend what she thinks caused the pain. It may have been lack of lubrication, which often diminishes after a first orgasm. Persuade her to try again, but don't push things: Let her initiate coitus—either by mounting you or by guiding you into her when she is ready. Cheerio.

Aural Sex

My lover says that she likes to be kissed in the ear. Indeed, she claims that aural stimulation causes her to reach orgasm. I've always thought that a woman required clitoral stimulation to reach orgasm. Is she pulling my leg? —T. R., Lyons, Illinois.

No, she's tugging your lobe. Perhaps you've heard the phrase "Stick it in her ear." It has physiological origins. Writing in *Medical Aspects of Human Sexuality,* Dr. George F. Melody notes that clitoral stimulation is not necessary: "Many women have a highly sensitive auriculogenital reflex, so that lingual stimulation of the external auditory canal—supplied by the nerve of Arnold, i.e., the auricular branch of the vagus nerve—will induce orgasm." We don't know who Arnold is, but the advice seems clear. If you've been avoiding this earogenous zone, it's time to whisper sweet nothings.

Cramps

Once a month, my girlfriend finds lovemaking intolerable. She has cramps during her period that are so painful, she is often paralyzed. She doesn't like to be touched, saying that her breasts also feel sore. Is this normal? Is there anything I can do to help? —M. C., Madison, Wisconsin.

A recent article in *Medical Self-Care* suggests the following: "Try to discuss how a lover feels about making love premenstrually or during her period. Some women prefer not to—pain or edema can interfere with the undivided attention lovemaking deserves. On the other hand, some women say lovemaking right before the start of menstruation, or during it, helps alleviate cramps. During orgasm, the uterus contracts and the cervix opens. This helps speed menstrual flow and reduces the duration of cramps in some women. Men should bear in mind, however, that this is a minority experience among women." For years, doctors have dismissed menstrual pain as psychosomatic, telling patients to take a few aspirins, et cetera. Unfortunately, aspirin doesn't work. However, in the past year, research teams have discovered a physical cause. A Cornell University Medical College team found that certain nonsteroidal anti-inflammatory drugs used to treat arthritis give good to com-

plete relief of menstrual pain in 80 percent of the cases. The drugs cited
were Motrin (generic name ibuprofen), Anaprox, Ponstel and Indocin.
Have your partner check with her doctor for more information.

Distracted During Sex

*Have you ever noticed how hard it is for some women to concentrate on sex?
My girlfriend has the opposite of a one-track mind—she can get derailed by noisy
neighbors, unfinished chores or the proverbial bread crumbs in bed. Once she
loses her momentum, it takes her a while to get started again and, frankly, I can't
always postpone my own pleasure for that long. Is her wandering attention a
sign that she is inhibited or that she just isn't interested? —E. Y., Portland,
Oregon.*

The man who said don't eat crackers in bed never dated anyone from
Georgia, but he did have a point—possibly the same one made by the
grim tale "The Princess and the Pea." Mistresses on mattresses are
easily distracted during sex. Psychologists may see the evasive action
as an "anxiety-motivated defense" or a "culturally induced inhibition,"
but Kinsey suggested that such behavior goes beyond the bedroom:
"Cheese crumbs spread in front of a copulating pair of rats may distract
the female but not the male. . . . When cattle are interrupted during
coitus, it is the cow that is more likely to be disturbed, while the bull
may try to continue with coitus." Furthermore, female cats have been
known to investigate mouse holes during intercourse. (We had a partner
who used to do that—damn irritating, but new baseboards broke her of
the habit.) Many women rate "privacy and freedom from intrusion"
second only to "quality of relationship with partner" as a factor in their
sexual satisfaction. Bear that in mind and find an appropriate setting for
your next tryst (bank vaults and fallout shelters are great favorites).
Also, you may find that if your girlfriend concentrates on something—
music or an erotic fantasy—she can "distract the distracter" and main-
line on the cannonball express.

Losing Consciousness During Sex

*My girlfriend has the disconcerting habit of losing consciousness at the climax
of sex. It's really starting to worry me. Is that a symptom of some kind of health
problem? —D. B., Dallas, Texas.*

Maybe it's your technique. Actually, there is nothing to worry about.
Sex therapist Avodah K. Offit describes this reaction: "Just as a penis
fills, so a woman's pelvis fills. Her vagina engorges; her large lips fill

their venous plexuses; the uterus may grow to twice its size because of all the blood in it. Climax expels immense amounts of blood from the pelvic plexuses. The literal amount of fluid that moves in and out of the orgasmic pool is enough, in some cases, to deprive women of consciousness, the same way that fainting does." The tide is high, so hold on.

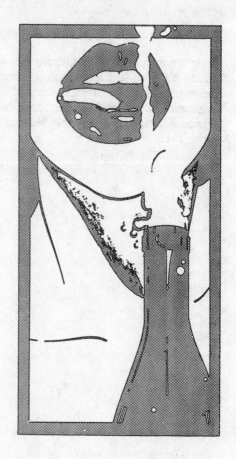

CHAPTER THREE

Sexual Pharma-copoeia

Alcohol and Orgasm

Some of the guys down at my local bar got into a debate on the effects of alcohol on sex. One guy pointed out that the ditty "Candy is dandy, but liquor is quicker" did not jibe with his own experience, that a few drinks can make you last longer. What's the straight info? —J. R., Chicago, Illinois.

You're dealing with two aspects of sex—interest and performance. There is no question that alcohol lowers inhibitions for some people and may speed the seduction process. But the time you save at the beginning of the evening can be lost in bed if you overindulge. Researchers at the University of Georgia found that in young male volunteers, there was a direct association between increased sexual arousal, decreased pleasurability and intensity of orgasm and reported difficulty in attaining orgasm. The results were very simple: The more a man drinks, the longer it takes to reach orgasm. That is great—to a point. The researchers also found that alcohol had the same effect on females as on males.

The more a woman drinks, the longer it takes her to reach orgasm. At that rate, you could start a nightly series, "Pleasure Held Hostage." The experiment was straightforward. Subjects would drink different amounts of alcohol and orange juice, watch erotic video tapes and masturbate. (Sounds like your basic frat party, right?) Whereas nondrinkers, on the average, reached climax after slightly more than five minutes, people who had a blood alcohol concentration of .03 percent took almost seven minutes. People with a blood alcohol concentration of .06 percent took more than ten minutes, while the .09 percent group averaged about twelve and a half minutes. (Note: Ten out of 24 subjects in the higher levels were unable to reach orgasm within 16 minutes.) For comparison—in most states, the legal limit is .1 percent—roughly equivalent to a 150-pound person downing four or five stiff ones. The moral: If you're too drunk to drive, you can always try parking; but don't expect the results to be much better. Moderation will produce the most desirable effects—both a loosening of inhibitions and the time to enjoy it.

Alcohol and Pregnancy

My wife and I are planning to have a child in the near future. We've been doing some reading and are somewhat worried. For example, we've read that women who drink have a greater chance of giving birth to an abnormal baby. Apparently, the problem is so severe, the Government is trying to force alcoholic-beverage companies into placing a warning label on bottles. Can you tell us more about this problem? —L. W., Miami, Florida.

Unless your wife has been drinking a pint of 80 proof a day and is already pregnant, you probably have nothing to worry about. In 1973, a team of doctors headed by K.L. Jones identified the Fetal Alcohol Syndrome. Children who were born to women who were heavy drinkers (150 grams of ethanol per day) displayed certain characteristics (facial abnormalities, deformed limbs, heart problems, stunted growth and delayed development). The study was not conclusive: Thomas D. Turner, dean emeritus of the Johns Hopkins University school of medicine, pointed out that other potentially damaging factors such as malnutrition, heavy smoking, drug usage and the age of the mother had not been taken into account. Also, the same symptoms have been found in the children of women who were teetotalers. The scientific community seems to be divided on the question of the effect of light or moderate dosages of alcohol. Studies have been done that indicate there is no significant difference between rare drinkers and moderate drinkers on the outcome of pregnancy. Dr. Ernest P. Noble and the National Institute on Alcohol Abuse and Alcoholism do "not endorse an abstinence policy for pregnant women because there is not clear-cut scientific data to support such conclusions. . . . In fact, major studies throughout this country and other international studies have indicated that small quantities of alcohol ingested daily are actually beneficial to the human system." The movement by government to put warning labels on alcoholic beverages seems to be an overreaction to slight evidence. However, the more we learn about pregnancy, the more we discover that everything seems to have some effect on the fetus, especially in its first weeks. It pays to plan ahead. A family should go into training for the big event. Consult your doctor for a complete list of forbidden fruits, recommended diets, et cetera, and then follow his advice.

Amyl Nitrite

Are poppers safe? A lot of my friends claim that amyl nitrite is a true aphrodisiac. I've tried some of the legal versions—the isobutyl nitrite—and all I end up with is a headache. What's the story? —L. S., Miami, Florida.

According to a report in *Medical Aspects of Human Sexuality*, some 500,000,000 doses of amyl and isobutyl nitrite were consumed last year for recreational purposes. Dr. Thomas P. Lowry explained the effects as follows: "When inhaled, the nitrites dilate the peripheral blood vessels (including the cerebral vessels), speed the heart and drop blood pressure about 20 mm/Hg. The EEG changes from alpha to beta with no pathologic patterns. Subjectively already pleasurable experiences are heightened, sexual sensations are enhanced, orgasm feels prolonged and exalted and activities that may have been repugnant or painful, such as fellatio or anal intercourse, become possible and/or desirable. Enthusiasts use terms like 'joy beyond words' and 'transcendent.'" Praise the Lord and pass the amyl, eh? The drug seems relatively safe: The Drug Abuse Warning Network has been unable to document a single death or permanent injury that could be traced to the use of poppers. Many users report that over-the-counter preparations of isobutyl nitrite produce headaches such as you experience. As for amyl nitrite—if you get caught, you may end up with a legal headache. Recreational use is frowned upon by the Feds.

Cocaine

Cocaine has become the counterculture's drug of choice and, although I haven't tried it yet, I've been collecting stories about the White Lady. I've heard that Freud was the first coke freak, that Sherlock Holmes indulged in the drug, that

New York narcs cut coke with ragweed pollen and sell it on the streets to turn people off, that the Ronald McDonald coffee stirrer is really a coke spoon and that the person who wrote "Coke is the real thing—what you want it to be" was not describing the beverage. Some of the routines are quite funny—I listened to one guy say that he had divided a purchase into two parts: "my gram and God's gram. I did my gram and then God did His" or: "Where do you buy a coke fork? In an empty head shop." In addition, I've been told that a dab of coke placed on the tip of the penis will retard ejaculation, while a dab placed on the clitoris before cunnilingus will drive a woman crazy. Can you confirm some of these stories, especially the one about the sexual characteristics of the drug? —S. K., Hartford, Connecticut.

The best source of information on cocaine is *The Gourmet Cokebook* from White Mountain Press. According to the authors, the drug "has historically been used as a climax inhibitor for both males and females as well as a sensory stimulant. This seemingly contradictory statement can be explained by the threshold theory of cocaine. If the drug is abused or overused during the course of a specific period of time, the strong sexually stimulative nature of the drug changes to one of sexual frustration, where erections and orgasms become almost impossible. Each person's tolerance must be determined by that person in order to prevent the unpleasant experience of sexual impotency, or frigidity." The authors point out that a fatal dose may range from 20 milligrams to 1.2 grams of pure cocaine. They also list the penalties for possession and intent to sell: Coke is a heavy trip.

Marijuana

I am a very healthy twenty-three-year-old female who thoroughly enjoys sex. The only problem is that I cannot have an orgasm with my partner unless I have smoked very high-quality marijuana prior to making love. When I do have orgasms, the feelings are incredible. They seem to last an eternity and my emotions are so intense that I am actually "inside" them. I can have orgasms while masturbating, but they're not quite the same. I know I have a dependency on marijuana, and I feel I must overcome it. Any suggestions? —Miss B. L., Big Sur, California.

Cough. Cough. Grass has been America's unofficial aphrodisiac for several years. Sin and Sinsemilla (the caviar of Cannabis) go well together. Woody Allen's film *Annie Hall* depicts a girl who shares your love of killer weed. There is a danger that an overanxious partner might object to your habit; i.e., are you getting off on your joint or his? But your friend sounds laid back, as well as laid. You don't mention what techniques you and your boyfriend use in your lovemaking. More and more women are saying that standard intercourse positions don't give them the clitoral stimulation that is necessary to climax. If you think this might be true in your case, don't worry about it. Just ask your boyfriend to give you a little more oral or manual attention. If the thought of a mechanical device doesn't offend you, invest in a vibrator and play with it together. We don't think how a woman climaxes during lovemaking is nearly as important as the fact that she does climax if she wants to. With patience, practice and love, you'll discover that to be true.

MDA

Counterculture chemists have come up with something called MDA—alias the Mellow Drug of America. Supposedly, it increases sexual excitement and generates a warm, diffused feeling of happiness: Take the love drug and no one is a stranger. I've heard it described as a combination of mescaline and speed, of mescaline and cocaine, of dehydrated Coors beer and champagne. Can you tell me more about the stuff? —B. S., Fort Lauderdale, Florida.

Methylenedioxamphetamine (MDA) was first synthesized in 1910. At various times, it has been tried as a cure for Parkinson's disease, as an appetite suppressant and as a potential cure for epilepsy. It proved ineffective and was put on the shelf but not, apparently, out of reach of drug-culture mad scientists. Chemically, MDA is similar to mescaline and speed. Officially classified as a hallucinogen, it stimulates the central nervous system and increases tactile sensitivity. (MDA freaks have been known to stand in the shower for hours getting off on the water. And who said hippies aren't clean?) The drug also creates a sense of euphoria, closeness, warmth and aesthetic enjoyment. It tends to make people talk, though the spontaneous reminiscences do not have the mythic or symbolic import of LSD raps. However, MDA is not a head of roses. As with any stimulant, an overdose can prove fatal. There is no evidence in drug literature of damage resulting from chronic use, but that may be due to the lack of tests. The drug is strictly street made and street sold—there is no pharmaceutical-quality MDA. A study conducted last year revealed that street MDA is relatively pure (only 10% of the samples proved to be something else, compared with a 38% counterfeit rate for LSD and a 68% rip-off rate for speed). Sometimes the drug is cut with atropine, LSD and amphetamine. If the bathtub chemist makes a mistake, the result may be PMA—a highly toxic and generally fatal drug. Enough said? The best love drug is a loaf of bread, a jug of wine and a cassette tape recorder singing beside you in the wilderness.

Saltpeter

Boys' schools and naval bases have always been the breeding ground of the idea that saltpeter can lower the male sex drive. I know that is nonsense, but several people at work say that there is now a chemical that diminishes the cravings of the horniest guy. True? —C. K., Houston, Texas.

Yes, there are several. Last year, *Forum Newsfront* reported on a British product (benperidol) that would undo the trick. Now the Schering Corporation of West Germany (where else?) has developed a form of chemical castration. Androcur (the company's trade name for cyproterone acetate) inhibits the function of the male sex hormone testosterone. Testosterone is a primary source of sexual desire—it activates the erotic centers in the brain and is a biological prerequisite for orgasm (i.e., it is vital to sperm production, erection and ejaculation). Sexual attraction can raise the level of blood testosterone. Anxiety, stress, defeat, humiliation and depression can result in low testosterone levels. Androcur does the same thing as the latter, with greater efficiency. The drug has been used to treat compulsive sex criminals in several European countries— after a few weeks on the drug, both the spirit and the flesh are unwilling, uninterested and unable. (Potency returns when the treatment is stopped.) The Germans believe that Androcur may be used to treat couples with unequal sex drives. A spokesman for Schering, Dr. A.W. Hircus, suggested: "There's no reason why a very small dosage of the drug could not be given to a hypersexual husband. It would reduce him to a 'once-a-week' man if, in fact, that is what his wife wants." Of course, if his once-a-week urge doesn't coincide with her once-a-week willingness, then there's trouble. The drug is not available in the United States—before it can be sold here, it must pass rather stringent tests. Since the male sex hormones also influence nonsexual behavior such as energy, appetite and aggressiveness, the side effects of Androcur might not be desirable. Imagine if the drug fell into the wrong hands. Radical guerrillas might dump a large quantity into the water-supply system of Pasadena and no one would ever know.

Strychnine

Can strychnine be used as an aphrodisiac? There was a reference to the drug in a movie (I think it was Harry and Tonto*) that led me to believe it increases potency. Is this true? —L. B., Kansas City, Kansas.*

Only for necrophiliacs. For many years, strychnine preparations have been used as tonics to stimulate the central nervous system. A combination of strychnine, thyroid and yohimbine is sometimes prescribed for "temporary psychogenic impotence," but the possible side effects (fainting, dizziness and vomiting) are a bummer. According to *Pharmacological Basis of Therapeutics*, strychnine is not for kicks: "To the drug have been ascribed properties which it does not possess, or which it exhibits only when administered in toxic doses." Strychnine increases excitability by selectively blocking neural inhibition; any stimulus then produces an exaggerated reflex—fatal convulsions. If you think this sounds like a "Masterpiece Theater" production of the pornographic murder mystery *Strychnine and Black Lace*, you're right.

CHAPTER FOUR

Make Love Not Babies

Birth Control—The Overview

My girlfriend is leery of using the pill, due to various reports of adverse side effects. I'm leery of becoming a father. Can you tell us the relative safety and contraceptive value of other birth control methods? —C. Z., Dallas, Texas.

We can do you one better. The Food and Drug Administration has a free chart that compares the different methods of birth control, including the advantages and disadvantages of each. Send a postcard to the Consumer Information Center, Department 692F, Pueblo, Colorado 81009, for a copy of *Contraception: Comparing the Options.* The chart points out that no nonsurgical method of contraception is 100 percent effective (unless you count abstinence or an exclusive diet of oral sex). The pill is still considered the most effective: If a thousand women took the pill for a year under perfect conditions, three or four of them would probably become pregnant. But conditions are seldom perfect, as figures for the other methods show. The differences in various field tests are staggering. For every 100 women using a given method for one year, 1 to 6 will become pregnant using a diaphragm with cream, jelly or foam; 2 to 29 will become pregnant using foam, cream or jelly alone and 3 to 36 will become pregnant if their partner uses a condom. The chart also gives interesting figures for various rhythm methods. The calendar method (in which the woman tries to calculate the time of her peak fertility from the time of her last menstrual cycle) is least effective: Of 100 women using this method, 14 to 47 will become pregnant. The temperature method is more successful: The woman keeps an accurate daily record of her body temperature using a special thermometer (body temperature rises after ovulation) and avoids intercourse during her hot days. Of 100 women using this method, 1 to 20 will become pregnant. The mucous method is almost as successful: The woman keeps an accurate daily record of vaginal secretions to determine ovulation. One to 25 will become pregnant. Variations on the temperature and mucous methods are more effective. If the woman abstains from lovemaking until ovulation has passed, she is fairly safe. Of 100 women using this approach, 1 to 7 will become pregnant. Of course, you can't make love for half of each month, but that's not a problem if you have lovers on different cycles.

Early Times

What type of birth-control devices were used in earlier times? I am particularly interested in the saloon houses of the old West. Am I wrong, or did cowboys end up using old socks as makeshift condoms? —W. J., Coraopolis, Pennsylvania.

You have your historical periods mixed up. Weren't you paying attention in school, or better yet, in the schoolyard? We thought everyone had heard the refrain: "In days of old, when knights were bold / And rubbers weren't invented / They tied a sock around their cocks / And babies were prevented." Cowboys had access to condoms and used them, if not for birth control, then as a V.D. preventive. The saloon girls of the wild West were a sophisticated lot. They were known to try douching, withdrawal and the use of a sponge as a primitive diaphragm. Douching supposedly was introduced to the American public in 1832 by Dr. Charles Knowlton in a work called *Fruits of Philosophy* (no jokes). The book sold thousands of copies and for the next hundred years or so, douching ranked right behind the condom and withdrawal (or coitus interruptus—as in "You better git, cowboy, I hear the sheriff coming"). None of those methods is particularly effective—which is why there are so many little cowpokes.

The Condom Comeback

Over the past few months, I've run into several women who have abandoned the traditional forms of birth control. They say that they no longer want sole responsibility for contraception, nor do they want to sacrifice their bodies to pills or I.U.D.s. If a man wants to have sex, he should carry a condom around in his wallet. I had one woman tell me that reluctance to use a condom is a sign of American male chauvinism. I am reluctant to sacrifice sensitivity. Any suggestions? —E. D., New York, New York.

Well, one thing you should not do is carry a condom around in your wallet for days. Body heat can cause the rubber to deteriorate. Better to keep them at bedside, or, better yet, have your girlfriend carry them around in her purse. As for American males' being less conscientious, your friend may have a point. Of the more than 250,000,000 people in the world using some method of birth control, about one out of three relies on male contraception, with 37,000,000 using condoms and 35,000,000 using vasectomy. Condom use is coming back. Sales in the United States grew from 300,000,000 in 1975 to nearly 500,000,000 in 1980. It's time to check them out: Condoms have a theoretical effectiveness of 97 percent and a use effectiveness of 90 percent. Some men claim that they limit sensation, but that seems to be a self-defeating prophecy. In Japan, where 79 percent of the men use condoms, one almost never hears that complaint. The attitude seems to be more the result of condom advertising than of condom use: Competing brands claim to deliver greater sensitivity, though the actual differences in thickness are negligible. We suggest that you find a brand you like and, er, stick to it. One writer has suggested that the primary benefit of condom use is that no one has to sleep on the wet spot.

The Quest for the Perfect Condom

With all the bad press the pill has gotten recently, I've decided to switch to condoms for birth control. I have found that the various lubricated condoms I've tried have too much or too little lubrication and that the unlubricated models are uncomfortable. Also, I find they cut down a bit on feeling. Any recommendations? —H. S., Miami, Florida.

Finding the perfect condom is purely a matter of trial and error. You'll have to go to the local pharmacy and buy one of every kind till you find something to your liking. A willing partner will make the experiment a lot more fun. If you decide on an unlubricated condom, to which you apply your own lubricant, remember to use K-Y jelly—not petroleum jelly. Petroleum products can dissolve the latex, with disastrous results. As for feeling: Condoms made from skin seem to enhance sensation by conducting body heat. A recent study suggests that the decrease in sensitivity may be an advantage. Twenty-seven percent of the people polled felt that the reduction in sensitivity helped prolong intercourse. While most people who use condoms report diminished feeling, some 8 percent of the women polled actually found that they increased sensitivity. It takes all kinds to fill the freeway.

Imported vs. Domestic

Condoms seem to be the only form of birth control that does not produce unhealthy side effects. What's more, they are readily available—you don't need to see a doctor to get them. My only problem with the damn things is size. I happen to be somewhat well endowed—not enough to make it as a porn star but enough to feel a tight squeeze when I slip into a safe. One of my best friends has the opposite problem—he feels lost in a normal condom. Does anyone market them in sizes? —H. V., Knoxville, Tennessee.

America is a democracy: It's one man, one vote and one size for all. Upright citizens at either extreme are left in the lurch. However, there are several solutions. The most intriguing involves international smuggling. (Government emission-control standards prohibit more than the importation of some foreign cars. The Food and Drug Administration refuses entry to imported condoms. Next thing you know, it'll be asking you to look for a union tag on your safes.) If you have a friend who flies to London, have him or her pick up Durex condoms. For some reason, British condoms are larger than American brands. (It may just be limey arrogance; those guys keep more than a stiff upper lip.) Those of you who feel lost in American condoms should try picking up Japanese brands, which are somewhat smaller. Also, they are one third the thickness of American condoms and thus are more sensitive. The thin condom is just as safe—the difference in thickness results in perhaps one additional pregnancy for every 2,500,000–5,000,000 acts of coitus. (If you're scoring *that* often, you deserve to have a kid.) Also, try experimenting with American brands. Condoms made of animal skin are larger than those made of latex—because they cannot stretch, they have to be more accommodating. (The lubricant keeps them in place.) On the other end of the scale, your friend might try Slims—which are 5 percent smaller in diameter than normal condoms. They are distributed by Population Planning Associates, 403 Jones Ferry Road, P.O. Box 400, Carrboro, North Carolina 27510. And remember, if the safe fits, wear it.

Condoms—How to Use

I'm an eighteen-year-old who has just started to enjoy sex. It's not half bad once you get the hang of things. My only problem is birth control. None of the girls I date seem to be taking any precautionary measures. (I always make it a point to ask.) So I've decided to equip myself with condoms. My question is this:

Is there any easy way to put on and take off a rubber? It never feels right. The moment is awkward and the flow of the evening is interrupted. In your eternal wisdom, do you know of a graceful way of handling the situation? —J. L., Memphis, Tennessee.

Well, we know of one guy who puts a condom on before he goes out on a date. We can't recommend that. Then there are the guys who pull out and slip into their safes shortly before ejaculation. They're called fathers. (The penis secretes seminal fluid long before ejaculation and impregnation can occur. It doesn't help to close the barn door after the come has gone.) The easiest and most graceful way to get into a condom is with a little help from your friends. The girl will be returning a favor and the added strokes can be a turn-on in themselves. What you do later is largely a matter of taste. We do not recommend filling your condoms with water and dropping them off the balcony of your high-rise. And don't flush them down the toilet. According to Barbara and Gideon Seaman, authors of *Women and the Crisis in Sex Hormones*, fish have been found strangled by the condoms wrapped around them.

And When

My girlfriend and I are in the midst of a heated debate that threatens our relationship. She was advised to go off the pill by her doctor. Since then, we have resorted to using prophylactics for contraceptive purposes. One night, we were enjoying a vigorous 69 session. After I had come in her mouth, she implored me to enter her. An argument ensued when I insisted on using a rubber. She said that there is so little sperm left after an ejaculation that there would be little chance of her getting pregnant. She was willing to take the chance of having intercourse with no means of contraception. I argued that there was enough sperm still active after my ejaculation to impregnate her. Who is right? —K. M., Tinley Park, Illinois.

It takes only one little bugger to make a woman pregnant—and there are more than that kicking around after an ejaculation. She may be willing to take the chance of pregnancy, but it is not her sole responsibility. You acted reasonably. You might tell her that she had overlooked the possibility of a *second* ejaculation (after all, she is good in bed). After you've made up, you can try for that second orgasm.

How to Buy a Condom

Like most guys my age (I am a college freshman), I suffer great embarrassment asking for prophylactics at the drugstore when there are little old ladies around or

when the salesclerk is a girl, or both, as is usually the case. Can you help?
—P. T., Hardwick, Massachusetts.

You might try the classic late Forties approach: Stand off to one side, memorizing the ingredients listed on toothpaste tubes and hair-tonic bottles, until a male salesclerk or pharmacist shows up, then shuffle over, stare at the chewing gum display and mumble your request. Pharmacists, who are adept at translating doctors' handwriting and adolescents' embarrassment, will supply the prophylactics, but they may ask loudly: "What size do you want, sonny?" (Don't fall for this professional "in" joke—there is only one size.) This ritual ordeal is senseless and ineffective; the result has been called the population explosion. We advise a straightforward approach. The sex of the persons behind or near the counter is irrelevant: There is nothing to be embarrassed about. Discuss with your doctor or a knowledgeable friend the different kinds of condoms and when you go to the drugstore, ask for them by brand name. Always buy more than you think you need—unabashed conspicuous consumption is one cure for what you *feel* is conspicuous. We can think of only two situations that require an alternate approach: (1) If you are planning to date the girl behind the counter, the quantity you buy may enhance or diminish your reputation; (2) if the pharmacist behind the counter is the father of the girl you are planning to date, you should consider going to another pharmacy. If that isn't possible, write to: Population Planning Associates, Box 2556, Chapel Hill, North Carolina 27514. They sell prophylactics by mail.

Should a Woman Offer a Man a Condom

What do you think of a woman who keeps a supply of condoms in her bedside table? The other night, I met a girl at a singles bar, went with her to her home, and as we were climbing into the sack, she pulled open a drawer and offered me "protection." I was so taken aback that I almost couldn't get it up. I thought maybe they belonged to her husband and I was in big trouble. She said that she had bought them herself. Have you ever heard of girls' doing this? —S. H., New York, New York.

If the safe fits, wear it. A spokesperson for the Planned Parenthood Federation of America says that it is becoming increasingly common for women to buy condoms. By combining them with a foam, suppository or other type of barrier method, a couple can nearly match the effectiveness of an I.U.D. or the pill without the side effects. They can also prevent the spread of dread social diseases. Your lady is experienced enough to know that many men are still too embarrassed to buy condoms (why do you think there are so many unplanned pregnancies?).

Our advice: See the woman again. Only this time, ask her to buy a couple of dozen. Maybe even a gross. You have plans for a big weekend.

The Golden Valve

I recall reading an article in Life *magazine years ago about a device that promised to be the new wave of birth control. Doctors were experimenting with little gold valves that could be inserted into the penis to control the flow of semen. Whatever became of the device? —R. C., Detroit, Michigan.*

Marc Goldstein and Michael Feldberg, authors of *The Vasectomy Book*, a report on birth control, describe the history of valve research: "At least two kinds of valves have been developed: one which must be opened and closed by a urologist through an incision in the scrotum similar to that required by a vasectomy and another which, in theory at least, can be opened and closed by passing a magnet across the scrotum.

"In the early Seventies, vas valves were thought to hold great promise as a reversible form of male contraception. But certain problems with the concept quickly became apparent. For one thing, switching the valves on and off has proved to be quite a problem, particularly in the magnetic types. For another, once implanted, the valves have not been able to guarantee that sperm will be able to flow through them freely. The surgical-implant site is even more prone to the problems of leaking and granuloma than are traditional vasectomy sites. Finally, like a conventional vasectomy, a closed valve produces back pressure on the epididymis and rete testis that can lead to tearing and granuloma in those areas that can render a man infertile even after his valve has been switched to open again. In short, while the concept of a vas valve is clever and appealing, the technology still has a long way to go." There you have it.

The Cervical Cap

My girlfriend would like to switch her method of birth control. We both hate the diaphragm and realize that our reluctance to use it has brought us very close to parenthood too many times. The pill is out and the I.U.D. seems to have more than its share of complications (though my girlfriend's doctor told her that many of the problems with the I.U.D. stemmed from multiple partners, not from the device itself). Several of our feminist friends have recommended something called a cervical cap. What is it? —J. L., New York, New York.

It's a little red thing with a tassel that Shriners wear. Just kidding. The cervical cap is a medical rediscovery, of sorts. Essentially, it is a thimble-shaped cap that fits over the cervix. It is held in place by suction and acts as a barrier to sperm. The method has been in use for centuries: According to one report, Casanova presented a prospective lover with half a squeezed lemon to use as a cervical cap. Other caps were made from molded opium, aluminum, gold, platinum, silver, ivory—but the one you're most likely to find will be made of rubber or plastic. The method fell out of use during the Thirties, for no apparent reason. Now, thanks to the feminist grapevine, and Barbara and Gideon Seaman's *Women and the Crisis in Sex Hormones*, various clinics are distributing caps to women who request them. The FDA has *not* approved the cap as a form of birth control, because the required research has not been done. Unofficial estimates, however, suggest that the cap is as effective as the diaphragm (without repeated applications of spermicidal jelly). It seems less likely to become dislodged during an especially active session. It can be left in place without discomfort. In short, it seems to have a lot going for it. Already, doctors are working on a better cap—one that allows uterine secretions to exit through a one-way valve. Neat. You may want to join the vanguard; or wait for the research to be completed. We'll keep you posted.

A Hot Time in the Old Town

I have heard that if a man exposes his genitals to heat by sitting in a sauna, warming them with a hot-water bottle or taking a steam bath, he will become temporarily sterile. It would seem to be an ideal method of birth control. Instead of taking a cold shower and abstaining, I could slide into the tub and boogie. Yee-hah! "Some like it hot" would take on a new meaning. Is there any truth in the theory and, if so, should I incorporate it into my sex life? —S. S., Neenah, Wisconsin.

Jack be nimble, Jack be quick, Jack jump over the candlestick and on top of the nearest consenting adult. Great in theory, but the practice leaves something to be desired. Heat has been known to diminish the production of sperm. Spermatogenesis takes place at a temperature slightly lower than 37 degrees centigrade (the testicles hang free for air conditioning). A slight prolonged rise in temperature can disrupt the process, but that is a far cry from foolproof birth control. Recently, scientists at the University of Missouri subjected goats, dogs, monkeys and rats to different forms of heat treatment—ultrasound (what a funny place to wear headphones), microwave (do you like your meat rare, medium or well done?) and hot baths, with varying degrees of success. For example, rodent Romeos who were given a fifteen-minute bath in water heated to 60 degrees centigrade, compared with a normal body temperature of 37 degrees centigrade, were unable to impregnate females for thirty to thirty-five days. The research looks promising, but scientists have yet to determine the temperature requirements for humans or the length of exposure to heat. Of course, if you take only one hot bath a month, you won't have to worry about birth control, but not for the reason you think. For now, keep to the more reliable methods.

Sex on the Rocks

One of my roommates claims to have discovered an effective method of birth control. An hour or so before engaging in intercourse, he exposes his testicles to extreme cold by applying an ice pack. He says that the sudden change in body temperature kills the sperm cells. Either he is right or he is incredibly lucky, because he is not a father. What is your opinion? —N. C., Knoxville, Tennessee.

A funny thing happens to people who employ unconventional birth-control methods—they become parents. This tactic has a few noticeable drawbacks: for example, we can't see carrying an ice pack around in our wallet on dates. Doctors believe that a decrease in temperature may slow down the movement of sperm cells, but it certainly won't kill them or prevent conception. Sperm banks keep their deposits in cold storage. If your friend wants to freeze his balls off, fine, but he should use more reliable contraceptive techniques when he thaws out.

Diaphragms

Because of the adverse publicity surrounding birth-control pills, my girlfriend switched to a diaphragm. I've heard that those devices can sometimes slip out of position during intercourse—with pregnancy a possible result. Is that true? —L. S., Dallas, Texas.

Dr. Mary E. Lane, writing in *Medical Aspects of Human Sexuality*, reports that diaphragms can be dislodged during sex. When the vagina expands during the excitement phase, the diaphragm may lose contact with the wall of the vagina and slip away. This mishap is most likely to occur when the woman is on top during lovemaking and her partner keeps losing his place, having to reinsert his penis. But don't be alarmed. Such displacements are rare: If a diaphragm fits snugly and is used properly in conjunction with a spermicidal preparation, the method is 98 percent effective.

Foams: Are They Safe?

My girlfriend recently switched from the pill to a combination of a diaphragm and spermicidal foam. I have a few questions. I enjoy performing oral sex. Is the foam dangerous? If spermicides kill sperm, are they poison? Do they pose a danger to me or my partner? —J. B., Boston, Massachusetts.

This reminds us of the philosophical question, At what point does meat tenderizer stop tenderizing? First the good news. According to an article in *Medical Self-Care,* spermicides do not kill sperm by poisoning them. Rather, "they alter the pH of the vagina, increasing its acidity to the point where sperm are immobilized. As a result, authorities say there is no reason to fear harm from vaginally absorbed spermicides, or from their inadvertent ingestion, except for the possibility of an allergic reaction (itching, irritation, rash)." In short, it is doubtful that you can ingest enough to do yourself in. (A simple suggestion: engage in oral sex before applying the foam.) Now for the bad news. While spermicides are safe for the people who use them, there is some evidence that they are not safe for children conceived while the parents are using them. A study by the Boston Collaborative Drug Surveillance Program suggests that children of women who use spermicides—children who were conceived in spite of the birth-control method—have a slightly higher incidence of birth defects. (About 2.2% of infants born to users develop birth defects, compared with only 1% in the offspring of women who do not use spermicides.) There is also a higher incidence of miscarriage. Scientists believe that the spermicide can damage both sperm and the egg, resulting in a less-than-healthy fetus. However, the results of the study are inconclusive. Our advice: Don't have children by accident. Plan your parenthood. Do it when you want to—not because you have to.

The Pause That Refreshes

My girlfriend and I have just switched methods of contraception (she thought she needed a rest from the pill). Our choice is to use a diaphragm and contraceptive foam. My question is this: How long is the foam effective? Sometimes we engage in marathons, with three or four separate sexual acts within a relatively short time. Is one shot of foam enough? —E. R., Boston, Massachusetts.

Sorry to break your rhythm, but according to a medical report on current concepts in contraceptive treatment, you should partake of a pause that refreshes: The active ingredient in foam becomes diluted and less effective with time. For maximum effectiveness, foam must be reinserted prior to each act of intercourse. The report also states that there is no clinical or scientific data to support the theory that it is necessary to take a rest from the pill. In fact, statistics show that unless another method is used during that time (the choice you made), a rest period is a primary cause of unplanned pregnancy. If the constant use of foam is a bummer, switch back to the pill.

The Rhythm Method

My girlfriend has decided to have her I.U.D. removed. We are currently debating what form of birth control to use. We've discussed the diaphragm, but all the women she has talked with say that they hate the thing, both because they have to stop sex to insert the rubber cap, and because the use of the spermicidal foam eliminates the attractiveness of oral sex. The other method we have in mind—one of the newer forms of the rhythm method, in which a woman takes her temperature and studies her mucous secretions to determine when she's ovulating—bothers me because it means we have to abstain for seven or so days. What do you recommend? —P. M., Dallas, Texas.

The pill spoiled everyone—we could make love and fall asleep. We didn't have to think about birth control. As a result, we've gotten out of practice (of thinking, that is). There is no reason that a rhythm method demands seven days of abstinence. How do you think Greek Week got its name? Or, if you aren't into anal sex, how about a week of oral sex? Probably the best solution is to combine the methods—and use the diaphragm and/or condoms during the peak fertility period. As for the diaphragm's interfering with the momentum of the sex act and eliminating cunnilingus—nonsense. The liberated couples we know simply engage in a few preliminary rounds of sex in various attitudes, and then, when everyone finally comes up for air, or for a postorgasm cigarette, a few minutes are set aside to prepare for the title bout. The point we are trying to make is that you should not let anxiety about your birth-control method interfere with your pleasure.

My girlfriend recently showed me an article on astrological birth control that claimed the method is completely natural and 98 percent effective. The article explained that a woman has two periods of fertility each month—one based on the menstrual-ovulation cycle and one based on the angle of the sun and moon at the time of her birth (i.e., a woman is fertile during ovulation and whenever there is a full moon, if she was born during a full moon). There usually are thirteen astrological fertile days each year. To prevent pregnancy, a woman abstains from sex for three days prior to, and for all the days of, peak fertility. In addition, she follows the ordinary rhythm method and abstains from sex from the tenth through the twenty-third day of her menstrual cycle. My girlfriend is eager to switch to this method, but I would like your opinion first. Is it effective? —A. C., West Orange, New Jersey.

The ordinary rhythm method is only 65 percent effective, primarily because women are not as regular as other heavenly bodies. Astrological birth control merely adds a few more forbidden days to the monthly calendar, so that you end up practicing near abstinence, which is a very effective form of birth control. We wouldn't call it natural. Unless you can find true joy in a lovemaking schedule that coincides with the appearances of Halley's comet, your girl had better avoid this gift to star-crossed lovers.

The I.U.D.—A History

My girlfriend switched from the pill to an intrauterine birth-control device. So far, she's had no problems, but I've heard that they can be dangerous and that some models have been recalled by the factory. How does an I.U.D. work and how would my girlfriend know whether or not her particular model is defective? —J. R., Chicago, Illinois.

I.U.D.s are based on a principle that originated with camel drivers. A pregnant camel would slow the progress of a desert caravan: it was found that a date pit inserted into the uterus of a camel seemed to prevent conception. (This may or may not have been the source of the phrases "dry humping" and "I've got a hot date tonight.") Actually, neither the date pit nor the I.U.D. is a true contraceptive: An egg can still be fertilized. However, internal organs tend to be sensitive to foreign substances: the presence of an I.U.D. in the womb causes an exaggerated uterine motility: the egg cannot adhere to the uterine wall and eventually is expelled. In some cases, the body will try to reject the I.U.D.; the uterine wall may be punctured, an infection may result, et cetera. Last year, the A. H. Robins Company indefinitely suspended sale and distribution of one I.U.D.—the Dalkon Shield. The process was similar to a Detroit recall. The company informed doctors who had used its product of the various problems that had come to its attention. Doctors then used their own discretion in passing the information on to patients (any woman using an I.U.D. should consult her gynecologist regularly). No doubt you've heard the story about the woman who made an appointment to exchange her shield on the same day her Buick was going into the shop to have its brake assembly replaced. She got the two confused. . . .

The I.U.D. and P.I.D.

Can you tell me what is going on with birth control? It seems that one by one the accepted methods have been getting the ax from concerned feminists. First the pill, and now I.U.D.s. My girlfriend is quite worried over reports that I.U.D.s can contribute to infertility and pelvic infection. She is thinking of switching to a combination of diaphragm and condoms—which sounds fine in theory but would rule out any spontaneous sex acts (in taxicabs or whatever). We'd much prefer a passive method that we don't have to think about every time we make love. How great is the risk of using an I.U.D.? —M. W., Portland, Oregon.

It has been estimated that between 2 and 4 percent of the women using I.U.D.s are susceptible to pelvic inflammatory disease, or P.I.D., a disease that can destroy the Fallopian tubes and ovaries and make pregnancy impossible at a later date. The statistic is somewhat misleading. Doctors view it as manageable, in the way that a 7 percent unemployment rate is manageable for the economy. But, as someone once pointed out, if you belong to the 7 percent, you are 100 percent unemployed, and if you are one of the unfortunate women who develop P.I.D., you can become 100 percent sterile. We are reluctant to throw out the birth-control device with the bath water, because it's not clear that the I.U.D. is the sole cause of pelvic inflammatory disease. More frequently, that condition is the result of an undetected case of gonorrhea. If caught early, P.I.D. can be treated with antibiotics. (Some of the symptoms are fever, menstrual cramps, increased bleeding and cramps during the menstrual period, an abnormal vaginal discharge and pain during intercourse.) In any case, no method of birth control should be considered passive. It is your job to be an informed consumer. Have your girlfriend ask her doctor for information about the I.U.D.—what the danger signs of P.I.D. are, et cetera. If he doesn't give answers, get another doctor, not another method of contraception.

The String—To Cut or Not to Cut

When my girlfriend switched from the pill to an I.U.D., we thought our troubles were over. Not so. Now, everytime we screw, my penis feels as though it's grinding against an emery board. The culprit responsible for the discomfort seems to be the stiff nylon cord attached to the I.U.D. The damn thing must be seven inches long. Does it need to be that long? And is there a way we can benefit from the I.U.D. without the damn string? As it is, pain is a very effective contraceptive. —J. E., Los Angeles, California.

Your friend's doctor is a bozo. When an I.U.D. is inserted, the doctor should trim the cord, so that it won't interfere with intercourse. The string is important, however, as a method of checking if the I.U.D. is still in place. But you can ask your friend to go back to the doctor and let him snip the excess footage. This procedure, we suspect, was the origin of the term pinking shears. May you have a smooth re-entry.

Vasectomy

I am thinking of having a vasectomy, but first I need to have a few questions answered. From what I understand, the body continues to produce sperm cells after the operation. What happens to the little buggers? I have this vision of my body becoming an Arlington National Cemetery of dead sperm cells. I've heard reports of microsurgeons reconnecting the severed ducts. I am curious: Is the operation reversible? —L. D., Madison, Wisconsin.

We can see a choir of angelic sperm cells singing, "Oh, that magic feeling, nowhere to go." In most cases, the body simply assimilates the sperm cells. However, in approximately half the men who have had vasectomies, the body seems to react to the sperm as foreign matter and produces sperm antibodies. There appear to be two kinds of sperm antibodies—one type causes the sperm to clump together; the other decreases sperm mobility. Neither type seems to be harmful, but you should be aware that antibodies have been found in nonvasectomized males with fertility problems: Even if you have the ducts reconnected through microsurgery, the antibodies that have built up will remain. There is a low incidence of fertility among men who have had the operation reversed. Most doctors still consider a vasectomy to be permanent.

I am considering having a vasectomy. Are there any complications after the operation? —N.P.R., Evansville, Indiana.

Vasectomy has fewer side effects than any other form of contraception. Minor discomfort can arise directly after the procedure (swelling and bruising of the scrotal skin), but it usually disappears without treatment. After any kind of surgery, hemorrhage and infection can occur. Two infrequent complications following vasectomies are epididymitis and sperm granuloma. Epididymitis is an infection of the tube at the back of the testes. Sperm granuloma is not some kind of kinky health-food breakfast but rather is an inflammation that is thought to be caused by sperm leakage from the cut ends of the vas. (Both conditions are not very serious and can be treated.) However, the over-all incidence of epididymitis is less than 2 percent and of sperm granuloma less than 1 to 3 percent. No hormonal changes occur after vasectomy: so there's no danger of your being a candidate for the Vienna Boys Choir. In less than 1 percent of vasectomy cases, the vas spontaneously reconnects, making unexpected fatherhood a possible, and embarrassing, complication.

Missing the Pill

What are the chances of my girlfriend's getting pregnant if she forgets to take her birth-control pill one evening? —E. T., Las Vegas, Nevada.

That's not something that Jimmy the Greek gives odds on, but here goes: The risk of pregnancy depends primarily on the type of birth-control pill being used at the time. If your girlfriend takes a combination of estrogen and progestin, the chances of pregnancy are slight (especially if she has been taking the pill for more than three months). The progestin creates an inhospitable environment in the uterus, so that should ovulation occur because of a missed pill, the egg will be unable to develop. If she takes a "mini" pill (with a smaller dose of progestin and no estrogen), the chance of ovulation and pregnancy is almost ten times as great. (If one to five pills are missed, the pregnancy rate rises to 7.2 %.) So if she forgets the pill one evening, she should take it the next morning, and then take that day's pill that night at the regular time. Then keep your fingers crossed, if not her legs.

The Pill and Desire

Over the past few months, I have grown very close to a woman who lives in my building. She and I see each other frequently and usually wind up an evening making love. Although our foreplay is great, she says she loses all desire as soon as I enter her. She is taking birth-control pills and believes that they may be the cause of the problem. Needless to say, I am quite concerned. Could the pills be to blame? —L. C., Memphis, Tennessee.

It may be a bitter pill to swallow, but some women lose their desire for intercourse after they've been taking contraceptives for a while. (This peculiar side effect brings to mind the old joke about the best form of birth control being a firm, polite "I don't feel anything.") We suggest that she ask her gynecologist to change her prescription to a pill with a different hormone level or that she switch to an I.U.D. or a diaphragm. Or you might start using condoms. If the situation doesn't improve, increase the amount of time you spend on noncoital sex play. She may simply be one of those women who respond to oral and manual stimulation but not to intercourse. Two out of three isn't bad.

CHAPTER FIVE

Venereal Disease

Gonorrhea

My girlfriend of a few months has just discovered that she has gonorrhea. It has been a year since she last saw her doctor and she had a few partners before finding me. Likewise, I led an active social life before meeting her—but, to my knowledge, never had symptoms of the disease. We are trying to act civilized about the whole thing, but it is very hard to avoid blaming one or the other. As we go through the cure, I wonder, is there some way to avoid this hassle? —G. W., Detroit, Michigan.

Over the past ten years, gonorrhea has increased in this country at a rate four times that of the population growth. Many cases (especially among women) are asymptomatic. The carriers do not know that they have the disease until their partners discover that they have it. Probably the only way to end the problem would be to line up every citizen in America, blindfold all of them and shoot them with antibiotics at the same moment. (Ironically, the Government is willing to spend millions on swine-flu vaccine, but not on social disease. But then, maybe politicians are more worried about something that can be contracted from pigs than from people.) In the meantime, it is your duty to help contain the epidemic. Women are taught to visit their gynecologist regularly. It strikes us as odd that men do not receive the same common-sense advice. Ask your doctor to check for V.D. at your annual physical or make it a point to visit a doctor whenever you expand your social circle and increase the chance of exposure. The routine would certainly help eliminate the embarrassment, the accusations and the tacky dinner conversations that follow this kind of episode. This approach may be cautious, but consider the alternatives: Cases of venereal complications are also on the increase. Doctors report a rash of gonorrheal arthritis, gonorrheal ophthalmia and partial or complete blockage of the Fallopian tubes in women. So do it now; the love you save may be your own.

Asymptomatic Gonorrhea

What's the incidence of invisible V.D. among teenagers? The latest locker-room tales warn of a kind of gonorrhea that has no symptoms. A person doesn't know when he or she has it and so can spread it through a whole class. How can you discover if you have it? And how do you break the news to your friends? —S. C., Atlanta, Georgia.

The actual frequency of asymptomatic gonorrhea is low. One study found that 1.9 percent of sexually active young men and 7 percent of sexually active young women had the disease. The men seem responsible for passing it along (24 percent had had more than one partner, compared with only 6 percent of the women). We have always felt that it was the responsibility of the individual to look after himself, to take care of the instrument through regular checkups. Not just when you have obvious symptoms. Not just when you come back from spring break in Tijuana. When it comes to telling your friends, you have a choice. You can be absolutely frank: "First the good news—it's not the dread Vietnamese Black Rose. It won't fall off and it can be treated." Or you can use the tried-and-true polite myth. Explain that you caught it from a toilet seat or a light switch. Of course, then you may have to explain what kind of kinky sex you were trying with the light switch. We prefer the frank approach. Maybe someday Hallmark will come out with a line of special greeting cards for the occasion.

Double Trouble

I lead a very active sex life and am finally facing the consequences. The last time I went to the doctor, he found I had gonorrhea (I thought I might have been exposed to it) and then proceeded to run tests for just about every other known venereal disease from syphilis to nonspecific urethritis. His comment was that if I had one, chances were I had two or three. Was he going overboard? It made me feel like I'd made love in a leper colony. —L. D., Los Angeles, California.

You have a good doctor. A researcher recently reported in *Medical Aspects of Human Sexuality* that he found that between 25 and 40 percent of gonorrhea patients are also infected with Chlamydia trachomati (the cause of about half of all cases of nongonococcal urethritis and over three fourths of all cases of post-gonococcal urethritis). Another study revealed that some 61 percent of the women who visited one V.D. clinic had two or more sexually transmitted diseases and 35 percent had three or more. The U.S. Public Health Service now recommends tetracycline—a wider-spectrum antibiotic than penicillin—as a first-line treatment for V.D., since it can also handle coincidental infections. Your chances of recovery are excellent. One of the best cures for the epidemic of venereal disease is information: The person who doesn't know enough to know that he has one disease is more than likely to be ignorant of a second or a third.

A Bug by Any Other Name

Recently, after a couple of days of loose living, I came down with a dose of clap, for which I got a shot of penicillin and I thought everything was fine. A few days later, the symptoms (such as pain on urination) returned. But I hadn't been screwing anyone but my live-in girlfriend. She's clean; and now she's mad because she thinks I've been unfaithful again. What's my best defense? —B. H., Evanston, Illinois.

It sounds to us as though what you have is not gonorrhea but a nongonococcal urethritis. Its symptoms are similar but different; instead of sharp pain during urination, the sensation is more of a tingle. Instead of a milky discharge, this nonspecific urethritis gives you a clear, sticky and lumpy discharge. Also, the little organism is a tough nut to crack. It does not respond to penicillin; tetracycline is needed. Also, whereas men suffer from the disease, women are its symptom-free carriers. Both you and your friend should visit a doctor who's well versed in V.D. esoterica and get treated at the same time. As usual with venereal disease, if left untreated, it could get very serious.

How You Get It

A month ago, my husband contracted gonorrhea. He told me about it as soon as the diagnosis was confirmed and we both received immediate treatment. The circumstances under which he contracted it were unusual. A bachelor blast for one of his oldest friends ended at a prostitute's apartment. He said that he was too bombed to have an erection, but the prostitute did try to arouse him orally. My gynecologist says that it is impossible to contract gonorrhea in this manner and that my husband is putting me on. I have always trusted my husband and felt that he was honest with me. The facts are that he did get gonorrhea (regardless of how) and that he told me anyway. Could my gynecologist be wrong? —Mrs. M. E., St. Louis, Missouri.

Trust your husband in this case, not your gynecologist. Gonorrhea is usually contracted through sexual intercourse, but the Chicago Board of Health told us that it can also be spread through oral contact with the genitals. If the prostitute had contact with the other men at the party, she probably infected them as well. Your husband would be doing his hostess and friends a favor by telling them what happened and by urging them to get a V.D. test.

Prevention

I'm planning a trip to Bangkok and it is extremely unlikely that I will be able to resist the pleasures of the local women. Unfortunately, I understand that there are several virulent strains of V.D. in Southeast Asia. What do you suggest? Are there any ointments or preventative tips that you can suggest that do not involve (a) condoms or (b) abstinence? —C. H., Kancohe, Hawaii.

Sure. You can wear a wet suit, stay home and wait for scientists at the University of Washington to perfect a vaccine against the six thousand or so strains of gonorrhea known to infect humans. That should take another two years or more. Of course, that won't protect you from the fourteen or so other sexually transmitted diseases for which there is little guard except knowledge. Acquaint yourself with the symptoms and try to avoid making love to someone who is obviously affected. If you're worried, wear condoms and pretend they're something else—like designer jeans, only smaller. If you do catch something, it probably can be treated—with the proper cycle of antibiotics, guilt and tall stories.

Prevention

I am planning to work in a ski resort this winter. Since there is an abundance of free and liberal sex for all, I plan to utilize my position to its fullest advantage. I am, however, worried about the chances of contracting a venereal disease. A friend told me that if you wear a condom during lovemaking, then wash yourself with a good antiseptic soap and urinate immediately after sex, the chances of contracting a dread social disease are almost nonexistent. Is that true? —J. D., Aspen, Colorado.

The technique won't ensure safety, but it will decrease the chances of your catching a venereal disease. Condoms have always enjoyed a reputation as a preventive measure, but they are actually effective only for intercourse and then only if used correctly. Still, that's better than having it turn green and fall off; so, by all means, follow your friend's advice.

Who Gets It?

One of my old Army buddies and I got into an argument with a sailor over which of the Armed Services has the lovers. The Navy guy said that he couldn't argue quantity but that he might argue quality. He's read somewhere that Army personnel lead the military in the incidence of gonorrhea. Is that true? —S. Y., San Francisco, California.

The highest incidence of gonorrhea occurs in the Army, followed by the Navy, then the Air Force. (Stay out of those foxholes, boys.) The highest number of sick-bay visits occurred at bases in Asia, with Europe a close second. Apparently, the home shores have been kept safe for intimacy: The lowest incidence of gonorrhea occurred among U.S.-based personnel. (Maybe the Volunteer Army is having a hard time finding volunteers.) For us civilians, it turns out there are regional and seasonal variations in the V.D. epidemic. The Pacific Coast states and the Southern states report the highest incidence of gonorrhea, followed by the mountain states and the Northeast states. (These figures may reflect a willingness to report the disease rather than an actual difference in the number of cases.) And, oddly enough, the highest incidence of V.D. occurs during July and August. So, if you're planning a vacation, try Maine in January. You may freeze your ass off, but the chances of catching anything are slight.

Trichomoniasis

Word has come back to me that several of my recent partners in bed have developed symptoms that resemble venereal disease. They have complained about an itching sensation in the genitals, as well as pain on urination. Some of them have experienced a gray-green discharge. I had myself checked for gonorrhea, but the tests were negative. If it's not V.D., what is it? Can I get it or, worse, am I the person giving it to my girlfriends? —H. W., Dallas, Texas.

Congratulations. You may be the proud carrier of a parasitic infection known as trichomoniasis. It is the most prevalent venereal disease in the country. Doctors estimate that there were 2,300,000 cases of trichomoniasis last year, compared with 1,000,000 reported cases of syphilis. The disease is caused by a parasite—the little bugger is tenacious but can be offed with a dose of metronidazole (Flagyl). Unfortunately, it tends to seek asylum in unsuspecting males. Men can carry the parasite and reinfect their partners without ever experiencing symptoms. The only way to prevent a Ping-Pong effect is to treat the male and the female at the same time. The treatment is relatively painless—you do have to go on the wagon for about a week (alcohol and metronidazole do not mix). If you and your girlfriend(s) go through this together, you won't have to go through it again, and that should give you something to celebrate.

Syphilis

One of my old lovers recently returned to town after a year away at school. She told me that during a physical, her doctor discovered that she had V.D.—specifically, syphilis. She did not know how long she had had it but suggested I see a doctor, as we had engaged in sexual relations during the time she might have been infected. I'm not sure I have to, since the symptoms should have shown up months ago. I haven't noticed anything, so I figure I'm safe. Or could I be sorry? —D. R. New York, New York.

See a doctor: Just because you haven't noticed any symptoms doesn't mean you're safe. According to an article in a recent issue of *Medical Aspects of Human Sexuality*, most people don't recognize V.D. Dr. Thomas A. Chapel writes, "For the last several years, approximately equal numbers of cases have been reported for infectious syphilis, early latent syphilis and late latent syphilis. This means that two out of every three patients with reported syphilis failed to notice a lesion or, if a lesion were observed, failed to recognize it as syphilitic chancre." Chances are the chances are. . . .

Herpes

Can you provide me with some information on herpes simplex, the venereal disease that has been called the grim reaper of the sexual Seventies? —M. A., Boston, Massachusetts.

Herpes simplex can be unpleasant, painful, aggravating and in some instances it is potentially dangerous, but there is no cause for panic. One of the reasons this venereal disease has reached epidemic proportions is that the clinical symptoms weren't deemed severe enough to warrant the full attention of medical science. The herpes virus is highly contagious. It can be transmitted through intercourse or oral sex. (Condoms are not an effective safeguard.) The virus is hard to detect—a person can be a carrier without displaying any symptoms. So far, doctors have identified two strains of herpes simplex. Type I usually affects the body from the waist up, producing cold sores and fever blisters that disappear after a week, only to reappear under conditions of tension, fatigue, indigestion, sunburn or menstruation. Type II usually affects the genitals—producing rash, swelling, itching, pain on urination, and finally clusters of blisters. At present, there is no medical cure for the disease: Once you have the virus, you keep it. Doctors treat the symptoms with drugs and antibiotics—in an attempt to make the patient comfortable and prevent further complications, such as infected blisters. Fortunately, outbreaks of symptoms tend to diminish in frequency and severity as the victim develops antibodies against the virus and may cease completely. (Interestingly, a person who had a Type I infection as a child is less likely to suffer a severe Type II infection.) Now for the bad news. An infant can pick up the virus if he is delivered through an infected birth canal—brain damage and death can result. (Caesarean sections can prevent the child's being contaminated.) Also, it has been suggested that there is a link between the herpes virus and cervical cancer in women: Herpetic cells have been found in tumors, but causality has not been established. Until more is learned about the disease, it might be wise to adopt a policy of self-discipline: If you have it, don't pass it on. Don't be afraid to explain the facts to a partner.

Danger During Childbirth

My wife is pregnant. The goods news is tempered by the disturbing fact that she occasionally suffers from herpes. We've read that women with herpes have to deliver by Caesarean section in order to avoid infecting the baby. Is that always necessary? We were planning to share the experience of natural childbirth. Anything you could tell us would be appreciated. —M. M., Los Angeles, California.

According to medical experts, your wife has a two-out-of-three chance of normal delivery. A Caesarean section is recommended only when the herpes virus is actually present in the birth canal. (That can be determined by culturing the virus or, in some cases, with a Pap smear.) Your wife should inform her obstetrician of the details and schedule the appropriate tests. Good luck.

Communicability

What's the latest news about herpes? I contracted the disease a few years ago and, consequently, my love life is in ruins. Are there any cures on the horizon?

Is it ever safe to go to bed with someone? You are the only one I can turn to for information. No one else writes about this disease. —S. F., Detroit, Michigan.

Probably the best news is the existence of an organization called HELP (Herpetics Engaged in Living Productively). To subscribe to its newsletter, send five dollars to HELP-ASHA, Box 100, Palo Alto, California 91302. As for communicability, HELP states: "In general the absence of active [herpes simplex] lesions means that no viral material is present on mucosal skin surface and the person can't transmit the disease. This general rule is thought to have an important exception. During the time before active sores appear, when there may be tingling or itching (this is called the prodrome), there may be herpes-simplex viruses present and the patient might be infectious. Therefore, it may be possible to transmit the disease from the time immediately preceding the appearance of sores until the sores are gone." HELP suggests that honesty is the best policy: A small percentage of victims (especially women) can have outbreaks without detecting any symptoms. It is best, therefore, to tell your partner that you have had herpes and let him or her decide. A condom will significantly decrease the possibility of transmission. And now for the bad news: According to the *Sexually Transmitted Disease Newsletter*, more than 90 percent of the U.S. population will have been infected with herpes by the age of fifty.

Coping

As a herpes victim, I've developed a lot of skepticism about cures. Having tried Lysine, oral zinc, smallpox vaccines, Virazole, et cetera, I've about given up hope. While I'm waiting for the government to approve the next miracle cure, is there anything I should be doing? I've never seen any suggestions for basic first aid or temporary care. Do guidelines exist? —T. W., Los Angeles, California.

A recent edition of *The Helper*, a quarterly publication of the Herpes Research Center, includes some coping strategies that have proved successful for some (but not all) herpes sufferers. Among the dos and don'ts are the following: "Don't use antibacteria creams or ointments indiscriminately to prevent secondary bacterial infection. The latest evidence suggests that these ointments will actually *prolong* the course of infection. Keeping the area dry and clean is the best way to avoid such infection." Similarly, the newsletter advises wearing loose-fitting clothing during an outbreak to prevent irritation of the lesions. Cotton underwear provides ventilation and dryness. Do not break the vesicles. Among the home remedies that have met with success: ice packs applied to the area during the prodroman (warning) stage. According to *The Helper*, "Some people find that this little trick is helpful in limiting the severity of the subsequent outbreak, while others have said it some-times precludes an attack altogether. No one's guaranteeing it will do either for you." Good luck. We'll keep you posted.

Alas, I have apparently acquired a case of herpes virus. Does that mean the end of my sex life? How do I go about telling someone that I have this dreaded social disease? —C. E., San Francisco, California.

We have heard of a lot of ways. One guy in Colorado wanted to manufacture battle ribbons for singles to wear. The color code would impart information such as "I do not have herpes," or "It's been two years since my last recurrence." The folks who publish *The Helper* have more sensible advice. They found certain guidelines that seemed to ease the anxiety of telling prospective bed partners. Choosing the right time and place are high on the list. Don't try to bring up the topic at a crowded party, while having dinner for the first time at his or her par-ents' house or after making love for the sixteenth time. Don't assume that your partner knows all about herpes, and don't try to disguise the topic in half-truths or complex medical vocabulary. Do stress that herpes is preventable, if precautions are taken. Attitude makes a big difference. Don't describe it as a nightmare or a terrible thing. *The Helper* stresses this point: "Never use the word incurable when explaining herpes to another person. Not only does this word have unfortunate connotations and imagery attached to it but it is descriptively inaccurate. Herpes is very curable—as a matter of fact, your body cures you again and again, each time a recurrence goes away. Unfortunately, the virus has the ability to hide out and escape the otherwise lethal effect of your immune system, and, therefore, the potential for recurrences exists. A better way to describe what is going on might be to refer to herpes as an intermit-tent, self-limiting condition that comes and goes more or less on its own, isn't particularly dangerous and can be dealt with by the body, unas-sisted by drugs of any sort. Sounds better—and it's more accurate." For more facts, contact HELP/ASHA, 260 Sheridan Avenue, Palo Alto, Cal-ifornia 94306.

Cold Sores

Your comments in the September Playboy *on the epidemic of herpes venereal disease have left me confused and worried. You mention that recurring cold sores and fever blisters are among the symptoms of Type I infection. I date two ladies: One gets a cold sore on her upper lip every winter: the other gets a fever blister on her lower arm whenever she is nervous. Are you saying that both are afflicted or that I may have become a carrier? —T. M., Chicago, Illinois.*

The most common form of venereal disease is the proverbial plague of doubts. One doctor told us that following the Dick Cavett special "V.D. Blues," every person with a pimple on his ass thought he had some kind of social disease. The doctor's favorite cases involve something he calls the front-seat syndrome: It seems that young men in the heat of passion sometimes get themselves caught in their zippers, wake up the next morning and don't recall where the abrasions came from. (The same thing can happen after a bite-size bout of oral sex.) Suddenly they are worried that they have "it." Don't be afraid to have a checkup: More often than not, "it" is something else, but better safe than a drooling idiot with tertiary syphilis. In your case: It is thought that all fever blisters and cold sores are caused by viruses but that not all of these are herpes virus. Only a virologist can tell for sure. Type I is troublesome but usually not serious, and the treatment is simple: Avoid infection and the sores eventually disappear. Also, for those of you worried about Type II infections—which can be serious—help is on the way. German doctors have had some success with a vaccine for Type II: If and when the FDA approves the cure, it will become available in this country.

I recall reading that one of the symptoms of herpes was cold sores or canker sores in the mouth. I have had canker sores off and on for several years. Does that mean I have herpes? —D. F., Portland, Oregon.

Canker sores share many of the symptoms of cold sores, but are not the result of the herpes virus. Researchers report, "It is estimated that anywhere from 20 to 50 percent of the population suffers from these sores, which, like herpes, break out in burning, painful ulcerations, singularly or in groups. Unlike herpes, though, canker sores rarely appear on the immovable mucosa (hard palate, attached gum)—a characteristic sufficient to differentiate them from primary or recurrent oral herpes lesions (which may occur concomitantly). Still, the small, oval, light yellow sores are painful enough that eating and drinking can be difficult. . . . Though the physiologic events that lead to canker sores are uncertain, physical trauma, slight injury, eating abrasive foods, emotional stress and nutrition all seem to play some role. As with herpes infections, it would appear that controlling stress and paying attention to proper diet may be of some benefit in decreasing the frequency and severity of outbreaks."

The First Cure

I have that god-awful curse genital herpes, and it is driving me nuts. For all the people who suffer from this disease, you would think someone would find a cure. A friend of mine who knows of my problem said he was watching a talk show one morning and a doctor was explaining some of the new wonder drugs. This doctor said that in three to six months, a drug would be on the market that would cure all types of herpes on the spot. What do you know about it? —M. L., San Diego, California.

The new drug is acyclovir (pronounced a-*cy*-clo-veer). It is *not* a cure, but it is a very important first step. The FDA recently gave its approval to Burroughs-Wellcome to market acyclovir as a topical cream prescribed under the trade name Zovirax. It should be in your local drugstore by now. The approved uses for the drug are relatively limited. Clinical tests show that the drug speeds healing time, reduces pain and reduces time the active virus is present in *initial* outbreaks of herpes. (Herpes is a chameleon. Initial outbreaks are usually severe and may last up to three weeks. Subsequent outbreaks are usually quite brief—two to six days.) Dannie King, project director at Burroughs, says that the only rule of thumb for the drug is this: The strongest effect is seen on the initial infection. Studies have shown that for recurrent outbreaks the drug is not as effective. It does cut down the duration of viral shedding, i.e., the period of infectiousness, by about 40 percent. At present, the drug is indicated only for initial sufferers. We are not sure how the drug will actually be used on the street. Doctors will probably prescribe it to all their herpes patients because they consider it the only weapon they have. We suspect that many herpes sufferers, when they feel they have a potentially effective agent in their pocket, will experience a self-cure: Stress is a crucial factor in the outbreak of herpes. Eliminate some of the stress and the body seems to be able to take care of itself. King pointed out that the topical ointment is only the first step. The emergence of acyclovir ointment reflects only about 10 percent of the herpes research being conducted by Burroughs-Wellcome. Also on the drawing boards are oral, ophthalmic and intravenous forms of acyclovir. One way of looking at it: Penicillin was the first effective form of antibacterial chemotherapy. Acyclovir is the first effective antiviral chemotherapy; there's still work to be done, but a whole new approach has been established.

The Pursuit of Pleasure

And now for the good part.

There is a rumor that the Playboy Advisor has access to something known as the Playboy Test Bedrooms. We don't want to dispel that notion. For what it's worth, we once tried to talk the IRS into declaring one of the bedrooms in our apartment a home office. Perhaps the single greatest reward in writing this column is checking out the techniques, the homemakers' hints submitted by readers. These letters are the war stories of the sexual revolution, the tiny acts of courage and bold experimentation by the true heroes of the age. We have told interviewers that we have never written about anything that we haven't personally tried. We'd like to thank our readers for improving our sex life.

The letters in this chapter reflect a changing attitude in the American way of sex. Marriage manuals at the turn of the century tended to view sex as a medical problem; it was not in woman's nature to enjoy sex. All the instruction was designed to cure a condition known as frigidity. After World War II, our attitudes changed. Some women were able to tolerate sex and on occasion able to enjoy it. But they were poorly designed physically and had to be brought along by careful attention. A generation grew up, brainwashed with the concept of *foreplay*, of Calvinist sex. If you did so much of "this," you got to do as much as you could of "that." Sex was work, foreplay a form of duty.

Masters and Johnson gave us a model of sex that was healthy: men and women are essentially equals, they are more alike than different, and everyone has the potential to enjoy orgasmic sex. Alex Comfort followed with two sex manuals that were not based on the assumption that one partner was inferior or needed to be fixed. There was no foreplay, only play.

Sociologically, the statistics have kept track of the change. Kinsey found that couples in the forties tended to have sex in the missionary position, with little foreplay. Americans were apt to view "oral-genital play, and even mouth to breast contact with suspicion, scorn or aversion" . . . but the mere publication of the Kinsey statistics gave Americans the permission to experiment. In the early seventies, *Playboy* duplicated the Kinsey research and found that the American way of sex had significantly changed. More people were doing everything. Instead of one position, couples were likely to have tried nine or ten positions. The majority of people had engaged in oral sex. Alex Comfort called it mouthwork and devoted two pages to the topic in *The Joy of Sex*.

A few years ago, we interviewed John Money, a sex researcher at Johns Hopkins Hospital, while researching an article on desire. He suggested that we acquire our attitudes about sex the way we acquire our native language. Indeed there might be an erotic equivalent to the standard I.Q. We could measure a person's sexual intelligence by how well he had mastered the vocabulary of sex. Reviewing these letters, I am struck by the avid curiosity our readers have about sex. If something has a name, they are willing to try it. And once they try something, they will write to the Advisor—to compare notes, to check in. They are looking for the words and acts to express themselves.

These letters are not problems per se. They are triumphs.

CHAPTER SIX

Secret Oriental Sex Techniques We Learned from Our Toyota Mechanic

Surefire Sex: America's Top Ten

If you read sex manuals, you get the impression that everybody is doing everything and enjoying it all. Yet I've found that, inevitably, my partner likes some things better than others. Are there any general guidelines for sexual preferences? —H. G., Los Angeles, California.

We tend to avoid generalities, but we came across an interesting claim in *The Book of Sex Lists* by Albert B. Gerber. According to the Association for Research, Inc., the ten sexual activities preferred by heterosexual women (in order of preference) are: "(1) Gentle cunnilingus (on the clitoris) by a man (much emphasis on the gentle); (2) gentle finger stimulation of the clitoris by a man; (3) sexual intercourse on top of a man; (4) sexual intercourse in a variety of changing positions; (5) receiving cunnilingus (gentle, of course) while performing fellatio (sixty-nine); (6) massaging a man all over; (7) masturbating a man; (8) being petted, kissed and stimulated manually and orally by two men, culminating in intercourse with one man while the other alternates between gently stroking the clitoris and the nipples; (9) masturbation; (10) performing simple fellatio." The key word, in case you missed it, is gentle. We can see *Billboard* publishing a weekly chart: "And #5 with a bullet . . ." For comparison, the list of ten sexual activities preferred by heterosexual men in order of preference, are: "(1) Fellatio by a woman to orgasm; (2)

intercourse with a woman in a variety of positions, changing from time to time; (3) nude encounters with two women in a variety of activities, changing from time to time; (4) petting the breasts of a woman; (5) anal intercourse with a woman; (6) performing cunnilingus while the woman is performing fellatio (sixty-nine); (7) performing sadomasochistic acts (mild, not severe) upon a woman; (8) being masturbated by a woman; (9) performing simple cunnilingus; (10) masturbation." Our suggestion: Show this list to your lover and find out her particular ranking, then work your way to the top.

Sensitivity to Touch

Just about every sex manual I have studied advises that the clitoris is the nerve center of the woman. Okay. Whenever I try to caress my girlfriend's nerve center, she complains that direct touch hurts her. Am I doing something wrong? She enjoys intercourse, so it's not psychological. —W. O., Boston, Massachusetts.

It's those rough, red dishpan hands. Perhaps you should switch detergents or let her do the dishes. Seriously, many women find direct stimulation of the clitoris to be abrasive. A nerve center is equally sensitive to pain and to pleasure; the clitoris can be as tender before intercourse as the head of the penis is afterward. The cure is relatively simple: Ask your partner to show you how she touches herself and follow suit. Go slow, be gentle and indirect. A tender massage of the entire area, followed by a tug at the clitoris, can be effective. When the area becomes engorged with blood and lubricated, you should be able to proceed to direct touch. Once your partner learns to relax, she will probably enjoy the experience. Let your fingers do the . . . uh . . . walking.

Positions

It seems there is a great dualism in the universe of sex, between doggy fashion and the missionary position. What the metaphysical significance of this division might be, whether it symbolizes alpha and omega, mind and matter or Masters and Johnson, I can't conceive. But as far as I know, the face-to-face, or missionary position does seem to be confined to human beings, while the rest of the animal kingdom goes to the dogs. Is this true? —R. S., Glencoe, Illinois.

Aristotle claimed that hedgehogs do it face to face, presumably to avoid stabbing each other with their spines. But Aristotle was a notoriously bad observer—he also stated that men had more teeth than women—and his immersion in Greek culture may have biased his views. No one else has ever seen hedgehogs lulling face to face. On the other paw, there is the two-toed sloth; a pair of lustful sloths were seen on one occasion getting after it eyeball to eyeball while hanging by their forelimbs—a feat we envy. A few primates also seem to enjoy a bit of the old tête à tête. Young apes and monkeys take that position, though with maturity they acquire a profounder view of life and approach sex from the rear. Gorillas have often been seen mating in the missionary position, but only in captivity; maybe zealots preach to them through the bars. The male orangutan, a chauvinistic and undignified beast, chases the female, wrestles her onto her back and then has his way with her while squatting on his haunches. The pygmy chimpanzee regularly commits head-on coitus: the female's vagina is located more toward the front than that of the common chimpanzee, facilitating frontal fucking. As for what it all means, there are those who think face to face is more appropriate for humans, since it aids conversation (and it's therefore recommended on the first date, when you're still getting to know each other). Among most animals, a preference for this form of copulation does seem to be a sign of evolutionary sophistication; however, in *Homo sapiens*, it appears to be just the reverse.

Heads or tails? After several months of making love to my girlfriend, I've reached an impasse. I prefer to make love in the missionary position. She prefers to make love in the female-superior position. She claims that the missionary is a male-chauvinist invention. I claim the female-superior position is a women's lib rhetorical device. We are curious. What is the most popular position? My girlfriend says that the missionary position is practiced only in America. I can't believe that. Do other cultures do it differently? —E. G., Boston, Massachusetts.

Yes. For years, the missionary position was America's chief export. It may be responsible for the trade deficit. In Kinsey's day, the missionary position was the *only* position used by 70 percent of the couples surveyed. Nowadays, the female superior is pulling its own weight at least in America. But neither position is world-wide. According to psychologist Frank Beach, face-to-face lovemaking is found in every culture, but most frequently it takes this form: "The woman lies on her back while the man squats or kneels between her legs, which are placed around his thighs. In the course of copulation, he may draw the woman close to him and she may lock her legs behind his back." In short, it's like the missionary position, only the man is praying to a different god.

Esoteric Positions: Take One

On a recent business trip to Hawaii, I met a Chinese woman at a disco. At the end of a pleasurable evening of dancing and drinking, we returned to my hotel room, at which time we made 'love in various ways. She introduced me to a position that was unfamiliar to me but that, she said, was the standard way of the Oriental. The position is as follows: The man squats and the woman mounts him from the front, with her thighs over his, while lying face up with her arms outstretched, supporting her. I am curious (and a bit sore) as to how and why this position originated. —R. P., Miami, Florida.

The position you describe is thought to have been developed in India. According to Alex Comfort in *The Joy of Sex*, "Indian erotology is the only ancient tradition devoid of stupid patriarchal hang-ups about the need for her to be underneath, and unashamed about accepting her fully aggressive role in reciprocal sex." Obviously, traveling ancient Indian sex gurus must have spread the word to discos in neighboring China.

Esoteric Positions: Take Two

The Joy of Sex and similar books advertised variety and more variety. My question is simple: Why? After a flurry of exploration a few years ago, my wife and I settled on, or into a few favorite positions and techniques that are reliable and rewarding. We can make love a hundred days in a row using the same position without getting tired of orgasms. When we try one of the new esoteric positions, there seems to be a greater chance of failure. We don't always find the right fit. If we can't make our regular performances, I'm not sure it's worth the effort to repeat our past mistakes. What do you think? —W. D., Fort Worth, Texas.

We think that you should abandon the scoring system that equates lack of orgasm with failure. We've heard of a few people who judge their lovemaking like an Olympic diving event, with separate scales for difficulty and execution multiplied by each other to give the score. A belly flop that results in orgasm may receive a 1.2 for intimacy and a 10 for success: total score—12. A rear flip with a half twist that lands one of you in the hospital might receive a 3.6 for intimacy and a 4 for success; total score 14.4 Trying that would get you around the orgasm hang-up, but you should recognize that sex isn't a contest. After all you're the only one entering. Alex Comfort gives a very good reason for systematically reviewing technique in *More Joy:* It's a good way to find sensations you've missed. He says that "some of them won't work for you, but don't write them off until you're sure it's preference and not inexperience which makes them fail. So take the plunge.

My girlfriend likes to make love standing up. She claims the position allows her as much control as the much-touted woman-on-top position, plus it has the added benefit of pressure: With her back to the wall, she enjoys the feeling of being caught between a rock and a hard place. I must admit that the position does have its advantages—we have made love in showers, in telephone booths, in self-service elevators, in hallways and in rest rooms on airplanes. When we experiment with bondage and discipline, instead of tying her spread-eagled on a bed, I handcuffed her to a chinning bar and did it in a doorway. As long as she gets off on it, I'm willing to go along, but it's gotten to the point that we almost never do it in bed. My question is this: Is she weird? —D. D., Detroit, Michigan.

No; she's just the right size. Obviously, the position doesn't work for everyone. If you were five foot one and she were six foot two, or vice versa, we doubt if she would be partial to the perpendicular. Go to it: What better way to ensure an encore than a standing ovation?

Erroneous Zones

Sex manuals inspire the reader to explore the primary and secondary erogenous zones of the human body. I have responded to the call, but sometimes I feel like I'm traveling through California with a map of New England. What is primary for one woman is secondary or nonexistent for the next. I enjoy variety, but the inconsistency is unnerving. Can you recommend a reliable tour guide for the young man on the move? —D.H.B. III, San Francisco, California.

We suspect that the variety you enjoy is the variety of the chain motel. Individual differences are the essence of variety, and discrepancies between text and touch are inevitable. Sex manuals, like road maps, tend to limit exploration to well-traveled highways, famous landmarks and tourist traps. Learn to travel without reservations (another word for expectations) and you may discover the pleasures of lesser-known avenues. In any case, the only reliable source of information is your partner; a native always makes the best guide.

Perhaps you can shed light on a delicate subject: Some of us at work were discussing sexual technique. We disagreed on how long one should continue a given activity. Most of us seem to follow the same pattern: We wait until our women start moaning and groaning and then we jump on board, hoping to bodysurf on the wave of her orgasm. One of the guys said it was bad to break rhythm: if the girl is moaning, it means she likes what you're doing and you should keep right on doing it. He said that diligence never fails to drive women out of their minds. You can see that the diversity of opinion has us stumped. Is there a right way? —K. P., Chicago, Illinois.

Each person's fingerprints are different, and the way each couple reaches orgasm is also unique. The first theory you mention suggests that there is a difference between foreplay and what follows. The mechanical model of sex suggests that a man has to earn his pleasure by preparing a woman. The drawbacks to that approach are well known. Catch the wave and all's well, miss and you may be washed up. The second theory you mention is potentially more rewarding: There is no foreplay, only play. If you are doing something and the woman likes it, keep doing it. Do it long enough and you'll come around to the same point again; then you can jump on board. Or maybe she'll take control of the action. When it comes to a discussion of technique, you should realize that everything works at one time or another. Try it both ways. Settle into the one that gives you and your partner more pleasure, and then, just for the heaven of it, break the pattern.

Afterplay

I am a young man of twenty-five who has been dating the same girl for the past three years. Our sex life is fairly good; though she doesn't always reach orgasm, it doesn't seem to bother her that much. Still, I would like to make our relationship better. If I had to work on one area, where should I start? —F. O., Dallas, Texas.

Well, we could give you a secret Oriental sex technique that we picked up from our Honda mechanic last week, but we haven't gotten the results from our test bedrooms yet. So let's talk general strategy. James Halpern and Mark Sherman, authors of a new book called *Afterplay*, did a study of several hundred people and tried to determine what most affected the over-all satisfaction with a relationship. For women, the factors ranged from the number of orgasms per session (10%), percentage of time orgasm occurs (19%), satisfaction with intercourse (21%), satisfaction with foreplay (21%) to satisfaction with afterplay, or the post-intercourse experience (40%). In other words, there was no significant relationship between the number of orgasms or the percentage of time orgasm is reached and satisfaction. The key, and probably the reason those two wrote the book, seems to lie in the postcoital experience. According to the study, the most significant Aspects of afterplay for a woman are her partner's attitude (does he want to remain close to her and cuddle or does he head for the kitchen for a beer?) and whether or not he talks to her after making love. If you touch and talk lovingly, and try to sustain the mood for the next hour or so, you will win her heart forever. That's it.

Maybe you can help. You see, I am very intrigued with acting out fantasies, with trying new things and learning how these things excite and affect my girlfriend. We both get into oral sex a lot. And the foreplay sessions last considerably longer than the actual copulation. In this there is no problem. My main concern deals with the period after the copulation is over—when the two people usually just lie there together and hold each other. My problem is that I cannot do this. It upsets my girlfriend a bit, because she is a true romanticist. She gets off on snuggling after we make love. I get a very different feeling, not about my girlfriend but about the situation. I will just get out of bed, get dressed and leave the room. I can't tell you how much this upsets her. In fact, she says she feels that she has just been laid like some two-bit whore. I hate to think that I make her feel this way, but my feelings won't allow me to lie there with her. This has happened with other girls. I would just want to take them home or do anything as long as I could get rid of them. The problem is really getting to me. I don't understand this feeling and it is very hard to describe. I'm wondering if there is anything I could do to change my feelings. What do you suggest? —B. P., Baltimore, Maryland.

A little bondage and discipline might help. If she ties you up, you can't leave. For a man who says he's into acting out fantasies and trying new things, you have an uncommon amount of guilt. You seem to be in a hurry to leave the scene of a crime. Or worse, a job. You view sex as a task. You try tricks to see how they affect your girlfriend—not how they make the evening more enjoyable for both of you. If you want to change your attitude, you'll have to stop treating sex as a one-act play. Next time you feel the urge to leave, get out of bed, put on your clothes, leave the room, then go back and climb into bed—fully dressed. When you get to the end, start all over again.

Autofellatio

How is it that I never hear mention of autofellatio in your column? It is my favorite form of masturbation. My accomplishments include not only putting my penis into my mouth but also sticking my tongue into my navel and placing my mouth against my lower abdomen and scrotum. Do many people have this degree of flexibility in their bodies? —J. W., Syosset, New York.

Don't Ouroborus. Although it's rare, we have heard of people with this talent. A few were fakirs, who managed the trick after years of training; others were born with the ability to make ends meet. And then there are those who are capable of a rectocranial inversion (sticking one's head up one's ass). Try that, if you haven't already.

Alka-Seltzer and Sex

Are you ready for this? A girlfriend and I have discovered a unique sexual turnon—Alka-Seltzer! She inserts one of the white wonders as she starts to get excited. When the juices flow, the tablet effervesces; the heat and tingling sensations that result are something else again. The Alka-Seltzer screw, as it is called, is spreading like wildfire among the swinging set in the Dallas–Fort Worth area. Is there any harm in what we're doing? —W.F.E., Fort Worth, Texas.

We were ready for your question. An oil-and-gas producer in your area has already written us about a dozen letters on this topic. We know that it must be hard to swing in the Lone-Star State—the trees are so far apart—but surely you have better things to do than to write to us. Still, we must answer: According to our medical expert, the lining of the vagina has a pH that must be maintained to prevent bacterial infection. A prompt and complete douching should restore the proper pH and ensure your girlfriend's health. Also, Alka-Seltzer contains aspirin; aspirin has been known to cause bleeding in the gastrointestinal lining after prolonged contact; the same thing might occur if vaginal contact was less than speedy. Again, this problem could be avoided by douching or, perhaps, by switching to one of those flavored fizzies. Then you would have a taste treat as well.

The Binaca Blast

Have you come across the Binaca Blast? It's something that every sex enthusiast should know about: Each partner places six to ten drops of concentrated Binaca Breath Freshener on the tongue before performing oral sex on his or her mate. The sensation is fantastic: What's more, you never have to worry about bad breath. —S. O., Copenhagen, Denmark.

There are some things even your best friend won't tell you. Obviously, this isn't one of them. Thanks for the tip. To borrow a line from another ad campaign—it's one way to improve the taste you hate to use twice a day. With moderation, there should be no harmful side effects.

Breasts vs. Buttocks

Perhaps you can settle an argument. For the past few months, I have been having lunch with one of the secretaries from work. Although we've never been to bed together, we enjoy comparing notes about what turns us on. She says that she really likes to be grabbed by the buttocks or by the inside of the thighs during intercourse—the maneuver heightens her sense of being back in the saddle again. Also, she finds that the area between her anus and her vagina is quite sensitive. She really gets off on men who attend to this erogenous zone; she even includes anal stimulation as one of her masturbatory techniques. (She calls it double clutching—one finger in each orifice.) I told her I thought that this was rather unusual; she responded that if something was pleasurable when done by other people, it would be pleasurable done all by oneself. Who's right? —M. F., Dallas, Texas.

You are both right, but your friend comes out ahead. Her logic is impeccable, even though it can't be supported by statistics. Men and women tend to be singleminded, if not singlehanded, in their masturbatory technique. For example, Kinsey found that approximately half of the women surveyed were somewhat sensitive to breast stimulation before and during intercourse, yet only about 11 percent of the women who masturbated bothered to fondle their own breasts. You friend's behavior may be uncommon, but it will do in a pinch.

Celibacy

My girlfriend and I have been trying to improve our love life, but we seem to have radically different ideas about how to go about it. She keeps harping on the importance of sensuality over sexuality. Apparently, she saw a therapist on TV recently who suggested that the path to pleasure came through celibacy. Her Rx. was this: "Throw your genitals out the window for two weeks." I don't think that avoiding sex is the way to improve your game. What do you say? —W. G., San Francisco, California.

We don't think sensuality is the same as celibacy: It might clear the confusion if you simply view sensuality as nongenital fooling around. The whole body is an erogenous zone, but most Americans create sexual ghettos—restricting sensory input to their genitals and their foreplay to lips, breasts and occasionally the clitoris. By most accounts, women prefer total body stimulation—hugging, cuddling, light massage, whatever. A lot of men respond negatively to requests for more foreplay (two weeks does strike us as being a bit extreme), because they feel the woman is trying to avoid sex altogether. Most therapists don't make a distinction among foreplay, intercourse and afterplay. It's all loveplay, and the longer you make the fun last, the better it is. As for throwing your genitals out the window, we live on the thirty-second floor of a high-rise. We're not sure what shape they would be in or if they would even be there after two weeks. And imagine the poor pedestrians.

The Chinese Basket Trick

Every now and then I get a letter from a friend of mine in the merchant marine relating his exploits in foreign ports. The last one came from Hong Kong and contained reference to something called the Chinese basket trick. He said that he had read about it in a book called The Rise and Fall of the Chinese Basket *and had finally gotten to try it. Apparently, it was exquisite, but he assumed that I knew what it was, and I don't. Can you give me details? —S. K., Hartford, Connecticut.*

Sure. Lovers suspend a basket from the ceiling of their bedroom with a block and tackle. The woman climbs into the basket and lowers herself until her genitals come into contact with her partner's. (By the way, the basket should have a hole in it, and the trick doesn't work quite as well with the man on top.) Some couples have the man raise and lower the basket, while the woman plucks the ropes as if they were the strings of a harp; the vibrations can be delightful. Other lovers twist the ropes before the woman gets into the basket: the gentle unwinding motion adds a new dimension to the phrase "getting turned on." We've heard of several variations of the Chinese basket trick. Persons concerned with birth control attach the basket to a catapult. When the man feels the approach of orgasm, he tugs a second rope to ensure a rather dramatic form of coitus interruptus. Also, single men sometimes combine the basket with a Chinese finger handcuff (one of those tubes of folded palm fronds that drove you crazy as a kid) for a unique form of masturbation. If you would like to experience the technique and don't happen to have beams in your bedroom, try the Chinese picnic-basket trick. Toss a block and tackle into a basket and find a secluded wood where the tree limbs are fairly thick. Make sure your equipment is secure and never raise your friend higher than you would like her to fall.

Daisy Chains

At a party not long ago, a drunken friend remarked that he felt like the last man in a daisy chain. He then tried to describe a daisy chain, but as he had lost command of the English language somewhere around his fourth martini, his explanation made little sense. What is a daisy chain and why should the last man feel anything apart from what his companions feel? —M. B., Portland, Oregon.

A daisy chain is a group sexual activity in which each participant simultaneously does to someone else more or less what someone else is doing to him or her. This concatenation of erotic contact usually is oral and almost always is circular. Technically, there should not be a last man in a daisy chain, which is endless, so to speak, but your friend may have been suffering from an inability to make ends meet. There is another possible explanation of his remark. A daisy chain with an even number of participants (e.g., 696969) can be completely heterosexual, while a daisy chain with an odd number of participants (69696) must be at least partially homosexual. In such cases, the togetherness of the chain must depend on the inclinations of the extra person. (A daisy chain is only as strong as its weakest link.) Consequently, your friend may have meant that he was the only unattached person at the party.

Aluminum Foil

A friend recently told me that wrapping one's erection in aluminum foil enhances the pleasure of oral sex. Is there any truth to that? —J.J.C., Staten Island, New York.

We sent your letter to our crew in the Playboy Test Bedrooms. Their report: Aluminum foil may help keep the meat fresh, but nothing more. Maybe Handi-Wrap would work better?

Feuille de Rose

Can you tell me what feuille de rose means? I came across the phrase in a short story. At first, I thought it might be a wine, but the French dictionary defines it as "rose leaf." In the story, a guy asks a girl if she has ever enjoyed some feuille de rose, and she follows him up to his apartment. If it's not wine, it must be a sexual act. Am I on the right track? —J. R., Boston, Massachusetts.

The phrase refers to lingual stimulation of the perineum, making it a brief layover on the sexual act known as "around the world." If it feels good, a Frenchman has a word for it.

The Emperor's Crown

Graham Greene's autobiography contains a line ("I remember how deftly the Emperor's Crown used to be performed by three girls at once in a brothel in Batista's Havana. Three can surely be as dangerous company as two.") that is paraphrased in his novel Travels with My Aunt *("There was a brothel in Havana where the Emperor's Crown was admirably performed by three nice girls"). Obviously, whatever the Emperor's Crown is, or was, it certainly impressed Greene. None of my friends has ever heard of the arrangement, but we've made some imaginative guesses: a form of fellatio for heads of state? What you wear after you've put on the Emperor's new clothes? —V. H., Megargel, Texas.*

The Cuban Revolution did more than cut off our supply of good cigars. According to a usually reliable source (one of our plumbers), pre-Castro Havana was noted for having the most outrageous sex circuses in the Western world. The Emperor's Crown was a favorite act (no, you didn't see it on the Sullivan show); it involved one man and (you guessed it) three girls. The first girl would sit on the man's face, the second girl would straddle his erect penis, while the third girl would kneel between his legs, taking his testicles into her mouth. The arrangement, seen from the side, was said to resemble a crown. We guess you had to be there.

Fisticuffs

The other night, I saw an X-rated movie in which a couple engaged in fist fucking. The man was able to put his entire hand into the woman; the woman seemed to enjoy it. Ever since, I've wanted to try the technique on my girlfriend. She's willing, but I need to know a little bit more about the activity. Is it dangerous? Does the size of the fist matter? —D. S., Minneapolis, Minnesota.

Penis size doesn't matter, so fist size shouldn't, either, unless, perhaps, you are a contender for the heavyweight crown. A vagina can accommodate a baby's head, so it should be able to take your hand. Trim your fingernails first. If your girlfriend is shy and dry, you may want to coat your hand with K-Y jelly. Add fingers as you and she see fit—the technique is known in some circles as cluster fucking and may provide a substantial thrill for your girlfriend. The extra thickness of several fingers stretches the lips of the vagina and tugs directly on the clitoris. Proceed slowly and with great care: Subtle movements are all that's required to floor her. As a variation on the five-finger exercise, you might try this trick while your partner uses a vibrator. The combination can knock her socks off.

Food

My girlfriend and I have seen several porn movies in which the actors and actresses used various fruits and vegetables to masturbate themselves. Is the practice safe? We couldn't tell from the film whether the implements were real or wax. —M. S., Camden, New Jersey.

If the vegetables are washed first to remove any dirt or chemicals, the procedure is safe and, indeed, a great fallback in the event that your vibrator breaks down in the middle of the night. (To avoid pesticides, you might want to buy your accessories at a local health-food store. And be sure that all of your playthings were picked by members of the United Farm Workers.) The favorite erotic fruits and vegetables seem to be cucumbers and zucchini for women, watermelons and cored apples for men. Tomatoes do not work well for either sex. Beyond that, it's pretty much a matter of personal taste: unpeeled versus peeled, et cetera. May we also suggest a tossed salad, with a light vinaigrette dressing?

Sex on the Rocks

Maybe I'm a little slow or something. My roommate and I double-dated to a double bill that included The Other Side of Midnight. *In one scene, a young lady satisfies her partner saddle style as he lies flat on his back. Just when it appears the poor fellow reaches his peak, the lady reaches down into an ice bucket and grabs all the ice she can handle with two hands and places it on her partner's crotch. The look on his face appears to be all but that of pleasure. Is this technique used widely? What are the sensations that result from a half pound of ice applied directly to the genitals? —T. P., Savannah, Georgia.*

The ice trick was first described in John Eichenlaub's *The Marriage Art*, which was published in 1961. (According to most survivors, the sudden shock produced an astonishing orgasm.) For a while after, snowballing was quite the rage. Couples would check into hotels, call room service and request a bucket of champagne minus the champagne. Bellboys would smirk knowingly. There's only one drawback to the technique: If you think sleeping on a wet spot is a drag, you should try it when the temperature is just above freezing. Still, it's worth trying. You probably won't get frostbite. If you do, you'll be in good company. We got more than one letter asking about the scene in *The Other Side of Midnight*. Just goes to show: In the worst movie, there is at least one worthwhile scene.

Hot Wax

Some of my friends have been trying to organize an orgy. The suggested party games include the old Wesson Oil tag-team wrestling match. Everyone would grease up and go at one another. I confess that the image of gleaming bodies slithering against one another—women's hands running up thighs to grasp erect penises, men's hands sliding from crotch to breast—is my idea of a good evening. One of the guys suggested that such antics are out of date. He recently read about something called a hot-wax orgy, where they drip candle wax over one another's bodies. Each drop of wax is a touch of warmth—to be removed after several layers have built up. The accompanying images—erections that look like the necks of Chianti bottles, breasts that look like ice-cream-shop concoctions—are kinky, but I have reservations. Isn't the hot wax dangerous? —S. M., Baltimore, Maryland.

Not really. Hold the candle high enough above the skin and the liquid wax will have time to cool off. And just think, you'll be saving a bundle on your electric bill.

Karezza

A while ago, you mentioned karezza—*the discipline by which the male postpones orgasm for hours. Is this technique effective under constant stimulation, such as thrusting, or does it require one to take breathers? I would benefit by any information on this subject, as would my fiancée. —D. S., Portland, Oregon.*

Philip Rawson, in *The Art of Tantra*, describes the philosophy behind karezza as follows: "Orgasm is in a sense an irrelevance, lost in the sustained and vastly enhanced inward condition of nervous vibration in which the energies of man and world are felt to be consummated, their infinite possibilities realized virtually on the astronomical scale of time and space." Somehow we don't think that's what you had in mind. Karezza is neither a cure for premature ejaculation nor a secret of the Orient leading to extended sexual play: it is the very opposite of the Western style of athletic, thrusting interaction. Many Americans who try karezza experience those nervous vibrations as impatience or frustration. The technique is part of a religious doctrine in which the sexual energy is first aroused, then channeled in consciousness-raising meditation. Lovers couple, then contemplate the male-female creative aspects of the universe. We've heard of folks who try to increase duration by thinking about other things—the Dow Jones stock index—or by chanting mantras such as "Gene Autry doing deep knee bends in a field of dead bats" or "Frenzied springboks capering their exasperations against the frogs that tickled them." We think they missed the point. If you want to try karezza or something like it, enter your partner, then sit facing her, comfortably. Forget your genitals. (Don't worry if you lose your erection; you don't need it if you aren't active, and you'll still enjoy yourself.) Study her face and body while she studies yours. When you realize that you are part of the same whole, you may have achieved your purpose.

The Knotted Handkerchief Bit

During an early scene in the play Lenny, *Bruce described his girlfriend with the remark "She even knows the knotted-handkerchief bit." The audience ranged in age from eighteen to eighty, but only a few persons seemed to know what he was talking about. What is the knotted-handkerchief bit? —W.J.H., La Jolla, California.*

The knotted-handkerchief bit is also known as the seven knots to heaven. According to one source, a knotted string or handkerchief is inserted into the male partner's anus prior to intercourse, then removed at the moment of orgasm. The anal region is almost as sensitive as the genital region: the abrupt stimulation is supposed to increase the intensity of orgasm. (It works for both sexes.) Now you know why your mother always told you to take a handkerchief along on dates.

Beads

No doubt by now you've caught the Saturday-night television show that features a weekend news wrap-up by someone you're not. I may be mistaken, but it's my impression that bit always begins with a subtle reference to sex. The camera zooms in on the newscaster, catching him in the middle of an obscene phone call to his war-torn girlfriend Angela. At least I think it's obscene. On one show, he was talking about whether or not a truck driver who passed them on the highway thought she was taking a nap in his lap. That went over my head. On another show, he made reference to the differences between the butterfly kiss and the butterfly flick. (Is it true love if she uses false eyelashes?) One line still bothers me; to wit, the not-quite-ready-for-prime-time conversation in which he said, "What I don't understand is who yanks out the beads." As a master of erotic esoterica, can you answer the question? Who does yank out the beads? —J. R., Chevy Chase, Maryland.

Someone who knows you very well—usually, but not always, the same person who inserted them.

The Local

On a business trip to New York, a friend and I spent an amusing half hour reading ads in the underground papers for so-called relaxation spas. The copy appealed directly, if ambiguously, to the libido. "What hasn't your woman done for you lately?" (Well, she hasn't brought me any twelve-year-old virgins for several months, but that's understandable. The neighborhood supply has been depleted.) Another ad offered magnificent handmaidens in assorted color combi-

nations—gorgeous blondes, ravishing redheads, and exquisite brunettes. (I suppose that if you asked for an exquisite blonde, you'd get turned down. "Sorry. No substitutions. Please order from the menu.") Apparently the basic form of pleasure at these places is something called the local. I am familiar with most sexual slang, but that one escapes me. Is it what I think it is? —N. B., Scarsdale, New York.

Probably, unless you think it's a branch of the Teamsters Union. In massage parlance, a local is a technique intended to produce a release from muscular tension via a body rub administered midway between the navel and the knees. It usually works. A local should not be confused with an express, the term for a patron who achieves a release from muscular tension as soon as he takes off his towel.

The Love Muscle

For five years, I have enjoyed an active sex life. I thought that I had the basics down, but now and then I discover my naivete. For example, Bitch, the story by Roald Dahl in the July Playboy, says that there are women with "an extraordinarily powerful muscle in a region where other women seem to have no muscles at all." My gynecologist advised me that by exercising my vaginal muscles regularly, I could strengthen them to the point where I could massage or even hold my man inside me—increasing the friction and intensity of feeling for both myself and him. He suggested that I tense the muscles at least ten times a day. He added that it would take a good six months, but the end would be rewarding. The exercise apparently tightens and firms all the related muscles supporting the urinary and reproductive tract—making pregnancy and recovery much easier. Why didn't someone tell me this five years ago? —Miss B. C., Austin, Texas.

You didn't ask. The training of erotic musculature is well known in the East, but American women have only recently become comfortable with or even interested in such an active role. If you want to go deeper into the subject, consult Alex Comfort's *Joy of Sex*. He suggests trying to draw a large Pyrex test tube into the vulva without using your hands (how's that for serious scientific value, judge?). Comfort also quotes English writer and adventurer Richard Burton as saying that any woman can learn to use her vaginal and pelvic muscles "by throwing her mind into the part concerned." We agree. Master this technique and your boyfriends will love you for your mind.

The Sound of Sex

Concerning the letter to The Playboy Advisor (Playboy, April) from the gentleman suffering embarrassment because his girl has to ask him if he has finished yet: Let it be known that the most dismaying turn-off for the female ego is the quiet corner. Nothing inspires more industrious attention to the subtle nuances of sensuous quirking and jerking than the thrilling reward of guttural male moans. If you want to improve a girl's oral-sex technique, just give her a little audio feedback. I would not waste my talents on a quiet corner. I would think him strangely inhibited and not ready or receptive to the kind of open, giving sex that I enjoy. —Miss J. G., Torrance, California.

We think the noises of lovemaking sound best in stereo—whatever the volume. Indeed, the only time we forgive a silent partner is when her mouth is full or we're trying not to disturb the couple next to us at the movies. But perhaps you should give some of those strong, silent types a second chance—maybe they need more attention. Use your fingernails, or maybe whips and chains.

A few months ago, my wife and I saw a film called 10 that had Bo Derek and Dudley Moore trying to make love to Ravel's Bolero. It was hysterically funny and launched a conversation about what kind of music was best for sex. I said that for a couple to have a good long-lasting relationship, the male and the female would have to enjoy listening to the same music while making love. My wife said that the two would work out the same way they worked out other sexual differences. Since she likes disco and I like rock, that could present some problems. What do you say? —S. J., Canton, Ohio.

We say what Tina Turner says: "First we're gonna do it nice and easy, then we're gonna do it nice and rough." Take turns. As for Ravel's *Bolero* —we added that one to our Frisbee collection in college. This is a serious moral question, and one of the few situations in which honesty is not the best policy. Tell your wife that there are scientific studies that show disco is not conducive to good sex. Indeed, that babies born to parents doing it to disco show a higher incidence of birth defects and may end up in government. If she does not respond to lies, buy headphones, and take turns playing "Name That Tune" in bed.

Help! It seems as though you are my last resort. Would you please tell me why 99 percent of the men I have gone to bed with, all seemingly worldly fellows who want to be able to do anything and everything to me while making love, and expect me to do likewise, look at me as though I am out of my mind when I ask them to make up a sexy story, or talk sexy, or even just talk? The best lovers I have had have been those with some imagination who are not afraid to express their fantasies. If they say they can't and ask me to express mine, does it ever turn them on! Am I wrong in wanting a fellow to talk sexy, to make up the wildest stories? I'm beginning to be afraid to even say anything, even though sexy stories turn me on so much. —Miss D. C., Culver City, California.

You're not wrong to want a sound track to accompany sex: There's nothing like a few cries, whispers and "Oh, God, don't stops" to tell you that you must be doing something right. But you should be aware that you're going up against a deeply ingrained sexual stereotype. Women make noise because men like them to. Men have viewed themselves as the active agent for so long, it is difficult for them to break down their inhibitions and reverse the process. A recent study suggests that there might be other reasons for silence during sex. Scientists observed a colony of baboons and discovered that only the dominant males vocalized loudly and frequently during copulation. The researchers suggest that silence is a safety precaution on the part of the inferior males: It allows them to score without attracting the attention of every dude in the neighborhood. On the other hand, the noisemaking on the part of the dominant males also prevents interference—in effect, the leader proclaims, "If you know what's good for you, you'll keep your ass on the other side of the savanna until I'm through." So tell your lovers that it's natural to go ape—if they are really dominant.

I have sex with my girlfriend often and we both enjoy it. However, something is missing. I want her to talk dirty. I want her to say things like: "I want to feel your giant cock in my pussy!" or "Cram your prick in and screw me!" We love each other very much and I've tried talking to her. I know she would do it if she could, and she wants to talk dirty, but when she tries, nothing comes out of her mouth and she gets upset with herself. What can we do? —T. N., Windsor, Connecticut.

Obviously, your girlfriend thinks that love means never having to say "Cram your prick in and screw me!" She should be reminded of her civic duty. The First Amendment guarantees freedom of expression—verbal, if not physical. (We have a hard time separating the two.) She's also missing something. The February 1978 "Playboy Sex Poll" found that 82 percent of men liked a good talking to in the sack. Seventy-eight percent of the women liked words of love. If she doesn't know what to say, try flash cards. Or, perhaps, find a suitably risqué novel and have her read aloud while you tuck yourself in.

The Flying Philadelphian

Unfortunately, I attend school in Philadelphia. Never mind the jokes: the facts are bad enough. Did you know that in this city, they put the clocks in the sidewalks under clear-plastic manhole covers, because everyone is too bummed out to look up at towers? Really. But to get to the point: What is a flying Philadelphia fuck? The phrase has become part of my vocabulary in the past year, but I don't know for sure what it refers to. Can you enlighten me? —D. O., Philadelphia, Pennsylvania.

Actually, it's a form of fellatio—a particularly gymnastic variety that's billed as the ultimate sexual experience, probably because it makes such a good story if you live to tell about it. The recipe includes a curtain rod or chinning bar, a rocking chair and a cooperative young miss (or whatever—Philadelphia *is* the City of Brotherly Love). Robert A. Wilson, author of *Playboy's Book of Forbidden Words*, describes the subsequent action: "The woman sits on the rocking chair, while the man, nude, stands upon its arms, holding on to the curtain rod with both hands. She fellates him by rocking herself back and forth and, at the crucial moment, he lifts his feet off the arms of the chair and hangs from the rod. Allegedly, because every muscle in his body is under maximum tension, his orgasmic spasms will be magnified most salubriously." Try it and you'll qualify for a Presidential Fitness Award. Now you may well ask what Philadelphia has to do with it—but not this month.

Popcorn Surprise

What is a popcorn surprise? I heard a folk singer do a parody of late Fifties rock songs called "Front Row Frenzy." I gathered from the lyrics ("Popcorn surprise/opened her eyes") that it had something to do with porno movies, but I'm not sure. True? —J. S., Portland, Oregon.

In the beginning was the folded newspaper and/or the derby hat. Placed in the lap, they concealed masturbatory action in adult moviehouses. (We heard of a dude who—in a classic display of one-upmanship—used a top hat instead of a derby.) Raincoats with slit pockets enjoyed the dark light of fashion for a while, but the emergence of mixed audiences precipitated the tactic called popcorn surprise. The male camouflages his erection in a container of popcorn (having first cut a hole in the bottom), then invites his partner to help herself—hence the phrase "coming soon in a theater near you."

The Silken Saddle

Have you ever heard of a practice called the silken saddle? One of my girlfriends glanced through my closet the other day and said that I was missing the essential ingredient for a silken saddle and that she would have to correct the situation. What am I in for? —M. S., Detroit, Michigan.

A delightful surprise, and we wish we could be there. A silken saddle is a nice bit of autoerotic stimulation. A woman draws a long silk scarf back and forth between her legs until she can't take it any longer. (The motion is similar to drying oneself, except that dryness is not the goal.) Terminally excited, she will fall into your arms and you ride off into the sunset. You may want to beat her to it and buy a silk scarf yourself. Not to your taste? We've found that, in a pinch, old school ties work just as well. For variety, so does a well-polished chain. Get it on.

Strokes

Different strokes for different folks is a fairly popular slang expression; one of my friends claims it is based on historical evidence. Apparently, some scholar devoted his life to a study of the average number of strokes needed to bring women of other nations to climax. Have you ever heard of such a study?
—H. H., Roanoke, Virginia.

Yes, from a Navy recruiting officer. Actually, there was a study of that sort conducted in the 1800s by Jacobus Sutor, a surgeon in the French army. (Men stationed at hardship outposts learn to pass the time in odd ways.) Sutor's findings were published in 1893; *L'Amour aux Colonies* included such erotic recipes as "Nine times shallow and one time deep" for Hindus, "Ten times shallow and slow, ten times deep and quick" for Japanese (repeat if necessary or possible) and, finally, "Forty times in and out will bring the majority of Chinese women to a climax," although the more responsive ones will get off after "eight shallow thrusts and two deep ones." Why the emphasis on shallow strokes? Masters and Johnson point out that the outer third of the vagina is the area most sensitive to stimulation—as a woman becomes excited, this area becomes engorged with blood and tightens around the penis, while the inner two thirds of the vagina expands. Shallow strokes, therefore, may tease and arouse a woman as much as or more than deep thrusts. So hire a coxswain and conduct your own study.

Toe Sucking

I am a devout heterosexual male of twenty years. I recently went to bed with a woman and a mutual male friend. Picture the three of us on a king-size bed, smoking herbs and drinking the toxic juices of fine grapes. Time progressed until my friend and I started to take turns rubbing and kissing the woman. The movements advanced to fast-ass foreplay and the removal of all garments. Well, after another joint, my true-blue color surfaced and I started to mount this luscious lass. I did not concern myself with our male friend, figuring he would wait his turn for climax. But, instead, he did the most unusual thing: He started sucking and licking the woman's toes. Yes, I will repeat that—toes. My female friend at first laughed, because it tickled. She started to kick at him to get him to stop. But because I had already penetrated those furry lips, she could not put up much of a fight. So our friend and I talked her into trying to enjoy it. To this day, I have never seen a woman enjoy herself so. Her vagina pulled and tugged on me—more than I do to myself when I masturbate. The more he sucked the girl's toes, the more she moaned and fought. Then she started clawing with those god-awful nails. My friend told me later that her toes curled up toward her head when she climaxed. I managed to climax twice without pulling out. The girl said she had a multiple orgasm and, believe it or not, our friend came all over the bed just from the excitement. What do you make of that? Is toe sucking an accepted technique? —N. L., San Francisco, California.

Is that what John Lennon meant by the phrase toe-jam football? After the big three (mouth, hands, genitals), your toes are probably your most sexually talented organ. They are responsive (as your girlfriend discovered) and they can also be aggressive. (Next time you're eating in a fancy restaurant, slip off a shoe and extend your leg under the table for an intimate caress of your date. Maybe she'll think it's not your toe.) The toes are directly connected to the sexual nervous system—when a person has an orgasm, his or her toes will involuntarily curl. It's possible to reverse the process: Play one end against the middle. It's fun in groups or as one-on-one foreplay.

Recently, a young lady spent the night at my apartment. After a strenuous session of tantric lovemaking, we collapsed backward and untangled ourselves. Lying there head to feet reminded me of the good old days in summer camp—I challenged her to a bit of Indian wrestling. Once. Twice. On the third count, we locked legs. As I started to pull her over toward me, she reached out and grabbed my penis, which became erect almost immediately. Shouting, "Foul!" I grabbed her below the belt and discovered, to her delight, that she was equally vulnerable. We lay there for several minutes, with our legs entwined, stroking each other lightly, getting very excited. We soon reached the point where our whole bodies ached to be involved. Not wanting to shift position, we began to suck on each other's toes, on the noninterlocked feet. (I know this sounds confusing, but imagine how it felt.) The climax was terrific, precipitated mainly by the oral sex on the toes. I'm freaked out; I had no idea that toes were sensitive. Have you ever heard of anything like this? —T. M., Des Moines, Iowa.

Yes. It's a favorite form of foreplay among politicians, although they usually go for the whole foot. The sucking is a popular sensory-awareness exercise in encounter groups. It is a novel way for couples to get to know each other intimately; also, it gets them turned around in the right direction.

Telephone Sex

My lover and I, both being rather hot-blooded, are in the midst of a long-distance love affair—literally. The situation is this: He calls me two or three times daily. Inevitably, the conversation turns to sex, which makes us horny. Lately, we've begun indulging in verbal masturbation—each of us talking the other to the point of climax. Is such behavior normal? Healthy? Legal? —Miss M. T., Washington, D.C.

This form of oral sex has become popular; for one thing, it allows lovers to communicate without resorting to the U.S. mails. (Interstate transport of obscene material is a Federal offense.) But you should be careful. One of our favorite research assistants used to engage in telephone high-jinks with her boyfriend. Late one night, her phone rang and she immediately went into her routine. After about twenty minutes, she suddenly realized that the stunned silence and/or the heavy breathing at the other end was not that of her boyfriend. Apparently, the poor guy had been trying to reach Dial-a-Prayer and just got lucky.

Undressing

When I get a girl in my bedroom and we are starting to enjoy ourselves, I get scared. I want to make love, but I don't know what to do or how to get her clothes off. I've heard that undressing is the most important stage in preparing for sex. Can you suggest a step-by-step method? —B. D., Fullerton, California.

Sure. Watch closely the person who dresses you in the morning, then reverse the process with your girl. (The item of clothing you don't recognize is a bra; it unhooks in the back or front.) We're only kidding; you are correct in assuming that undressing is important, but there is no set way to approach the subject. The method should vary according to the mood. New lovers almost naturally savor a slow disrobing—after all, you see another person's body for the first time only once. Each piece of clothing removed imparts an erotic friction and a sense of release to the encounter. Consider a blouse edged across a collarbone, a dress bunched just below an expectant breast, the descent of a pair of Levi's down an inner thigh or the moment a woman arches her back to allow the removal of an undergarment. Now take a cold shower. Bare in mind that later, an economy of expectation may dictate a sudden strip-tease, with both partners overcoming the obstacles between themselves and what they know is about to happen. If you think it might be worth the expense, buy your girlfriend a light cotton dress and literally tear it off her body. It's like splitting firewood—her nakedness is immediate and will certainly kindle your fires. You're on your own from there on in.

Who Has the Best Time in Bed?

A couple of my frat brothers have placed a bet on which sex receives more pleasure from orgasm. I'm holding the money and have been entrusted with the task of finding out the facts. Can you help us settle the question? Who does get more kicks from sex? —V. W., Madison, Wisconsin.

Whoever is on top? Physiologically, male and female orgasms are similar. Subjectively, it's even harder to tell the difference. Over the past year, researchers have conducted several interesting studies to determine which gender enjoys sex more. In one, E. B. Proctor and N. Wagner distributed forty-eight written descriptions of orgasm to a group of obstetricians, psychologists and medical students, then asked the group to guess which sex had written which descriptions. The professionals could not identify the sex of the authors—which suggests that the pleasure response is essentially the same for both men and women. If you want to settle the bet in public, why not repeat the experiment at your next fraternity get-together? Have all the brothers and their guests describe an orgasmic experience in twenty-five words or less on a 3-by-5-inch index card. Then ask the party to guess the sex (and perhaps the identity) of the authors. Keep the descriptions on file: you can perform magic tricks: Take a card, any card.

A few of us were debating the old question: Who has more fun during sex— men or women? One of our group suggested that men were anatomically equipped to have more fun, since they have more nerve endings in their genitals. Could this be true? —C. B., Madison, Wisconsin.

Your friend may have a point. According to Dr. F. Brantley Scott, "The glans of the clitoris does have fewer nerve endings than the glans of the penis, because the surface area of the glans clitoridis is smaller than that of the glans penis. Anatomic studies have shown that on a per-square centimeter surface area, the number of nerve endings in the glans clitoridis is equal to that in the same surface area of the glans penis. Other anatomic studies, however, have shown that the prudendal nerve, which is the main sensory nerve root supplying the glans penis and the glans clitoridis, is significantly smaller in diameter in the female as opposed to the male. This would corroborate the suggestion that there are fewer nerve endings in the glans clitoridis than in the glans penis." We tried to verify his conclusion in independent research conducted in our *Playboy* test bedrooms. Do you have any idea how hard it is to count nerve endings when your partner keeps moving?

CHAPTER SEVEN

Oral Sex

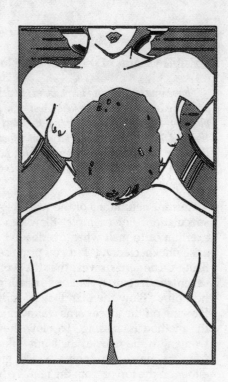

The Origins of Oral Sex

After many years of indulging in the most basic form of sex—intercourse—I met an uninhibited girl who introduced me to the fine art of fellatio. She was surprised that I had never before experienced that particular delight. After all, she said, it's been around forever. Curiosity got the better of me: How old is oral sex? Certainly, the unsung heroine who first gave head ranks with the inventor of the wheel, bread and pants. Kenneth Clark somehow missed this point in his history of civilization. Can you enlighten me? What is the earliest mention of fellatio? —L. P., Cambridge, Massachusetts.

We brushed the cobwebs from the shelves of our favorite adult bookstore and came up with a candidate for the earliest representation of oral sex: The *Papyrus Ani* of the Egyptian *Book of the Dead* shows the goddess Isis performing fellatio on the mummified god Osiris—apparently in an attempt to call him back from the world of the dead. (If this doesn't get a rise out of the old boy, nothing will.) The practice goes back to the dawn of man. If prostitution is the oldest profession, then fellatio—the stock in trade of the ladies of the night—is the oldest trick in the book. Or the mouth. But one thing you should know about old tricks—they don't get to be old if they don't work the first time. Or the second time. Enjoy.

Possible Origins of the Term Blow Job

I have undertaken an independent, in depth survey to determine the origin and accuracy of the term blow job. Most of my subjects report that the actual act of blowing—i.e. puckering the lips to direct a stream of air at the object in question—does not do too much for them. However, reversing the direction of the air flow does wonders, as you can imagine. My question is this: Why, if men like it so much, did they choose such a misleading adjective? —Miss E.A.E., St. Paul, Minnesota.

Current definitions of the word blow offer seeds for some intriguing speculation. For example; Blow can mean to put out of breath with exertion or to melt when overloaded. Hear, hear! Blowing in means to arise unexpectedly. ("But you promised . . ." "I couldn't help myself.") Slang dictionaries reveal that the word had sexual connotations in the seventeenth century, but none relating to oral sex per se. The old sailor's hornpipe "Blow the Man Down" indicates the end but not the means. Blowing off the loose corns was akin to getting your rocks off; but again, the method is missing. To blow the ground sells meant to lie with a woman on the floor of the stairs. Blow referred to an act of copulation from the man's standpoint, which, given the seventeenth century, was either on the top or from the rear. To hit the blow was to steal the goods. ("Where did it go?") And, finally, a blower was a harlot or the mistress of a highwayman. Our guess is that, since most men do not visit prostitutes for regular sex, the term came to mean an act of fellatio. But that's just word of mouth, so feel free to continue your research.

Words of Love

How's your Latin? My current boyfriend is a former divinity student, who gave up the cloth for the carnal. He seems to be making up for lost time in bed and, to the best of my abilities and inclinations, I have tried to help. Recently, after a bout of oral sex, I asked if he liked the way I performed fellatio. He said, with what sounded like disappointment, that actually I had performed irrumatio. Can you tell me what it is? —S. H., Cambridge, Massachusetts.

Ah, yes. We recall now that our high school Latin teacher promised us that studying a dead language would improve our vocabulary. It didn't, but it may help your sex life. The Romans had two words for oral sex. *Irrumationem* indicated a form of buccal copulation in which the mouth is a passive receptacle. In *fellationem*, the mouth is actively stimulating the male organ. The fact that of the two words, only *fellatio* entered the English language may indicate a preference. Move to the head of the class and try again.

Reveille

The other morning, I rose before my boyfriend and spent several minutes watching him sleep. I noticed that he developed an erection just before he woke up. I remember reading that this is one of the indications that a person is dreaming—rapid eye movements being another. Do you think he would mind if I performed fellatio on his sleeping organ some morning? —Miss C. W., Kansas City, Kansas.

Go ahead and blow reveille—then you'll really see some rapid eye movements.

The Basic Ingredients

I've just finished reading Erica Jong's Fear of Flying, *in which she recounts an anecdote about a woman who was on a strict diet but who still didn't lose weight. The doctor asked her to list everything she ate, then, unable to figure out where the extra calories came from, asked her if she was sure she had listed every mouthful. "Mouthful? I didn't realize that had calories." The woman turned out to be a prostitute who swallowed ten to fifteen mouthfuls of semen a day. Supposedly, "Ten to fifteen ejaculations [a day] turned out to be the equivalent of a seven-course meal at the Tour d'Argent." Is this true? A lot of women are reading that book, and I'm afraid that some of them will use the information as an excuse to forgo fellatio. What are the ingredients, caloric count, etcetera, of the average ejaculation? —M. R., Phoenix, Arizona.*

All right, you clowns—this is the last time we answer this question. Take notes: A short quiz will be given: pass the written part and you get to take the orals. The chemical composition of ejaculate varies from individual to individual and within the same individual from time to time. Semen is essentially seminal plasma and spermatozoa. Approximately 8 percent of the substance is dry weight. According to the fine print on the label, it contains minute quantities of more than thirty elements—such as fructose, ascorbic acid, cholesterol, creatine, citric acid, urea, uric acid, sorbitol, pyruvic acid, glutathione, inositol, lactic acid, nitrogen, B_{12}, various salts (sodium, zinc, calcium, chloride, magnesium, potassium, phosphorus, ammonia) and enzymes (hyaluronidase, spermadine, choline, spermine, purine and pyrimidine) and deoxyribonucleic acid (DNA). Blood-group antigens are also present. The caloric content is minimal (perhaps one or two calories per ejaculate) and the nutritional value practically nonexistent. In other words—it won't blow a diet. And, since semen does not contain any artificial flavoring, meat by-products or monosodium glutamate, your organically inclined friends can continue their inclinations toward your organ.

Just in case Jong writes another book: semen does not cause cavities, does not improve the voices of opera singers, does not clear up the complexion (even when applied directly from the tube), nor does it cause the growth of facial hair on the recipient. It does cause babies. If someone can still find an excuse not to perform fellatio, we suggest you take up where the woman who wrote the next letter left off.

Oral Sex and Breast Size

Last month, I went to Florida and saw my cousin. I really got a surprise. The last time I saw her, we were both the same size—34B—but in the past two years, she has grown to a 36C. (We are both 21.) I told her I had tried exercise to increase the size of my bust but that nothing had worked. I asked her secret and she said that she had read an article suggesting that women who frequently swallowed semen experienced breast enlargement. According to the article, semen contains some substance that stimulates growth. My cousin said she liked oral sex a lot, that when she gave oral sex, she always swallowed the semen, and that after about five or six months, she noticed that her bust started to get a little larger. Now she tries to give oral sex at least twice a week. She told another girl about what she learned, and that girl's bust went from a 34B to a 35B in one year. Is there any truth to this theory? —Miss C. J., New York, New York.

It's questions like this that make people think we invent these letters. Ahem. For the record, semen contains minute quantities of more than thirty substances—such as fructose, ascorbic acid, cholesterol, creatine, citric acid, urea, uric acid, sorbitol, pyruvic acid, glutathione, inositol, lactic acid, nitrogen, B_{12}, sodium, zinc, calcium, chlorine, magnesium, potassium, phosphorus, ammonia, hyaluronidase, spermidine, choline, spermine, purine, pyrimidine, deoxyribonucleic acid (DNA) and blood-group antigens. None of those is known to permanently increase breast size. (We suspect that your cousin is a later bloomer; that or she's taking birth-control pills—which do cause breasts to swell.) However, we are willing to conduct further research ourselves. If you know of any volunteers who would like to further the cause of science, please have them contact us.

How Long Should You Last

I have been under the impression that a good lover has the ability to maintain an erection for a long period of time. Now my girlfriend says that if I climax quickly during oral sex, she knows that I am really turned on and that turns her on even more. How can I learn to last and blast? —D. C., Carbondale, Illinois.

The original Kinsey study on male sexuality found that 75 percent of the men in the sample reached orgasm within two minutes of penetration during intercourse. However, later reports based on the same raw data suggest that the average self-report of duration was between six and seven minutes. It turns out that Kinsey's data showed three clusters of self-report estimates—at one to three minutes, six to eight minutes and ten to twenty minutes for a 6.68 minute average. Those are figures for intercourse. There are no comparable figures for oral sex. And that is where statistics cease to be of use. If you are concerned with premature ejaculation during intercourse, you may or may not find solace in those figures. One sex researcher points out that even if you last longer than seven minutes, you do not noticeably increase the chance that your girlfriend will have an orgasm. (Ironically, Kinsey found that the women in his study were a full minute off in their estimates of how long sex lasted—their average was 5.65 minutes.) The notion that sex has to last a certain amount of time is limiting: Some of the best sex in the world has been on the fly—in telephone booths, taxicabs, elevators. In this instance, your girlfriend is correct. She is giving you pleasure. You do not have to exhibit control. Why would you want to? Indeed, the point of oral sex is to attain complete abandon. And if she gets off on seeing you lose control—terrific.

Lockjaw

This may sound like a stupid question, but how do you keep your jaw from aching when you give fellatio and try to keep your teeth out of the way? I like to make the pleasure last for my husband, but my jaw muscles get so tired that sometimes I just try to get him off fast to ease the fatigue in my mouth. —Mrs. C. K., Montpelier, Ohio.

No, your question isn't stupid at all. Many women experience similar discomfort in prolonged fellatio. The only solution we can suggest is to take it slow. Alternate fellatio with licking, kissing and gentle biting. If you sometimes get too tired to take it slow, then take it fast. We're sure your husband won't mind.

Difficulty Reaching Orgasm

I have been married for ten wonderful years and have enjoyed many wondrous sexual experiences. My wife is a fantastic bed partner and pleases me in every way but one. I have tried for years to come via fellatio with no success, much to my dismay and her feelings of inadequacy. The real mystery is that she gives the best head I've ever had. She can deep throat and knows all the tricks that should result in a tremendous orgasm, and probably would in a normal man. That is my concern. Am I ever going to reach orgasm through fellatio? —R. M., Zanesville, Ohio.

First of all, we suggest that you relax. Stop making such a big thing out of your inability to reach orgasm during fellatio. Probably, neither your responsiveness nor your wife's technique is inadequate. Rather, you may be holding back because you subconsciously think that coming in a woman's mouth is somehow dirty or wrong. (You are absolutely right. That's what makes it so much fun.) There are still a lot of taboos surrounding oral sex in our society. You may simply be trying too hard. Performance anxiety is the main cause of most sexual problems. Often, the more one tries, the less successful he or she really is. Both you and your wife should try to dispel any of the nervous tension that might arise during fellatio. Learn to enjoy the pleasurable sensations she gives you, without worrying about the outcome. Finally, you might try switching to fellatio in midstream, interrupting manual stimulation or intercourse for the coup de grâce.

This problem may not be unique, but as far as I'm concerned, it might as well be. I'm disturbed by the fact that it takes an inordinate amount of time to achieve orgasm when my wife and I have intercourse. What's more, save for one time (I neglected to jot down the date, time and atmospheric conditions) I have never been able to achieve orgasm from oral sex. And this is The Age of the Blow Job! What disturbs me most about this condition is that it takes me almost no time at all to achieve orgasm when I masturbate. Is this problem physical or psychological? What can I do about it? It would be nice if I could climax within a reasonable time. —C. M., Nashville, Tennessee.

This is "The Age of the Blow Job"? We're always getting those Chinese New Years confused. Oh, well. You don't have that much of a problem. It's obvious that you require fairly rough handling in order to achieve orgasm. (Nothing like a case of dishpan hands to get someone off.) In comparison, intercourse and fellatio are fairly mild forms of stimulation. You could ask your wife to combine manual and oral—that might whip you into shape. During intercourse, have her reach down and give you a few strokes with her hand. As for duration: When it comes to sex, there is no such thing as reasonable time.

Reluctant Lovers

I've started dating a woman who seems almost perfect. When it comes to making love, she is sensuous and unrestrained—as long as we are engaged in intercourse. After several loving encounters, I am very conscious of the fact that she never takes control, that she never performs oral sex. I am faced with an interesting contradiction. Could someone so uninhibited in bed have a hang-up about oral sex? —A. B., Chicago, Illinois.

It takes all kinds to fill the freeways. We recall reading that while 45 percent of wives performed oral sex in a marriage, only 15 percent did so in affairs. We assume that there is a similar breakdown in unmarried relationships. For some women, oral sex is the last gesture—something they perform only from the heart, with someone they are intimate with. For some women, it is an easy way to dispense with strangers without taking their clothes off. There are mixed signals. As someone once said: Life is not fair. When everything is permitted, you take your chances. . . . Our advice: At the next opportunity, raise the issue, preferably out of bed—over lunch, or Scrabble, or whatever. Take a sexual history. Ask about her experience, her upbringing. You might get a revealing answer.

My boyfriend and I have gone round and round about this and have finally decided to leave the matter in your hands. Every time we make love, I first perform fellatio, because he enjoys it tremendously and it turns me on knowing that he loves it. But he obviously doesn't believe in the golden rule of doing unto others as others do unto you. We have talked about his performing cunnilingus—he said that the day I tasted like a strawberry would be the day he'd enjoy it. To say the least, I was hurt. My other lovers never complained and, indeed, they enjoyed my reaction to the act. Any solutions? —Miss R. J., Reno, Nevada.

Lovemaking works only when it is a reciprocating engine. Anyone who doesn't make the effort to please a partner deserves a pie in the face—make it a strawberry one. Your boyfriend sounds like a lost cause, who at best has no tact. Reject part of a person and you reject all of the person. You are beautiful; if he doesn't appreciate it, find someone who does. (You've got our address, right?)

I'm convinced that cunnilingus is among the most pleasant nonspectator sports around. This is not to say that I survive on a steady diet of pussy, but I do think that once a week would be nice. Since my wife seldom fails to climax when I chow down on her clit, one would assume that she felt the same as I do. Not true, sports fans. For some strange reason, she allows me to munch her muff only about twice a year. I've tried reason, I've tried logic, I've tried anger, but she isn't close to changing her habit. Box lunches are addictive and I'm in danger of death by starvation. What do you suggest? —L. T., Providence, Rhode Island.

Ropes, chains, whips and a bib. Your wife for some reason (maybe religious upbringing or some psychological difficulty) must withhold from you what you crave most. It doesn't sound as though she gives a damn what you want, nor does she want to allow herself what she enjoys, either. Gentle persuasion seems in order. If that doesn't work, throw her out of the house. Then place an ad in your local underground paper that reads something like: "Man who loves giving head wants women who enjoy same." Your phone will be busy. Unless, God forbid, you give incredibly bad head, and that's why your wife was turned off. No teeth, please.

Help! I have tried everything and you're my last hope. I am very open to any kind of sex and have always enjoyed experimentation. I recently married (my husband and I had lived together for several months). Now, here's the shock. After one week of marriage, he informed me that he can't stand to go down on me, or any other woman, for that matter. He claims that the "fishy" smell of the vagina is distasteful. I've tried douching, but then he says that the smell is soapy. What do you suggest? My husband doesn't bother to get into any kind of foreplay. He just lies back and expects me to kiss and lick him from head to toe, front and back. Then he's ready to go and I'm as dry as a bone. Even my imagination doesn't help anymore. He seems to think it's my problem, that I'm just oversexed. —Mrs. D. H., Chicago, Illinois.

First: Visit your gynecologist. The most common cause of vaginal odor is a bacterial infection. The characteristic fishy smell is symptomatic of a *Hemophilus vaginalis* infection. A vaginal smear will indicate the presence of the bacteria. Treatment consists of both you and your partner taking antibiotics. (Both partners need treatment to prevent a Ping-Pong reinfection pattern.) In addition, you may use a sulfa cream for a few days. However, it sounds to us as though this problem is in your husband's head, not yours. If the doctor gives you a clean bill, you're going to have to tackle the problem of communication with a reluctant spouse. There is nothing distasteful about a natural woman in good health.

After several halfhearted attempts, my girlfriend now refuses to perform fellatio—a kind of sexplay I especially enjoy—on the grounds that she finds the act distasteful. She claims that it is her right to abstain from any form of sex that she finds offensive. Otherwise, lovemaking becomes an obligation, et cetera. Lately, she's taken to wearing one of those buttons that announce, I JUST SAID NO AND I DON'T FEEL GUILTY. Needless to say, I am bothered by her position—it strikes me as the old ultimatum: Respect me, respect my inhibitions. What should I do? —P. G., Portland, Oregon.

Look for someone wearing a button that announces I JUST SAID YES AND I DON'T FEEL GUILTY. Or unbutton the girl you already know:

Talking is an incredibly persuasive form of oral sex. Try to create an atmosphere of trust in which she can shed her images of "foul fellatio." Inhibitions melt in the mind, not in the mouth. (It doesn't hurt to practice what you preach, either. Do onto others as you would have them do unto you.) There is nothing inherently distasteful about oral sex, provided you are clean and relatively healthy. If she is bothered by the flavor, have her try an erotic hors d'oeuvre: artichokes. No kidding. Scientists at Yale found that eating artichokes improves the flavor of whatever follows. Dousing the old swizzle stick in brandy or a flavored liqueur will also help. (Why not try artichoke liqueur?) Also, suggest an aggressive approach to fellatio—if the orgasm occurs far enough back in the throat, it will completely bypass the taste buds. She won't notice a thing, but you will. Yes, indeed. Aggressiveness and practice are a great cure for reluctance of any kind. The more you do something in sex, the looser you get, the more inventive, the more comfortable and, in general, the more willing to try it again. Full speed ahead.

Fear of Kissing After Oral Sex

I need your opinion. My girlfriend and I enjoy a fantastic oral-sex life. However, I have a strong taboo against kissing her after she's performed fellatio (for obvious reasons). How do I tell her "Thanks for the oral sex, but there's no way I'm going to kiss you" without hurting her or ending our evening prematurely? —A. S., Towson, Maryland.

If it's just the evening that ends, you'll be getting off lucky. We suspect that your girlfriend might find your revulsion toward kissing a shocking incongruity. If you find part of your body distasteful, how can you realistically expect your partner to continue her performance? The best sex occurs when you meet as equals, taking the same risks, and the same pleasures. Examine your taboo. Where did it come from? Does it really deserve to have that much power over your love life? Ask her what she thinks of the taste. The reality is always better than your lack of imagination. If the taste offends her, maybe she would appreciate a glass of water, mouthwash or wine on the bedside table.

Flashbacks

I'm writing to find out what you can suggest as a solution to a slight sex problem I'm having with my wife. She had some terrible experiences when she was a child living at home with her mother and father. It seems that her parents' bedroom adjoined hers. My wife has said that several times she heard her mother choking and gagging in the bedroom and never knew just what was going on. She later found out that her mother was giving her father head. Now we come to my slight sex problem. My wife won't give me head unless I wear a condom. You know how much fun it is to wear a condom during oral sex. If you rated it on a scale of 1 to 50, it might score a minus 75. My wife lets me perform oral sex on her and she has some really great orgasms, but she claims that she doesn't really like it. I feel cheated whenever I talk her into giving me head, because I must wear a rubber. I believe that my wife more or less relives her childhood listening to the sounds she makes when she gives me head. She and I love each other very much and I would do almost anything short of divorce to get some great head from her. What do you suggest? —F. K., New York, New York.

Ahem. We do not know what it is like to get head while wearing a condom, but we can guess. Sort of like taking a piss in a wet suit or getting a hand job from someone wearing a strait jacket. Your wife obviously has a problem: It sounds like you've discussed it. The problem isn't that she refuses to listen—in fact, it is just the opposite. We suggest earplugs. Or headphones. (How do you think headphones got their name?) They will provide an alternate sound track and you both should come around.

The Virgin Lover

On our most recent weekend together, my boyfriend proposed sexual intercourse, which I categorically reject until we are married. After my refusal, he convinced me to have oral sex with him. I wanted to give my virginity away on the marriage bed, not before; but now I'm wondering whether I can still think of myself as a virgin. Can I? —Miss C. V., Allentown, Pennsylvania.

Why not? The definition of virginity pertains to the breaking (or, rather, nonbreaking) of the hymen. Personally, we think you're playing silly games with yourself and that you'll be a lot more comfortable when you stop trying to find labels for your sexual status.

Deep Throat

My husband and I were inspired by the feats of fellatio that we saw in Deep Throat. *We watched in awe as Linda Lovelace took into her mouth and throat all of a penis that must have been nine inches long. Although I try, I have been unable to achieve her total grasp. An article in the April* Playboy *mentioned that she shared certain skills with professional sword swallowers. I was under the*

impression that sword swallowers used collapsible swords. What is the secret?
—Mrs. R. C., Burlington, Vermont.

A professional sword swallower, who swallows real swords, says: (1) Throw your head back as far as it will go. This opens up the throat and allows you to accept an elongated object without gagging. (Lying on your back with your head over the edge of a bed is the most comfortable way to maintain this position.) (2) Hold your breath. (Impractical in this context; we suggest that you breathe through your nose. Linda Lovelace says that she breathes around the penis on the outstroke.) (3) Practice with a blunt object before you try a real sword. (Linda says it was three weeks before she believed she could eat the whole thing.) A collapsed sword is the end, not the means of this particular trick.

The Carnal Cough Drop

My girlfriend suggested that I write to you about our favorite lovemaking technique. She really gets off when I give her head with a menthol cough drop in my mouth. The cough drop doesn't spoil the good taste—it just adds a cooling and tingling sensation to her most sensitive region. The trick is particularly effective if one stops every so often to blow on the affected area to aid evaporation. My girlfriend says that her clit has never been so hot and so cold at the same time. She thinks your readers would enjoy trying it. What do you think?
—S. T., Teaneck, New Jersey.

We thank you. Our readers thank you. But the first person you should share this information with is your girlfriend. The cough-drop caper works just as well with fellatio. Indeed, the glycerin content of the cough drop can go a long way to comfort sore-throat pain.

Water into Wine

Have you ever heard of a sexual practice known as "changing water into wine?" My girlfriend asked me if I had ever had it done to or for me. Not really knowing what it was, I answered flippantly that I had not had it done since the days I was an altar boy. She looked at me sort of funny. Did I say the wrong thing? —N. W., Corpus Christi, Texas.

Probably not. The water-into-wine trick is yet another variety of that diner's delight—fellatio. The woman fills her mouth with water, then slides her lips around the nearest thing that looks like a swizzle stick. Carefully, so as not to spill a drop, she swirls the water. The motion is that of a connoisseur testing wine or someone using the taste you hate twice a day. The results are substantial. Other beverages can be used—liquors, fruit punches, coffee (pass the cream, please), even wine—although you will have to decide whether the dish deserves a red or a white.

The Hum Job

My girlfriend and I have heard about a technique known as the hum job. It's a form of fellatio in which the girl puts her lips around her partner's testicles and hums "The Star Spangled Banner." The male immediately comes to attention. We tried it and nothing happened, even though my girlfriend hummed every song she knows. Now she's worried that she did it wrong. Any hints? —M. H., Madison, Wisconsin.

"What would you do if I hummed out of tune, would you get up and walk out on me?" Ahem. There is no standard repertoire for people who like organ music. The technique (allegedly of Arabic origin—cf. the snake charmer's flute) may require hours of concentrated effort to bring about an orgasm. Since your girlfriend's a cappella effort didn't seem to work, she might try a little instrumental accompaniment with the lip, tongue and two-handed quartet.

Gift-Wrapped

There's a letter in the September Playboy Advisor from a couple complaining about lack of success with a technique known as the hum job. May I suggest a variation: the gift wrap. Have your girlfriend mold some aluminum foil around your testicles and, with her teeth lightly touching the foil, hum her favorite song. The metallic vibrations should produce the desired effect. —A. V., San Diego, California.

We always appreciate household hints from enlightened readers. You are absolutely right: Every straight man deserves his foil. And now, take it from the top, Felicia.

Sauces, Jams and Preserves

My lover is partial to oral sex that includes side orders of sauces, jams, preserves and even peanut butter (not the chunk style). We often proceed directly to intercourse and these foods inevitably end up inside me. By the way, preserves make an especially fine lubricant or sealant. The increase in friction is sublime.

However, I'm concerned that some of these substances might not be removed by douching and that I am sitting here quietly fermenting. Is there any harm in this menu? —S. W., Birmingham, Michigan.

Probably not. Tell your lover that he has to join the clean-plate club before he gets dessert. That will settle the question of what to do with the leftovers, and you can get in a few licks yourself. Foodstuffs do make interesting lubricants, but stick to something like honey that washes off easily. Then you won't have to worry about giving birth to an eight-pound peanut-butter-and-jelly sandwich.

The Chinese Basket Trick

I've been going steady with a guy for over two years now. We make love frequently—though for the past few months, we've indulged in oral sex more often than in intercourse. We really like it. I seem to please him, but sometimes I wonder: Is there anything I could try that would improve the basic act? I would really like to surprise him with something new. —Miss J. M., Louisville, Kentucky.

We never met a girl who didn't give great head, if she gave it at all. So there is no reason to worry about your performance. However, if you want to try something radical, how about a variation of the Chinese basket trick? We recently saw a movie in which a man attached a pulley to a beam in the ceiling, then attached his girlfriend by the heels to a rope running through the aforementioned pulley. (Her hands were bound behind her back, but that lack of touch is optional.) Lying on his back, he positioned the girl over his upright member and alternately twirled, raised and lowered her until the blood rushed to her head, his head and hallelujah.

Headphones

My girlfriend and I recently discovered something that should give new meaning to the word headphones. I bought one of the new tiny cassette players with the ultralight headphones and that night, the stereo went to bed with us. While receiving head, I was listening to Michael Jackson's "Don't Stop 'Til You Get Enough." Then the idea struck me. I pushed the Talk button on the cassette player. (That overrides about 50 percent of the music and allows the headphones wearer to pick up sounds through a sensitive condenser mike.) I placed the unit down by my lady's lips and cannot describe the erotic effect it had on me. A few minutes later, we switched places and she was obviously as turned on as I had been. Being able to hear every detail of oral sex is like having three lovers at once—one giving head and one on each ear. Thought I'd share this discovery with others, but first I'll buy some stock in the company that made the cassette player. —M. M., Oceanside, California.

We thought of sending this letter along to the editors of *Playboy Guide to Electronic Entertainment*, but what the hell. Let them find their own letters.

The French Lesson

Last month I met a delightful French girl. We started dating and soon began to enjoy intercourse. I would like to further our relations and I wonder how to ask her in French if I may perform cunnilingus. —N. L., Brooklyn, New York.

We took your question to one of our French cousins at *Oui* who is bilingual as well as cunnilingual. The phrase is: *Est-ce que je peux sucer ta chatte, chérie?* She wondered why you have to ask.

Practice

The mechanic who works on my motorcycle reads all the new sex manuals and he claims that practice is the key to success. To prepare and perfect his cunnilingual skills, he removes corks from champagne bottles with his tongue. To refine his knowledge of nipples, he has carnal relations with a grape. He insists that these exercises have improved his technique, but I'm skeptical—mechanics as a rule aren't known for their credibility. What do you think? —L. B., Del Mar, California.

Football players who run through rows of old tires get better at running through rows of old tires. The exercise does little for their broken field running (opponents seldom behave like rows of old tires), but it is one way to pass the time between games. In short, why practice with an inanimate object when you can play with an animate partner? A grape cannot tell you what you are doing wrong or, for that matter, what you are doing right. Your girlfriend can and will, if you ask. Save the champagne for a victory celebration and open it the regular way.

Are Gays Better Lovers?

Gay ladies say that only a woman knows how to please another woman. My lover doesn't exactly go out of her mind with ecstasy or multiple orgasms when I perform cunnilingus with her, and I'm beginning to think I need lessons. (Neither of us had done it before.) I feel like a dunce sitting in the corner looking at two walls. Maybe I could find a lesbian to give me tips on oral sex. What do you suggest? —D. H., Des Moines, Iowa.

The gay claim is a classic example of word-of-mouth advertising—the people who believe something are the people who spread it. We are reminded of a similar proposition: that you can never find a person who makes love as well as you can masturbate. Logic like that could keep a good man down. Fortunately, a little feedback will improve any situation, and feedback is one thing you get a lot of in oral sex. There is one truth in the lesbian love rap: A woman can have fun without getting shafted. Cunnilingus is the perfect complement to coitus; what your genitals can do, the rest of you can do as well and more reliably. Face it and you'll find it is a pleasure to give pleasure without being worried about impotence, premature ejaculation or size. Who cares if somewhere in the world there is a Frenchman with a 12-inch tongue who can hold his breath for twenty minutes? If you want to use your tongue as a substitute penis, or approach your partner like an oxygen mask, go right ahead. It makes more sense, though, to explore and exploit the differences between cunnilingus and coitus. Save the penetration for later and focus (lightly) on the clitoris. In terms of pressure, less is more. Flickering touches with the tongue, nibbling, tugging or sucking motions with the lips, in combination with manual stimulation—just about everything works at one time or another. Duration is open-ended. A few minutes is fine as foreplay, but the event is fantastic in and of itself. Don't stop until your partner asks you to. If you miss a few days of work, it will be worth the effort. If she asks you to stop before you get started, you may have a problem, but one that is easily overcome. The recipient of oral sex should never be passive or reserved. If she wonders why you are doing it, chances are she won't find out. At the very least, she must pay attention. The shift in attitude can be subtle or dramatic. One woman told us that the first time she got off, her lover simply lifted her by the buttocks so that her pelvis was the highest point of her body. The blood rushing to her head, or away from it, increased and focused the erotic tension. Possibly your partner is worried about the act's being distasteful. If she is healthy, that concern is usually fictitious. Tell her that you enjoy what you're doing. As Nathaniel Bynner, the Brooklyn bard, says: "Distaste is da best taste in da world."

Your Face or Mine

There is one very basic sexual activity that I have never tried. When a man says he wants me to sit on his face, I have always hesitated and steered the activity to more familiar ground. Why? I have never understood the actual position of the man and the woman. Please explain the delicate details of this maneuver. —Miss N. J., Dallas, Texas.

If only we could make house calls. Oh, well, here goes: Chances are if a man asks, he knows what he is asking for and will be perfectly willing to lend a helping hand. Perhaps you should take a gander at Gershon Legman's classic work *Oragenitalism*, in which he reveals the following: "All the motions of her hips and torso that the woman can use in coital postures where she lies, kneels, stands or squats over the man can also be used when she is in the same position over the man for cunnilingus or the 69. In particular, the woman can use—and should make a real effort to try to learn, and learn well—the superb pelvic motion or mysterious gyration . . . La Diligence DeLyon (The Lyons Stagecoach) . . . a rapid and continuous forward and backward rolling motion of the kneeling woman's hips, similar to that known in horseback riding under the name of posting or 'broncobusting,' where the rider's body sinks and rises rhythmically forward and backward to match the motions of the galloping or bucking horse." Yee-hah. The simplest way to begin: Your partner should assume a reclining position. You may choose to face his feet, as in the *soixante-neuf* position, or reverse direction. The latter allows better contact between the clitoris and the tongue. You support most of your weight with your thighs and arms. Raise and lower yourself as the spirit moves you.

On the Job Training

Various sex journals have left me with the impression that cunnilingus is something so good women just come naturally to it, whatever the technique. Not so. My girlfriend doesn't seem to enjoy oral sex, no matter how hard or how soft I try. Do women have to learn to appreciate the act, or is my girlfriend minus a few nerve endings? —S. L., Detroit, Michigan.

Both men and women have to learn their sexual responses. It is possible that your partner will have to overcome her reservations before she can enjoy herself completely. Other cultures have discovered that cunnilingus is not immediately pleasurable. According to Ivan Bloch, in the society of Ponape (which is not, as you might think, a resort in the Catskills), "Impotent old men are employed to lick the clitoris with their tongues or else irritate it by the sting of huge ants, so that gradually the organ of voluptuousness is made more susceptible. At coitus, too, the men, at the desire of the women, must use not only their tongue but also their teeth to produce a local stimulation of the female genitals." No doubt they use those army ants that will eat anything in their path. It's not our idea of a picnic, but, by all means, persevere.

Pleasure During Period

I hope you can clear up a little disagreement between me and my boyfriend. We always go down on each other when making love. However, one weekend excursion to a ranch really blew my mind. It was a bad time for me, as I promptly started on the rag the night we got there. Then, to make things worse, I noticed that he wouldn't go down on me. None of my past lovers ever let this come between us—but my current boyfriend seems to be hung up about it. My question is this: Is there any harm in going down on a girl while she's having her period? This question is for his benefit, because I know myself that there's nothing wrong in it, but he won't believe me. Besides, if a girl's only half good for five days of the month, then she's no good at all. —Miss S. B., Tucson, Arizona.

Down, girl. You are partially correct. The blood and tissue passed during menstruation is sterile and poses no threat to the health of anyone who comes into contact with it. Lovemaking and gentle oral sex are generally safe. However, vigorous oral sex during menstruation does pose a slight problem to your health. During menstruation and pregnancy, air may pass through the lining of the placenta into the blood stream. The resulting embolism can be fatal. Admittedly, that is a rare occurrence (it can be avoided simply by not forcing air into the vagina. Your lovers should never blow the woman down). Meanwhile, back at the ranch: You may have a problem you don't realize. You say that you always go down on each other. When someone breaks a rigid pattern, the partner usually takes it personally as a sign of dissatisfaction, boredom or neurosis. Try to be more flexible and your boyfriend may respond in kind.

It's the Motion

Maybe it's a pattern, maybe it's me. The last few women I've dated have been very vocal about what pleases them. One could come only by touching herself. Another had to have a vibrator present. I'm currently seeing a woman who has such distinct ideas about sex. For one thing, she prefers that I come first. She will then rub against me with gentle motions until she comes, as I lose my erection. During oral sex, she does not like me to flick my tongue or aggressively stimulate her; she will move against my tongue until she comes, treating her clitoris as a tiny penis. I feel stymied. None of the moves I thought I had down pat seems to work with this woman. This is not the way I heard it should be. I keep asking myself: "What did you do for her?" What would you do in this situation? —N. B., Chicago, Illinois.

Probably have the time of our lives. Over the past decade, there has been a shift in our concept of sexual responsibility. It used to be that a man thought he was a man by *making* a woman come—via intercourse. Thrusting in the missionary position. The old in and out. It didn't always work, and *that* drove a lot of men crazy. Nowadays, women are more upfront about declaring what works and what doesn't. If a woman is bold enough, or honest enough, to tell you what excites her, you should feel privileged. She is giving you the keys to the kingdom, the power to please. Just remember, it was as hard for women to admit that traditional intercourse didn't work as it was for men to realize that they weren't threatened by other options. Forget your old notions about what is right and wrong. We define love as the willingness and ability to please. At the same time, you should discuss your feelings—your needs have equal weight. Try for something more. A compromise could be astonishing.

Contraceptive Foam

I recently went off the pill and got a diaphragm with which I use a spermatocidal cream or jelly. Since then, I have had sex with a friend who greatly enjoys the oral approach. (He's not the only one!) But, "Alas," he cried, "you taste awful!" I was, needless to say, greatly dismayed by this comment. I tasted some of this evil jelly and he was right, it was pretty bad. So the question is: Is there any flavored jelly cream on the market that tastes good and prevents one plus one from equaling more than two? —Miss A. H., Seattle, Washington.

Unfortunately, most of the companies that make jellies, foams and creams consider them contraceptive substances, not condiments or party dips. Hence, they have done very little to improve the palatability of their products. The companies are, however, gradually becoming aware of the need for such a product and enough consumer pressure could see results soon. By the way, there are no harmful side effects (other than the taste) when these products are ingested in small quantities, so you can feel free to sample them to your heart's content. It might help to have a carafe of good tequila nearby when you do your tasting, though. It makes a most pleasant chaser.

Foam: A Matter of Taste

I would like to offer a suggestion to Miss A. H. in Seattle (The Playboy Advisor, September) and to everyone else who has experienced the unpleasant taste of contraceptive jellies currently available. Because I don't enjoy the taste, I usually have oral sex before my partner inserts her diaphragm. We make insertion of the diaphragm part of our lovemaking. The sex is better and much more intimate than if she were to slip off to the bathroom by herself. Also, we like to have oral sex without intercourse (and subsequent birth-control hassles) once in a while. —E. B., Cherry Hill, New Jersey.

We like your attitude: You've got a good head on your shoulders. Other readers wrote to offer solutions to the problem of contraceptive-jelly aftertaste. A number recommended Koromex II by Holland-Rantos—claiming that it has a neutral taste or, better yet, for some palates, a slight raspberry flavor. The perfect thing for toast or biscuits.

Dueling Scars

Not long ago, I brought a new lover home for a weekend of sexual delights beyond my wildest expectations. So much for the good news. The morning after she left, as I was brushing my teeth, I noticed a cut, or sore, on the underside of my tongue (on the tiny vertical fold of skin that attaches the tongue to the mouth). I'm afraid to go to the doctor. Is it herpes or some other dread venereal disease? —W. L., Chicago, Illinois.

Bite your tongue. It's not a case of the dreaded Tyrolean waffle stomp or the black rose of Calcutta. It's something better. Not long ago, a *Playboy* reader (who happens to be a dental student) sent us a copy of an article published in *The Journal of the American Dental Association* titled "Lingual Frenum Ulcer Resulting from Orogenital Sex." Don't you wish you got our mail? It seems that in the heat of passion, a man sometimes extends his tongue in such a fashion that said tongue is lacerated by the mandibular incisors. (Down Fang.) The first cut is the deepest—the phenomenon you noticed is mechanical, not infectious (like catching yourself in your zipper). The wound should heal within seven to ten days. Of course, long before then, you should invite the woman back, show her the damage and invite her sympathy. It's not the same as a Prussian dueling scar, but in this day and age, it comes close.

The Advanced Lesson in Oral Sex—A Reader Survey

The other night, my lover mentioned that he had experienced great head only a few times in his life. Mind you, he wasn't complaining about the quality of our daily diet, it was just that there were one or two episodes that stuck out in his mind, if not his pants. I didn't follow up the conversation at the time, but since then, I've been wondering: How can I improve my technique? I've read The Joy of Sex, More Joy, Xaviera's Supersex. *All the sex manuals tell you is that oral sex is okay and fun, but none of them really goes into detail. Can you give me any pointers?* —Miss S. B., Seattle, Washington.

We love questions like this; it gives us a chance to convene the Playboy Advisor Advanced Tutorial on Wondrous Sex and spend hours in the test bedrooms confirming our data. Ahem. You might ask your boyfriend to review those peak encounters, to see if he can find anything particular that distinguishes great head from the merely incredible. He might be able to define the secret ingredient, but you should be warned that a lot of the people with whom we talked said that when it comes to oral sex, not having to give directions was a blessing. Surprise is more important than suggestions, improvisation more pleasurable than obedience or duty. There were a few techniques that were cited: Men seemed to recall with special fondness their partners who swallowed the ejaculate, who performed deep throat or some other special trick (adding hands or teeth, handcuffs, feathers, whipped cream). Women liked men who did not stop at the first orgasm, who bopped till they dropped. Both sexes seem to like oral sex when it is done for its own benefit and not as some halfhearted form of foreplay. It seems that timing is more important than technique, though. Where and when you perform oral sex will make more of an impression than the specific combination of saliva and sensation. Oral sex is to intercourse what guerrilla warfare is to trench warfare: It's best on the fly. Hit and run. Just remember the scene in *Dressed to Kill*, in which Angie Dickinson engages in a little zipless head with a stranger in the back seat of a taxi. We think it's safe to say that the event was special. It's getting awfully hard to find an empty cab these days. Other than that, it pays to notice how a lover performs oral sex on you—it seems that people tend to do onto others as they want others to do onto them. Since this is a matter of national concern, we think we ought to open the discussion: If any of you have a special technique, or episode, why not drop us a letter? We'll publish the best tips in a future column.

This is in answer to the March Advisor's request for letters concerning oral sex. I say examine the attitude, not the procedure. I've found that the best oral sex is just that—a form of expression in itself, not just another method of foreplay, though there's nothing wrong with that, either. The really remarkable episodes in my mind always involve aggressive, enthusiastic women who aren't at all self-conscious about expressing desire. What seems to make the difference are the enthusiasm and timing. A woman walked up to me in a saloon once and simply said, "I was just sitting over there wondering what it would be like to suck you off." You'd better believe the evening ended in great head. Of all the really good times, it's not the method that stands out but the motive. For the purpose of suggesting ways of making it better for Miss S. B. and her lover, I can only bring out a few points, such as they are. First: Have some idea of what you're doing, so the poor guy doesn't have to direct the whole episode as if it were a scene from a movie. I'm all for the communication of likes and dislikes, but it detracts from the spontaneity if every step has to be requested. Open up and just enjoy yourself. He'll probably enjoy it, too. Also, it's quite endearing to the man when the woman swallows the ejaculate. Lastly, my suggestion is to pick some really surprising time and/or place. For the other side of the coin, I've noticed that those same things make for good sex for the lady. After all, feeling good isn't dependent on gender. Unusual places and/or impromptu timing does the trick here, too. I seem to get more response from going slowly, almost as if I were seducing her, even if we may have been lovers for a long time. Rather than use oral sex as a prelude to intercourse, just keep going. Don't get so rhythmic your moves are predictable. Stagger the times and places you place your tongue. Bounce from clitoris to vagina in a random pattern and use her quickening breath as a guide to her likes. The biggie, though, seems to be keep going. Go for an orgasm or spend the whole night trying. Go for two. Go for three; what the hell! If she's enjoying herself, save screwing for another time. You'll have a very happy lady with you right now, and that's pretty nice. Time for a little more independent study on my part. —E. J., New York, New York.

What is this? You must be after my job. Thanks for your insight. By the way, what was the address of that saloon?

Fingers

My girlfriend has this great oral sex technique that makes me climax within fifteen seconds to two minutes. Her approach is something like this: While she is sucking my penis, she uses her thumb and index finger in an up-and-down motion on the blood vessel that runs along its underside. Then she uses the same two fingers under the sac of my balls, with each finger manipulating a ball in the same up-and-down motion. It's dynamite: The motion is similar to milking and produces an intense orgasm, which drains my sperm and leaves me moaning. I would like to know if you have an explanation for the success of this technique. I have not found too many women who can duplicate it. I find other forms of fellatio—particularly 69—to be less satisfying. Is this normal? —W.H.C., Mill Valley, California.

Thank you. We have just returned from our test bedroom and, yes, the technique is truly fascinating. We'd give it a 95 (a good beat). If there is an explanation for its success, it is this: The penis is more sensitive on the underside than on the top. (Doctors believe that this is related to the thinner ventral skin.) Aficionados of fellatio have noted that the sexual nerve center of the male is the frenulum —the little flap of skin on the underside of the penis beneath the cleft in the glans. This spot is hard to reach during 69, and, while we are not one to complain of neglect, it can make a difference. When a woman plays skin flute, she should put her fingers where they'll make the most music.

After reading your request for comments on the style of fellatio, I finally gathered enough courage to write (not that I think you will publish it). I agree with what you said about attitudes, since this plays as much of an important role as do true emotion and the openness of the couple involved. When you combine those qualities with a truly polished technique, you can't fail. It is very important to become fully aware of your partner's body. Know what he likes, where he likes it to be touched, kissed, caressed, squeezed, licked and bitten. This is achieved by spending as much time as possible in bed together, just feeling each other in a lazy sort of way. After you feel confident that you know some of the things he likes, do them. I enjoy kissing the inside of his thighs first and moving upward to the groin. He likes me to trace a line with my tongue from his groin, under his balls to his back. When I tease the anal opening with my tongue, going in and out, then quickly move away, it drives him crazy. His deep inhalation and the tightening of his abdominal muscles make me know he really is enjoying it, so I enjoy it and want to continue. I enjoy running my tongue from the base of the penis to the tip on all sides, then teasing the head by making circular motions around the glans with my tongue tip. Then, when he least expects it, I dive down the full length of the shaft and suck like crazy, moving my head around and up and down, so that he gets two or three movements at once. By then, I am so overflowing with my own juices I find that I like pulling his leg closest to me right up between my thighs and slowly hunching. He gets the message and moves his leg slowly back and forth while he reaches down and flicks my nipple and squeezes my breast. If I am between his legs, facing him, I can suck and massage his penis with my tongue in a way that, should I choose to, I can make him have an orgasm whether he's ready or not. (It's really hard to explain it; you just have to be there.) Then I swallow all his juices and reach for a drink while he recovers.

Another thing we have discovered is that if he enters me almost immediately afterward, which he often does because I am squirming so violently by then, he can have a second orgasm in a very short time, with no recovery period needed. I think it is partly because he recognizes my needs and wants to satisfy me, and partly because I keep my vaginal muscles in such good shape that I can create such a suction that I can drain him dry. He says I'm like a fourteen-year-old virgin, even though I am thirty and have a child. What I am really trying to say is that, in my opinion, successful fellatio or cunnilingus, for that matter, takes

some homework. Thanks for the opportunity to write, and we love your maga-
zine. —*Miss N. M., Milledgeville, Georgia.*

Ahem. Thanks. We needed that.

When I read the Advisor letter last March asking about oral sex, I intended to
write to you immediately but put it off till I read E. J.'s letter in the July issue. I
agree with your response in March. You covered about everything I've found
that men like—and I appreciated what E. J. said; but here's a woman's side of it.
I just found out that oral sex is fun—I think a lot of women are afraid of it.
And I think a lot of men are afraid to ask for it, to indicate that that is what they'd
like, when they should. *Sixty-nine is not my favorite position, because I like to*
be able to concentrate on what I'm doing without being distracted by what my
lower half is feeling. Oral sex is a lot more pleasant than most women are led to
believe—the look on a man's face while you suck his cock is one of the most
beautiful sights in the world. To begin with, for me, starting off slowly is
important: slow kisses or brushing my hair along a guy's belly, and then a little
tongue around the tip of his cock. Using my hands (as you suggested) is always
important, to give the man the feeling that his whole cock and balls are involved
without doing "deep throat" immediately. As I begin to take more and more of
his cock in my mouth, it gets easier and easier to enjoy for both of us. I try to suck
and use my tongue at the same time, concentrating with my tongue around the
head. And all the time using my hand to either go up and down with my head or
(for a little contrast) go up with my hand while going down with my head. When
a man gets close to orgasm, he gets harder and the noises he makes say it all.
Swallowing "it" is not as horrible as we are led to believe. (And I think men are
responsible for this belief.) Swallowing and sucking are part of the same reflex,
and it works. And it is delightful. *And easy.*
A P.S. for men and oral sex—slow and gentle to begin with is much more
stimulating than hard and rough. And fingers should always be included (and
inserted)—the clitoris is not the only thing that needs stimulation. —*Miss*
K. A., Detroit, Michigan.

Great sex is all in the head, right folks?

CHAPTER EIGHT

Anal Sex

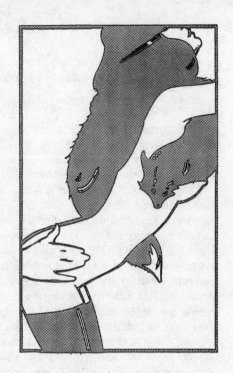

For Gays Only

I have been trying to introduce my wife to the joys of anal sex. She says that any man who would prefer that method of sex must have latent homosexual desires. She's got me worried. What do you say? —W. G., Memphis, Tennessee.

Bend over and spread. We used to hear that same charge made about men who wanted their partners to perform oral sex. Anything that was unusual was queer, and anything that was queer was. . . . Oh, well. Fortunately, the male prevailed and the objections diminished. (Women couldn't talk with their mouths full.) By definition—anything that a man and woman do together is heterosexual. As Dr. William Cantrell, writing in *Medical Aspects of Human Sexuality*, points out, "Homosexuality has to do with the matter of preference regarding the *person* with whom one shares a sexual experience and not with *what* is done." Amen. You might try that line of reasoning on your wife. Patience has unraveled many a repression. Judging from your wife's remark, though, her attitude is deep-seated. You may have a hard go of it. Just remember: Communication is the K-Y jelly of life.

Why Is It Enjoyable

Why should a female find anal sex enjoyable? As a medical student, I can understand why gay men who engage in sodomy get off on the practice. The rectum is adjacent to the prostate gland, which is very sensitive to stimulation. Any massage is felt as pleasure. But a woman does not have a prostate and the rectum is—as far as I can tell—not adjacent to any sensitive tissues. (For example, the inner two thirds of the vagina lack nerve endings.) Is a woman's pleasure purely psychological? —D. K., Houston, Texas.

A woman's ability to enjoy anal sex just has to be ranked as one of those tiny wonders that let us face each day with renewed vigor. (There are a lot of people who don't understand why a woman enjoys regular sex.) You are correct in saying that the lining of the vagina does not have nerve endings, but the muscles surrounding it do have nerve endings that are sensitive to different strokes. This fact has led sexologists to suggest that exercising these muscles will improve the tone of coital orgasms. Anal sex engages these magic muscles as well as the peritoneum—the sensitive membrane that lines the abdomen. Finally, any contact between humans is potentially pleasurable. Try massaging your partner's neck, or feet, and see what kind of response you get. If, by some slim chance, she doesn't like such attention and tells you to put it where the sun don't peek . . . go right ahead.

An Overview on Anal Sex

Two popular films—Last Tango in Paris and The Devil in Miss Jones—have stressed anal eroticism, depicting acts up to and including anal intercourse. My wife and I are curious about this form of sex, but we have reservations. Reports on the subject are contradictory: Some say that sodomy is unnatural, unhealthy and painful, while others say that it is intensely pleasurable. What is the truth and can you suggest an approach? —N. M., New York, New York.

The "Playboy Sex Survey" found that approximately a quarter of heterosexual Americans have experimented with anal sex and that many of them include anal foreplay and intercourse in their sexual repertoire. Why? Because the entire human body is potentially an erogenous zone. Freud called this phenomenon "polymorphous perversity," but don't take his word for it. The modern view holds that pleasure is healthy and natural; the term polymorphous perversity is neither an indictment nor a diagnosis. Be aware that the taboo against nongenital sex is quite strong. Proceed slowly; you'll have to cultivate the pleasure response.

For openers, try postillionage, an erotic touch that can turn you both on. Simply press a finger, or a small vibrator, in or near your partner's anus just prior to orgasm. The surprise can precipitate an intense orgasm. When (and if) you become comfortable with this form of pleasure, advance to anal intercourse. Your partner's body may resist entrance even when she is willing. Don't respond with a vigorous thrust. Press lightly with the head of the penis; it should feel as though you're being drawn in, rather than forcing your way. The anal passage does not secrete a natural lubricant, so you'll have to supply one. Coat the glans with K-Y jelly or wear a lubricated condom. The first few tries are likely to be painful for both of you, but after a break-in period, anal intercourse can be its own reward. Some women enjoy the different form of penetration and experience overwhelming orgasm; some men find the unaccustomed tightness exciting. You'll have to evaluate your own response. In any case, observe certain precautions. Never move from the rectum to the vagina without washing first; you risk transmitting bacteria that can cause severe infection in the vagina, uterus and Fallopian tubes. The same bacteria can enter the penile passage and cause prostate, bladder and kidney infections (the condom is a safeguard against this danger). One final warning: It *is* sodomy, and it is illegal in most states. If you do it, don't advertise.

The Physiology of Anal Sex

Please, if possible, draw from your knowledge and experience and tell us the true facts about anal love. My husband and I want to have sex this way, but we are afraid of physical damage to me. We tried anal sex once and it was painful. In fact, I bled slightly, though he did not even penetrate me. We used a lot of petroleum jelly, but I think the fact that I had wholeheartedly agreed to do this (after years of coaxing on his part) led him to try to enter me "headlong," which, to me, is a physical impossibility with the average-sized penis. I have refused to attempt it again, thus far. But I'm curious. Are there any specific instructions we should follow? Would a condom help or hinder? If he gets into me, can I accommodate the full length of his penis? Will it hurt me if he thrusts or when he starts to withdraw? Will it hurt if he comes in me? How long should we fuck that way per session? Will frequent anal fucking be harmful? What are the ill effects? Will I have an orgasm? —Mrs. M. B., Trenton, New Jersey.

You sure ask a lot of questions for someone from New Jersey. But we like your spirit. It doesn't take a lot of hindsight to figure out why your first attempt failed. According to Masters and Johnson, some pain is inevitable, but with experience, the pain diminishes—to be replaced by pleasure. What happens is this: When rectal intercourse is attempted, the anal sphincter contracts in an involuntary protective reaction. If you're new to the game, the spasm can last a minute or longer. If you enjoy anal sex regularly, the spasm can be short-lived, with involuntary relaxation of the muscle occurring within fifteen to thirty seconds. Once relaxation occurs, the penis can be accommodated with relative ease, and full penetration can be accomplished without incident. Masters also notes that after penetration, and with the onset of a maintained thrusting pattern, the sphincter usually reverses its relaxation reaction and constricts lightly around the penile shaft. (You can tell when that happens—your partner will be screaming in ecstasy, pulling his hair out and making other subtle endearing comments—if you can hear any of that over your own erotic sound track.) As to your other questions: A lubricant will facilitate penetration. Your partner should refrain from entry until the sphincter has relaxed (via manual stimulation at first). A condom is recommended—it can prevent bacteria from entering the penis and infecting the urethra and the prostate. (Similarly, if you engage in any kind of anal sex, wash before returning to the vagina—the front and rear tenants are not compatible.) If you follow those simple precautions, you should be in for a good time.

A Word of Warning

I have a feeling that I am a little bit behind the times concerning anal sex. I had never heard of heterosexual anal activity until my fiancé (now my husband) proposed it. I put him off until I could find out enough information to be comfortable with the act, but I still don't know anything. I tried asking my doctor and he just got uncomfortable and did not say anything. Help! My husband is getting impatient. Do I have to make any special preparations? I know I must sound rather innocent, but actually, I am rather eager, too. Would you just tell me a little bit about it? —Mrs. F. L., Seattle, Washington.

The key to enjoying anal sex is relaxation on the part of the woman. A good lubricant is essential. K-Y jelly or various oils are most frequently recommended, but avoid petroleum jelly, because it isn't water-soluble. The male should use a well-lubricated finger to gently probe and prepare the female anus for penetration. When the anal sphincter has relaxed sufficiently, penetration can be attempted, but that, too, should be done slowly and gently. If there is anxiety or pain for either partner, stop at once. You will need to experiment with different positions to see which is most comfortable. You might start with the common one of the female kneeling and bending slightly forward. Or the male can lie on his back, with the woman sitting astride him, which allows her to control the depth of penetration. In any case, do not move from anal to vaginal penetration without first thoroughly washing the fingers or the penis. If caution is exercised, there should be no bleeding during or after anal intercourse. Take your time, and we hope the experience is pleasant for both of you.

A Word of Warning

Concerning your response in the May issue to Mrs. F. L., of Seattle, Washington, regarding anal intercourse: Your advice on technique is excellent; however, there is one bit of expertise you've omitted. It pertains to the risk of infection. I believe it would have been helpful to advise the wearing of a condom to prevent fecal bacteria (E. coli) from entering the male urethra and wreaking havoc in the bladder and prostate. Also, a lubricated condom can be used to facilitate entry. Lovers can then easily move from anus to vagina without stopping to wash—just slip off the sheath before doing so. As an educator and a counselor, I appreciate the helpful information your column provides to the Playboy readership. Keep up the good work. —Miss L. F., Arlington, Texas.

Thanks for the household hint.

Love Lotion #9

My girlfriend and I enjoy a wide variety of sexual hi-jinks, including anal sex. For the past few years, we've been searching for the perfect lubricant to facilitate our slipping and sliding. Wesson Oil, Vaseline and K-Y jelly aren't quite right—we end up feeling like we've just had a ten-thousand-mile oil change. Can you recommend something? —B. N., Orlando, Florida.

Tired of that greasy kid's stuff? It just happens that one of our close friends—a lady college professor who shall remain nameless until tenure—has discovered what may be the greatest aid to getting it on since the Self-heating Shaving Cream Sandwich. The magic balm is called Albolene Cream and is available at cosmetic counters everywhere. One of our local folk singers has even written a song commemorating the product ("Albolene, Albolene, prettiest stuff I've ever seen/Women, they won't treat you mean in Albolene"). It is not the policy of this column to endorse specific brands, but for Albolene we'll make an exception. Of course, if the manufacturer wants to send us a case, it will be appreciated by all concerned.

Fingernails

Several of my co-workers were discussing their sex lives over drinks not long ago, when my secretary announced that she had found the perfect lover. When we asked her how she knew that her partner was a perfect lover, she blurted out, "He stuck his finger up my ass while we were screwing." Well, for the past few weeks, I have had to resist a temptation to duplicate that gesture with every woman I've taken to bed. I feel like Dr. Strangelove trying to control his artificial hand as it inches toward the forbidden target, as though it possessed a will of its own. Is anal stimulation the sign of the perfect lover? —E. G., Portland, Oregon.

Obviously, it is for your secretary. Unfortunately, what works for one person may not work for another. For that matter, what works for one person may not work for the same person the next time around. There are no guarantees in this business; we know because we run the complaint department. The perfect lover is the person who pays attention to his partner's moods and needs, who finds out from the partner what feels good and then does it. If you are taking that secretary to bed, by all means give in to your Strangelove impulse. But wait for the right moment (i.e., not during dictation or at a board meeting but later, when she's half expecting it. A container of Crisco or K-Y jelly left on the bedside table should give her a hint). Trim your fingernails first.

Bad Vibrations

My girlfriend and I like to experiment with sexual accessories. Perusing a catalog of erotic devices, we noticed a tiny battery-powered vibrator. It is evidently intended for anal stimulation. My girlfriend says that she has heard that phallic-shaped objects are dangerous if used on the anus. True? —T. C., Portland, Oregon.

True. One of our favorite books of the past year was B. Kliban's *Never Eat Anything Bigger Than Your Head.* A similar axiom goes for anal sex: Never sit on anything smaller than your ass. According to the *British Medical Journal,* vibrators are being used increasingly "to gratify anal eroticism and may easily be inserted beyond the anal sphincters. These tend to close and to force a foreign object up the tract out of reach of the user, so that it has to be retrieved by surgery." Apparently, the little buggers are hard to hold on to in the excitement and they tend to slip away. Our advice: If it doesn't have a handle on it, don't use it.

The Big Apple

On a flight from New York City, I overheard a conversation about sex accessories. One gentleman said that he had finally uncovered the true meaning of Fun City's nickname the Big Apple—while visiting a high-class house of erotic delight. I didn't catch all the details, but it seems that he had been subjected to some

kind of device that was inserted into the anus and then inflated at the moment of
orgasm. Could you shed some light on this reportedly ecstasy-producing ac-
cessory? And can you tell me where I can buy one, provided I still want one after
I find out what it is? —D. G., Minneapolis, Minnesota.

Basically, you've got the details down pat: The Big Apple is a rubber
balloon that is inserted into the orifice of your choice (usually anal, his or
hers) and pumped up by means of a remote-control squeeze bulb. Supposedly, it heightens the effect of orgasm and, used once a day, keeps
the doctor away. (Fist-fucking aficionados have been known to train
their muscles with the device.) The Big Apple is available from the
Pleasure Chest, 120 Eleventh Avenue, New York, New York 10011.
Before you buy one, though, you should be aware that the device may
be hazardous to your health. Previous Playboy Advisor answers have
warned about the dangers of forcing air into any body cavity, particularly the vagina. Also, just imagine what would happen if the Big
Apple became disconnected from the pump. Your partner would go
ricocheting around the room, propelled by a sputtering balloon.

Turnaround Fair Play

A few weeks ago, I was in bed with a woman with whom I'm having a casual
affair. After foreplay, I found myself turned on by the idea of anal intercourse. I
performed the job on her to the satisfaction of us both. Then I had an overwhelm-
ing urge to know what it felt like to her. She selected a phallus-shaped object from
her collection of erotic toys and, after some initial gentle probing with her
fingers, turned the tables. It was extremely pleasurable. The only thing that
bothers me about the whole experience is that now I find sex with my wife rather
uninteresting and am afraid that sooner or later she'll notice my lack of enthusi-
asm. I desire to repeat the episode of anal sex and have even contemplated using a
vibrator or a dildo on myself. Does this indicate that a latent homosexual ten-
dency is beginning to surface? —B. A., Seattle, Washington.

There's no reason a man should not find anal stimulation pleasurable:
It would be a sad state of affairs if only females and male homosexuals
enjoyed themselves in so free a fashion. The episode does not indicate
that you are a latent anything. (Never mind the graffito that declares: "If
God had meant you to be heterosexual, He wouldn't have given you an
asshole.") Relax. You are not responsible for the distribution of nerve
endings through your body. If you are intrigued by this technique, don't
be afraid to suggest it to your wife. The very worst that could happen is
that she might tell you where you can put it.

Oral, Anal and Manual or Three into One

Several years before we met, my boyfriend visited a massage parlor. As he tells the story, the lady in attendance performed a rather strange combination of oral sex and manual stimulation, which he claims was the most startling turn-on he'd ever experienced. While she gave him head, one hand masturbated him, while the other hand was busy finger-fucking his ass. He says that the experience at first disturbed him ("Why did she think I would enjoy that?") but that eventually the attack proved successful. Now he wants me to try the same technique. My question: Is this practice abnormal? If not, how should I go about it? —Miss J. L., New Orleans, Louisiana.

When you've been doing what we do for a living for as long as we've been doing it, nothing strikes you as abnormal. Certainly not this. The reason the lady in the massage parlor did what she did is simple—the technique works. The trick is a fairly standard form of play in the gay community—there's no reason that two devout heterosexuals can't get off on it. Our suggestion: Use a lubricant. Treat him as he would treat a virgin (i.e., somewhat gently). Fingernails should be clipped. You might consider purchasing a pair of surgical gloves. This will keep you from fretting about cleanliness. Also, the lubricant will last longer on a glove than on skin. The reason for buying a pair—you can wear one and he can wear the other. If you want a touch of class, you can always treat each other with kid gloves.

Making Ends Meet . . . Proceed with Caution

I feel I must protest the letter in the May Playboy Advisor *in which you tell a man whose lady dislikes oral sex to keep at it until she sees the error of her ways. I have a similar problem with anal sex. My husband likes it and keeps on trying. But I want him to stop. In spite of numerous attempts, all I get from it are tears, pain and bleeding. He brought the letter in question to my attention, saying the problem was in my head. Now, really. I have tried. There are so many beautiful ways to make love, why insist on the one technique that I find so painful and disagreeable? I feel that love and respect for each other's feelings should go together. And since I love him and never refuse other things he asks of me, why shouldn't he simply respect what I ask in this matter? I resent being made to feel guilty. You let me down. I hope you publish this with a word in my defense. —Mrs. C. D., Omaha, Nebraska.*

Tell your husband to back off. In traffic court, he would be penalized for following too closely. In this context, he should be reprimanded for misquoting our advice, which is about fellatio, not anal sex. There is a difference, though some folks can't tell their ass from their other bodily orifices; for these free souls, sodomy is a pleasurable experience. However, even couples who are willing to engage in sodomy approach the act with care. The woman has to be relaxed or it hurts like hell, even when the man has taken the proper precautions (K-Y jelly or a lubricated condom, or both). Tension increases the chances of discomfort and injury, but the problem is not in your head. Your body may not be made for the act. We do not feel that a person should undergo pain to please a partner. Unless he or she is into it. Enough said?

Around the World

While perusing an underground paper, I came across an ad for a massage parlor that offered the "ultimate erotic trip around the world." Unless I'm mistaken, that's a double-entendre for something very sexy. Am I right? If so, how do I perform the trick at home? —Miss C. B., Kansas City, Kansas.

Actually, it's a single entendre in the tuck position with a half twist: Around the world is a slang term for a sexual technique that involves fellatio and anilingus (or cunnilingus and anilingus) but also includes short stops and layovers at other parts of the body. To take this trip, begin a tongue massage around your partner's eyes, ears, throat and chin, move across the collarbone to the region of his breasts (yes, they are sensitive, too). A few licks, and then on to the midriff, the sides of the body and on around to the back (neck, shoulders, sacral dimples, buttocks, etc.). Then it's time for a slight respite at the back door of the dangling diner (unlike cunnilingus, anilingus is better brief—a fleeting hit-and-run thrill, as opposed to diligent attack). Continue down the back of the legs to the arches and toes of the feet, then slowly work up the inside of the thighs. Stay in a holding pattern over the genitals until you reach your destination. Then switch roles. One of our friends, who is particularly fond of this form of tongue-lashing, points out that it's better after a bath. (He also says that his cat is totally fascinated by his and his girlfriend's odd habit of immersing themselves in water before going to bed. The cat does not recognize that activity as a bath. What they do in bed, the cat recognizes as a bath.)

Postillionage

My question concerns the female anal erotic, if, in fact, there is such a thing. I'd heard vaguely about this but was never sure, since I had had no personal experience. Now, however, I'm beginning to doubt my former doubts. A few weeks ago, I took to bed a perfectly delicious little black-haired beauty who was, unfortunately, very unhappy with her husband and with sex in general. She claimed she had never in her life had a real orgasm. And, to my dismay, she seemingly didn't have one with me, either. She was well worth another try, though. And that time, a strange thing happened. It was almost, if not quite, accidental on my part. As I slid into her, with a hand behind her bottom to hold her close, my fingers pressed into the crevice of her buttocks and found her anus. A sudden impulse seized me and I thrust my forefinger through and up into the channel beyond. She arched her back, gave a long, shuddering gasp and went into an explosive climax that was unmistakably the real thing.

Was this only happenstance, or are there really some women who respond instantly and uncontrollably to anal stimulation? —E. M., Arlington, Virginia.

The term female anal erotic is rather quaint but is needlessly sexist, as this technique is equally effective for males. It is called postillionage and is popular in French erotic novels. Alex Comfort defines it as "putting a finger in or on your partner's anus just before orgasm." Comfort goes on to say that "most prefer firm finger pressure just in front of the anus; in men this can produce an erection used alone. . . . Firm pressure with a heel behind the scrotum or between the anus and vulva works as well in some postures." Although this technique won't work on all of the people all of the time, it will work on some of the people most of the time. One cautionary note: If you have inserted your finger into the anus, do not put it into the vagina afterward, as this can cause bacterial infections.

Real-Life Reactions

Being a fellow New Orleans gal, I feel qualified to reply to Miss J. L. (Playboy Advisor, November 1978) regarding anal stimulation of her boyfriend. An Austrian guy once asked me to stimulate him with my finger while we had intercourse. I was rather shocked but soon found I enjoyed it almost as much as he did. Since then, I have used this technique on about twenty guys, and only two didn't enjoy it. (One guy freaked out and never called me again.) If cleanliness bothers you, promise the guy a treat and fetch a hot washcloth. Use it on his prick, his balls and finally his anus. I guarantee he'll like it too much to be offended. Then muster up your courage and visit the area with your tongue. You'll both enjoy it. —Miss J. B., New Orleans, Louisiana.

And New Orleans used to be known for finger-snapping jazz. How times change. Thank you for sharing this homemaker's hint with us.

About a year ago, I tried anal intercourse for the first time, liked it and have been fairly heavily into it ever since as part of the variety I like in my sex life. I

*wasn't a total stranger to the sensation. I'm lucky in having a doctor with whom
I can talk frankly, and during a physical, I asked him about anal intercourse. He
said there's nothing wrong with it, if both partners are willing, and that all I had
to remember was to wash my partner off afterward if we also intended to have
vaginal intercourse. He also suggested using a lubricant, which I did the first few
times. But I've learned that most times it's not necessary unless a guy has an
unusually thick penis, and then saliva works fine. Recently, at a wedding shower
for one of my friends, the conversation got into some fairly private aspects of sex.
Of the fourteen girls there, nine of us had tried anal intercourse. Those of us who
had done it agreed that it's a marvelous variation and that there's no other feeling
quite like it. The problem is that a lot of guys are really reluctant to try it. I've
been with some who have been outstanding lovers in every other way but who
simply wouldn't try anal intercourse. I think most of the myths about it have
been dispelled as far as women are concerned, but for some reason, the men in our
lives are still playing by obsolete rules. All of the guys I've done it with have
really liked it once they got started, but sometimes getting a guy to do it is almost
more trouble than it's worth. Perhaps you can say something to your male
readers that will help them past their shyness and maybe give females who enjoy
it some tips on getting our guys to at least try it. —Miss J. M., Rockford,
Illinois.*

What are you doing next Friday night? Never mind. Your problem
stems from one of society's most ridiculous taboos: Women talk with
women about sex (witness your bridal shower) but never bother to
convey their curiosity to men. How did you initiate the conversation
with your female friends? Try the same tactic with your next date. You
might say you read this great letter in the Playboy Advisor about anal
sex. What does he think of it? You may be surprised at his response. We
have learned this about sex talk: The greater the detail, the greater the
sex.

Masturbation, or Love the One You're With

Tying One On

Over the past year, I've developed a masturbation technique with my boyfriend. First, I apply baby oil to the head of his penis—this prevents irritation and creates a different sensation from what he does for himself. Then I slowly stroke him with one hand—occasionally giving a slight twist or pinch for variety. My free hand traces his thighs, scrotum or stomach muscles. (I can usually tell from the tension in the last when he is close to orgasm.) My boyfriend claims that the climaxes brought about by this technique differ from the orgasms brought about by normal intercourse—they are almost excruciatingly genital. Lately, he has consented to being tied down, so that he can thrash about in feigned helplessness as I continue to masturbate him to a second orgasm and fellate him to a third. After several of these marathons, he has told me that he felt he was going to have a heart attack. Am I hurting him by doing this? —H. J., Cincinnati, Ohio.

If your boyfriend is in reasonably good shape, you shouldn't have to worry about his coming to meet his Maker. He may have been describing physical ecstasy rather than distress—he did wait until you had finished before saying anything, right?

Mutual Masturbation

*I've been following The Playboy Advisor for quite some time and I have been
enlightened on many subjects that really have helped me and my friends. I have
recently come upon a problem myself and I don't know who to go to. I enjoy
sexual intercourse with my many lovers, but I have found that I would rather be
jacked off by my girl than anything else. I also find myself getting into violent
masturbation sessions, once, twice and even three times a day. I often fantasize
about this act during class, and sometimes I have to imagine myself whacking off
in order to come with my girl! I need to know if I have a problem. Am I different
from everybody else? Will masturbation, in my case, hurt my sex organs? These
are very difficult questions to answer, but I feel sure that the answers to them
will help many people in similar situations. —S. T., Atlanta, Georgia.*

You're not that different. We heard about someone who was really
kinky. He was into bondage and masturbation—he had to tie himself up
first. Neat. It is common knowledge among sex researchers that both
men and women can experience more pleasure from manual stimulation
than from intercourse. Autoeroticism is pure pleasure—you have only
yourself to blame if you do it wrong. Liberated lovers often exchange
tips on touch—many women can orgasm only from manual stimulation
of the clitoris. Some men prefer this form of touch—the increased friction—to the more subtle pleasures of intercourse. No harm in that. In
addition, many people have favorite fantasies that act as catalysts to
orgasm. If something works, don't fix it.

A Little Strange

*I'm a happily married male of forty. My wife and I enjoy a beautiful sex life.
My problem, if it is one, is that I'm a compulsive masturbator. By compulsive I
mean almost daily for as far back as I can remember. I have fantasy fucked
virtually every desirable female I've ever met, regardless of her age. I jerk off at
home, at the office, in my car or just about anywhere at any time. I love to feel my
throbbing meat explode. I've used about every known lubricant from cooking oil
to artificial pussies made from various meats. Some of my most thrilling orgasms
have taken place in, of all places, the shoe of a female co-worker. (I squirt hand
lotion all over the inside and use the shoe to erupt in.) I then wipe it clean, place
it back in her desk and can't wait to see her wearing that shoe again. One of my
favorite hobbies is to spend hours creating paste-ups using pictures of females I
know. I neatly cut out their heads and paste them onto other pictures of sexy
female bodies. I get so aroused doing this that I always end up jerking myself to a
violent orgasm. Am I sick, or is my behavior within the limits of normal sexuality? —L. F., Indianapolis, Indiana.*

It's not every day that we get a letter from someone who can type one-handed. Sex researchers have discovered an interesting thing about masturbation. Everyone does it. Everyone who does it thinks that his own pattern (two or three times a week or whatever) is normal but that anything more is suspect. It's obvious that you've taken self-abuse and carried it to a hobby that will reward you with hours of pleasure, if not to an art form. The bit with your co-worker's shoe sounds a little whacko. It's not the kind of sex with a consenting Gucci that we recommend. Keep it to yourself and you'll do okay. If not, you'd better see a shrink.

Well-Hung? Not Really

Have you ever heard of anyone intentionally strangling himself during masturbation to heighten the orgasm? One of my friends has confessed to a strange form of autoeroticism. He throws a soft velvet noose over the bar in his closet and slowly increases the tension while stroking himself. The closer he comes to passing out, the better his climax. It strikes me that it would be easy to go too far. How common is this practice? —R. S., Chicago, Illinois.

Yet another bizarre sexual practice comes out of the closet. This form of self-abuse has been around for years, which is more than we can say for some of the people who have tried it. Supposedly, the momentary oxygen starvation increases the intensity of the orgasm—the same thing can happen if you hold your breath. It's dangerous to do alone—pass out and you may well pass on. There are a number of documented cases of boys and men who have died this way. Even with supervision, the practice may be unsafe. English brothels in the 1600s experimented with the technique: Apparently, some enterprising madam noticed that when a convict went to the gallows, he often died with an erection and/or an ejaculation (hence the praise, "He was a well-hung man"). Seeking a cure for impotence, ladies of the night sometimes played the part of high executioner. The madam would let the aging lord dangle from the chandelier until he developed an erection; then she would cut him down. Accidents were known to happen. To avoid a scandal, the death would be explained as a suicide. There are better ways to go—or come.

Does it Change Your Anatomy?

Not long ago, I took my girlfriend to a porn movie. She noticed and later commented on the variety of shapes in women's genitals. Many of the women had protruding folds of skin. We wondered what might cause this; she suggested that it was the result of excessive masturbation or perhaps an overactive sex life. What do you say? —T. L., Kansas City, Kansas.

Next thing you know, they'll be blaming masturbation for the state of the economy. Singlehanded people throughout the country are forever saying, "We must be doing something wrong." Autoeroticism is the original sin: If you're going to feel guilty about something, it might as well be something that feels good. The fact is that the only result of masturbation is pleasure, pure and simple. The anatomical differences your girlfriend noticed are just part of the great diversity contained within the genetic code. There's something for everyone, no matter what your taste.

Clitoral Increase

Whenever some time goes by without sexual intercourse, I masturbate. I've heard that masturbation can increase the size of the clitoris. Is this true? Also, I would like to know the size of the largest recorded clitoris. —Miss F. A., Redondo Beach, California.

Masturbation does not increase the size of either the male or the female genitals. Although no records are kept, one of the largest clitorises known to man belonged to a John Dillinger. It was 19 inches long and is currently on display in the Smithsonian Institution. Ask the guard for the exact location. Contrary to popular belief, Dillinger (nee Joanna) was not a man. The rampant chauvinists of the FBI were loath to allow a woman on the ten most-wanted list and so perpetrated the rumor that Dillinger was a man. If you think this answer is tongue in cheek, you're wrong: That's not our tongue.

Once Is Not Enough

For the past few years, I've been reading all sorts of feminist PR for the multiple orgasm. You know, once is not enough, and all that bullshit. The multiple O has become the measuring stick of a successful night—or, for that matter, of a failure. Tell me this: Can a woman be satisfied with only one orgasm per session? —E. D., New York, New York.

Is the Pope Polish? Shere Hite (bless her little survey) found that only a small minority of the women who answered her questionnaire needed or wanted more than one orgasm per session. Almost half were satisfied with whatever came their way. A more telling statistic involves what women do to themselves. Psychologist Ruth E. Clifford asked seventy-four college women who masturbated whether they stopped at one orgasm or continued. While thirty of the girls said they often had more than one orgasm in rapid succession, only four responded that they needed more than one orgasm to be satisfied. The rest of the group said that additional orgasms added to their pleasure but were not essential to their satisfaction. So it appears that there are three ways to measure an evening's sexual performance—unsatisfactory, satisfactory and "As long as you're at it, dear, how about another one?"

Unabashed Dictionary

My wife of ten years has just discovered the joys of masturbation. I find it a terrific erotic high watching her get herself off, and her discovery has greatly improved our sex life. One evening, while discussing this matter, it occurred to us that we could not think of a single euphemism or slang expression commonly used to refer to female masturbation. Male masturbation, of course, is well represented in this area: There is the ubiquitous jacking off and its variants (jerking off, jerkin' the gherkin, tickling the pickle, etc.), several S/M-like variations (pounding the pud, beating the meat) and a favorite from my college days, falling in love with Mother Thumb and her four daughters. There must be several dozen others. But what about female masturbation? Is there a slang phrase in common currency? Is the absence of such a phrase a sign of the sexual repression of women by the larger society? —J. W., Amherst, Massachusetts.

You've hit the nail on the head. We conducted an informal poll of the ladies in our life and couldn't come up with an accepted slang term for female masturbation. Some nice tries—diddling, the old five-finger discount, getting off—were obviously borrowed from the masculine. What are you going to do—sue them for copyright infringement? Women only recently discovered masturbation. Some of them even go to seminars to learn the basics (clear evidence of a difference in intelligence between the sexes). If they talk about it at all, they tend to use the simple term: masturbation. Give them time and they'll invent euphemisms. Then again, as masturbation becomes acceptable (and guilt-free), it won't be necessary to use slang.

Love and the Proper Orgasm

Your magazine has got me through many a hard time in the past, and I hope you will be able to help me now. My girlfriend seems completely unable to reach orgasm in normal intercourse. I do not believe there can be a psychological block, as she can come while masturbating and when I stimulate her clitoris either orally or manually. These orgasms are pretty earth-shattering. As far as I can tell, she is anatomically normal, the clitoris being uncoverable and about an inch away from the vagina. She finds it difficult to understand how sufficient stimula-

tion can be applied to the clitoris during intercourse, given this setup. We are both convinced that there must be a solution to this problem. We have tried everything we could think of, from cognac to spanking to dirty talking. Long an avid reader of Playboy, *I am not short of ideas. But it doesn't seem to be a question of horniness or technique, as all the necessary conditions, including mood, have come together many, many times. We have tried abstaining—very difficult—and extreme frequency, both without calculation. We have also used floors, pillows, walls and chairs, all spontaneously and in the heat of the moment. I am beginning to lose faith. Any suggestions? —D. T., Buffalo, New York.*

Your problem is not as serious as you make it sound. (How can a person who uses floors, pillows, etc., have a problem?) There is no *proper* way to have an orgasm and, consequently, those your girlfriend does experience are not inferior substitutes. She has pointed out the major design flaw in the female body—that the clitoris is not exactly situated on Main Street and receives no direct stimulation during intercourse. (Several studies have reported that only 30 to 45 percent of women regularly climax during coitus.) The answer is at hand. There is no rule against self-stimulation during lovemaking. Unless you're into bondage and she has both hands tied, she should be able to add to her own pleasure. There is another solution. Two researchers in Nebraska studied 281 women who were unable to experience orgasm during intercourse and found that they had poor vaginal muscles—specifically, the pubococcygeus muscle, the one a woman clenches to control urination. The pubococcygeus muscle does not receive a lot of exercise in the normal course of affairs. Isometrics (contracting the muscle for ten seconds at a time, several times a day) may remedy the problem. There's no explanation for the relation between fitness and fun, but if it gets results, who cares?

Is It Addictive?

For some reason, my girlfriend cannot achieve orgasm during intercourse. I have suggested that she learn to masturbate, but she doesn't feel comfortable with it. She says that she has read that masturbation makes a person dependent on one kind of stimulation. Can you settle this argument? —D. W., Dallas, Texas.

You've seen the motto on dollar bills: In hibition we trust. Most sex therapists feel that if a person is too anxious to masturbate—because of parental guilt or whatever—then he or she will be too anxious to reach orgasm during intercourse. Kinsey found that women who did not masturbate were three times as likely as masturbators to have problems achieving orgasm. Feminists suggest that self-help is the only cure. If nothing else, all your girlfriend has to lose is a couple of hundred orgasms. She seems to have encountered what we call the masturbation backlash. Some shrinks do feel that too much masturbation will make a woman dependent on clitoral stimulation. Consequently, she will be unable to reach orgasm during normal intercourse. That sounds like sour grapes. We define intercourse as *everything* that happens between two people in bed . . . including touching, watching "The Tonight Show" and playing with Black & Decker vibrators. Go to it.

Is It an Orgasm?

I'm twenty-two and have had only one sex partner in my life. I went out with the guy for two years but finally broke up with him because he was incredibly selfish as far as sex (and everything else) was concerned. That was over a year ago. Recently, I've discovered the pleasures of vibrators. They really get me off as nothing else has. However, I still don't know if I've ever experienced an orgasm. Friends tell me that if you have one, you know it. Well, I'm not sure that's true. When masturbating, I work myself up to a very pleasant yet tense state. My stomach muscles get supertight. At that moment, I feel like I want direct and constant contact on my clitoris, but it's difficult to keep from jerking the vibrator away because of the tension. Then I usually get a warm, tingling sensation down my legs and throughout my torso. Is that an orgasm? If it is, it's not all it's cracked up to be. If it isn't, can you tell me how to get one? —Miss J. C., Vancouver, British Columbia.

Well, you could try ordering one from J.C. Penney. (Sorry about that.) Since you've had only one sex partner, you've got some catching up to do. Don't try to go it alone. Orgasms, like good dinners, are best when they are shared. Frankly, it sounds to us as though you have reached what Masters and Johnson describe as stage two of the three stages of the female orgasm. But don't worry. Enjoy. We tend to agree with your friends, though; when you do have an orgasm, it will make its presence felt. Substitute some patient and attentive young man for your vibrator and you'll be surprised at how soon your confusion disappears.

Is It Normal?

I'm a nineteen-year-old girl who has indulged in masturbation since I was around ten years old. That's also probably about the age my boyfriend started. Neither he nor I have any trouble reaching a climax that way. When we have intercourse, he has an orgasm but says the feeling, though pleasant, is not as intense as when he masturbates. As for me, I can't reach orgasm at all, no matter how slowly he takes it. Neither of us is inhibited. We're very much in love and we enjoy sex immensely, but we feel a little incomplete (especially me). I'm beginning to wonder if what I thought was a myth—that masturbation interferes with sexual satisfaction later—is really true. I realize that this is a whopper to advise someone on by letter, but we hoped you could suggest a therapist who could deal with our problem more extensively. —Miss D. L., Phoenix, Arizona.

Don't panic. You may not have so serious a problem. The fact that you have already masturbated to orgasm greatly increases the chances that you will learn to do so during intercourse. (Kinsey found that women who had taken things into their own hands in childhood were more orgasmic in marriage.) As for the relative quality of the pleasure, your experience is not unique. Masters and Johnson found that the people in their lab generally reported that the orgasm derived from masturbation was more intense than the one achieved during intercourse. It is easy enough to explain. You have the situation under total control and no one else to be concerned with. As for attaining orgasm during intercourse—it is less a matter of how slow he takes it than of how he takes it slow. Find a position that gives you a little more control, that lets you direct the attention to where you need it most (usually, but not always, the clitoris). Use your hands—and/or a vibrator—while he's inside you. Try oral sex. In short, you probably don't need professional help, just a little amateur-hour enthusiasm.

Is It Normal: Take Two

My boyfriend and I have been living together for a year and a half, and I have always felt we had a very good sexual relationship. Several times, without his knowledge, I have caught him masturbating in the living room, after I have retired to our bedroom for the night. I ask him to come to bed with me, but he says he wants to stay up awhile and watch TV. I have rarely turned down his sexual advances. I don't want to embarrass him by confronting him, but after these incidents, I feel betrayed and inadequate. I feel I am to blame, because he must not be getting enough satisfaction from me. Is it normal for a twenty-seven-year-old male to do this when he has easy access to sexual relations whenever he wants, or is there something lacking in our sex life? We get along well in every other aspect of our relationship, but I'm to the point that whenever he wants to stay up and watch TV, I think he's making up an excuse to masturbate. —Miss F. C., Springfield, Illinois.

Masters and Johnson and other surveys of male sexuality report that the physical intensity in a masturbatory climax frequently exceeds that of intercourse. Many women experience that same intensity. (You should try it yourself.) This is not to say that masturbation can or should replace intercourse; it's just another form of sexual enjoyment. Since 72 percent of married men (who admit it) masturbate regularly, you shouldn't think your boyfriend unusual, nor should you feel unappealing. It is unrealistic (and probably unhealthy) to assume that you are the sole proprietor of another person's sexuality. There *is* a problem in your relationship, though. Communication. You and your boyfriend have retreated to neutral corners out of ignorance or inhibition. If the most you can say is that you rarely turn down his advances, you have a lot to learn about sexuality—his and yours.

Does Masturbation Affect Virility?

Shortly after my husband and I were married, I discovered that he derived great pleasure from reading pornographic literature, viewing erotic films and masturbating. It was probably the most devastating feeling I have ever had. I was naive enough to believe that I was his only sexual outlet. This practice has continued over the years, even though we have had a good sex life. Somehow, I feel as though I have been robbed of a great deal of sex. Now that we are older and my husband is no longer quite as virile as he used to be, it makes me very sad (and not a little bitter) to think of all the sex I missed as a result of his actions. What would you recommend to someone in my situation? —Mrs. N. W., Chicago, Illinois.

Sex is not a limited commodity. It is not something that should be put into a joint checking account, with both partners having to cosign bed checks. Your husband did not steal anything from you by masturbating—he was merely dealing with his own sex drive in an acceptable adult fashion. According to Morton Hunt, author of *Sexual Behavior in the 1970s*, 72 percent of husbands and 68 percent of wives masturbate with some regularity. The change in your husband's virility is not the result of masturbation—it comes as a natural result of the aging process. As males grow older, it takes longer for them to become erect and longer for them to ejaculate. They are still capable of getting it up and getting it on. If you want more sex, the responsibility is yours. Make up for lost time, kid. The alternative is divorce, and we've never heard of anyone naming Mary Fist as corespondent.

Water Works

With my boyfriend and me living under the same roof, it seems that we have less sex than before. And since he has recommended on several occasions that I masturbate (which I prefer not to do), I have found a way in which to enjoy myself between lovemaking sessions. I wait till he has gone to work, then I deadbolt the door. Then off to the bathroom I go. First I take a hot shower and get relaxed, then the excitement begins. I turn on the faucet and get a good, steady, powerful stream of water going and, in a sitting position, with my feet on the edge of the tub, I center it on my clit. I don't think that receiving oral sex from any man could even come close to the excitement, because it is so intense, stimulating and ecstatic. This beats masturbation by a head. Even though I would prefer to make love with my boyfriend, episodes like this keep me going between the times we share with each other. And I can actually say that this bit of drama has saved our relationship. —Miss S. K., Clearwater, Florida.

Cleanliness is next to horniness: Your relationship should last as long as the local water supply. Our only suggestion: Share your new hygiene with your friend. We're sure he'll enjoy the show.

For a year, I've been dating a twenty-year-old divorcée. We've been open about our past experiences and about what turns us on sexually. Our sex lives have been about the same, though she has had fewer partners but longer affairs than I. I've never doubted my ability in bed, but our frankness has given me cause to worry. Recently, my girlfriend admitted that she could attain a greater orgasm through masturbation, using a stream of water from the bathtub faucet, than she has had with any man she has known. I contend that I should be able to bring her to the same heights. Am I right? Can a man bring a woman to as strong an orgasm as she can receive by artificial means? So far, she has not complained and swears that our lovemaking has been fulfilling. I know that I should be happy with her contentment, but I have no desire to lose her due to a lack of ability on my part. What should I do? —L. M., Detroit, Michigan.

Masters and Johnson found that women frequently achieve more intense orgasms through masturbation than they do through intercourse; the researchers also reported that some women said that these orgasms were subjectively less satisfying. It's hard to beat singlemindedness in matters of efficiency. A self-made woman can apply exactly the type of caress that excites her most; in intercourse, she has less immediate control—there's the rub. But the greatest pleasure in sex comes from having only half the fun. Don't try to compete with plumbing; performance fear is a primary cause of impotence. Ask your girlfriend if you can watch her next affair with the faucet. You'll find that it's not a difficult act to follow and you may learn something about your partner's pattern of response.

But Is It Dangerous

My husband and I recently installed a wonderfully sensuous Jacuzzi hot tub in our back yard. It certainly has transformed our sex lives, as well as those of our neighbors. Our back yard is now the "in" spot in the area. I have one concern, though: I recall reading that air forced into the vagina could cause an embolism. One of my favorite pastimes in the Jacuzzi consists of letting the water jet caress my clitoris—to the point of orgasm and beyond. The water jet is part water and part air. The bubbles contribute to the erotic massage. Should I cease this titillating turn-on, or should I perhaps limit my geyser to just gushing water? —Mrs. M. M., Seattle, Washington.

Dear next of kin: Just kidding, folks. It is true that forcing air into the vagina can be fatal, especially during pregnancy or menstruation. Even in those circumstances, the chances are slight that the water jet in the Jacuzzi could build up enough pressure to do you in. As long as you don't impale yourself on the jet, you should be safe. So enjoy the bubbly.

CHAPTER TEN

Fantasy

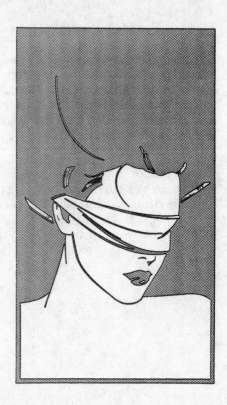

Better Loving Through Fantasy

I'm a twenty-year-old woman. I don't want to suggest that I have a dirty mind, but I fantasize like crazy when I masturbate. On occasion, I will drift off while making love to a real person. I've read Nancy Friday and The Hite Report. *All those books tell you that women have fantasies and that there's no such thing as weird or normal. But I wonder. Is there such a thing as too much fantasy? Shouldn't I be able to get off on the real thing? What effect does my fantasy life have on my love life? —Miss T. S., Dallas, Texas.*

There is some evidence to suggest that the more you fantisize in bed on your own, the easier it is to be aroused in other situations. Researchers at the State University of New York at Stony Brook asked women how frequently they fantasized during masturbation, then tested their response in a laboratory situation. The subjects indulged in a fantasy or listened to an erotic tape. Instruments measured genital arousal. Among the top ten responders in the fantasy condition, nine reported use of masturbatory fantasy at least 75 percent of the time. Among the lowest of the responders in the fantasy condition, six used masturbatory fantasy less than 25 percent of the time, and two never used fantasy. Apparently, it's what goes on in your head, not your hands, that counts. The more you think about sex, the more you bring to the actual event. Fantasy is definitely a factor in sexual arousal; if you are having any problems in bed, you should spend some time in private reverie, going over old memories, trying out favorite fantasies.

First Night Fantasies

I've been dating a girl for several months. We finally got around to talking about what went on in our heads during sex, what we liked, and so forth. I mentioned that I sometimes fantasized during intercourse. She asked me if I had had erotic daydreams the first time we made love. I said yes, which was a mistake. She grants that fantasies are normal but thinks I must be pretty weird to drift off in the middle of a completely novel encounter, when I should be totally absorbed in my new partner. Am I strange? —K. R., Madison, Wisconsin.

Depends on what you were dreaming about. Baseball? The Dow Jones? A psychologist at the University of Michigan polled 421 college students and found that nearly 60 percent reported fantasizing at least sometimes during intercourse. Over 35 percent of the males reported erotic fantasies during their first coital encounter—so you have some company. (In contrast, only 18 percent of the females were in fantasy-land on their first night.) The reasons given for fantasizing varied: "Thirty-eight percent of the men said it facilitated sexual arousal; 18 percent spent their time thinking of sexual activities that they had yet to engage in with their partners; 30 percent used fantasy to increase their partner's attractiveness, 3 percent to relieve boredom. An honest 10 percent said they had no idea why they did it. Next time you have this discussion with your girlfriend, just paraphrase the old art critic: I don't know if it's normal, but I know what I like.

Fantasies During Sex

The other night, my girlfriend and I were discussing sexual fantasies. She mentioned that she frequently slips into an erotic daydream state during sex. She started doing that with her first lover and confessed that the longer she knew him, the more she fantasized about other people, places or whatever during sex. Now that she has met me, she is somewhat worried that she will go through the same cycle. Is her worry justified? —S. O., Boston, Massachusetts.

According to a report in *Medical Aspects of Human Sexuality*, erotic fantasies during intercourse are quite common. Among college students, for example, some 60 percent said they experienced the x-rated accompaniment, with 6 percent of the females saying that they almost always added a silent movie to sex. Older women turned in slightly higher figures—65 percent reported fantasies, while 37 percent said they occurred frequently. It seems to be the natural outcome of age, continued exposure to the same partner and increased knowledge about sex. The more you do it with someone, the more there is to fantasize about.

Same Sex Fantasies

I am a woman in my mid-twenties. Over the past three years, I've had some very sexual dreams, sometimes with men and sometimes (the part that's really bothering me) with women. I even fantasize about people I know. I can't stress to you how badly I feel when I wake up. Sometimes it upsets me for days. What I want to know is, why do I sometimes have sexual dreams that involve women, when I'm revolted by it afterward? Even the thought of its being a subconscious desire upsets me terribly. Does it mean that deep down that is what I want? I'm on the verge of going for professional help. Has anyone else ever had this problem? —Miss D. L., New Haven, Connecticut.

Relax. Sex researchers found that everyone has fantasies about sex with a member of the same gender at one time or another. In other words, we have all had this problem. It is important to realize that it isn't a problem. Dreams and fantasies are not symptoms. View them as an expression of the mind's awareness of possibilities rather than as desires. Think of them as a kind of TV programing that is not always ready for prime time.

A Woman's Wet Dream

My wife and I have been married for almost two years. We are both in our early twenties, enjoy sex, have done some swinging now and weren't virgins when we met. My wife has started to have highly erotic dreams. In her dreams, she has intercourse with one man while other men or a mixed crowd look on. The dreams are so intense, she awakens with her body sweating, swept away by the feeling that she has just had a cosmic climax. She claims that she never feels like that during real sex. What is puzzling is that she cannot remember the identity of her lover or any of the faces in the crowd. Does she secretly desire another man? Please advise. —W. C., San Francisco, California.

Her dream is a fairly common one: The crowd of anonymous admirers defines her own desirability. And it is quite possible that her dream produces physical orgasm (Kinsey found that 20 percent of the women he interviewed had experienced nocturnal climaxes). Our advice: Don't engage in armchair analysis—proceed directly to bed and remember the old adage: The person who wants to make a dream come true doesn't sleep.

Playing Doctor

Some years ago, my wife was hired by a company requiring that she have a physical examination before starting her new employment. Since the company doctor's office was some distance from our home, I volunteered to drive there and take her out to dinner afterward. She was apparently the last patient for the night and after a short wait, she was called into an inner office. About ten minutes later, I felt a call of nature and went looking for a rest room. Upon entering, I found that the doctor's w.c. had two doors, one a main entrance and the other connecting with the examining room. That one was slightly ajar. My first thought was to close the door and go about my business, when I looked through the crack and saw my wife getting undressed to put on a hospital gown. I had never seen my wife undress without her knowing about it; the thought of secretly doing so and of her now-naked body prompted me to look on. Only minutes after she had the gown on, the doctor came into the room and began a complete physical examination. During the next half hour, I watched as he had her partially remove the gown for some things and completely remove it for others. Throughout the examination, the doctor acted serious and completely professional. I, however, was extremely turned on watching him examine my wife's naked breasts, have her strip down for x-rays and lie with her legs spread for her vaginal examinations. It has been eight years since this incident, and although I occasionally think about it, I have never told my wife what happened. I would, however, like to have another such experience, since it was one of the most stimulating that I can remember. My questions are these: Do I have more than normal voyeuristic tendencies, or are there some people who get extremely turned on by watching a doctor perform a routine examination on a woman? Is there any reason why a doctor should not want a patient's husband present during consultation? —D. T., Springfield, Massachusetts.

Your fantasy is surprisingly common. (How else can you account for the popularity of "Marcus Welby"?) A few years ago, we heard of an erotic hotel where couples could rent various fantasy rooms and videotape themselves making love in a Polynesian setting, a space capsule, a torture chamber, whatever. One of the settings was a Victorian doctor's office, with an antique examining table. On second thought, maybe your fantasy is rare: The hotel closed for lack of business. Maybe you can check local flea markets for an examining table and set up shop at home. Unless you're enrolled in a natural-childbirth program, the chances are slim of finding a doctor who will let you share the fun.

Masked Ball

Being a twenty-year-old male, I have my share of sexual problems—acting out fantasy being the main one. Recently, I saw a movie that presented a novel form of seduction. A guy met a girl in the park. Both were wearing masks. Not knowing who she was, and vice versa, they made wild, passionate love, then departed without a word. The idea of such an encounter appeals to me. I can imagine the scene: A mere glance between complete strangers and we would get it on, weather permitting. I feel that by doing it with masks, I would have the freedom to make love the way I want. I would not let her facial expressions rule my actions. Could you tell me if this is a good idea? —A. K., New York, New York.

The editorial *we* is divided on this issue; *we* think it's a great idea (having had the same fantasy ourself), but it has to be put in perspective (for example, the time the Lone Ranger and Tonto were surrounded by hostile Indians and the Lone Ranger said, "It looks like the end for us" and Tonto said, "What do you mean *us?*"). The fantasy has its place, but not in public. The police have been known to take a dim view of people walking into Central Park wearing masks. Actually, masking is an ancient tradition. Eastern potentates often had their concubines and wives wear masks; it saved them the trouble of keeping track of all those names. The carnivals of Rio are occasions for celebrating impersonal sex. Go there or find a cooperative accomplice and try a masked ball in the privacy of your own bedroom. She won't find your mysterious-stranger routine that strange; she's probably had her own fantasies of Zorro leaving his mark. A plain mask will provide anonymity—you'll feel like Everyman making love to Everywoman. Or if you desire a change of face from come-as-you-are parties, try celebrity sex. We recall an orgy (described in *Trashing* by Ann Fettamen) where bedfellows wore the masks of politicians (Richard Nixon, Henry Kissinger, Shirley Temple Black, Martha Mitchell, et al.). Now that's strange, but it goes to show: different folks for the same old stroke.

Special Effects

While making love to my girlfriend a few nights ago, I had the strangest experience. I was riding atop, looking down at her and, as I approached orgasm, I seemed to see the faces of several of my former girlfriends superimposed on top of hers. It really spooked me. Later, I tried to explain the phenomenon—the ladies have certain similarities, the pleasure of the event brought back old associations, et cetera. I've talked with several of my buddies, and some of them confessed to having experienced the same "special effects." Is this a common phenomenon? Is it normal? —D. G., Burlington, Vermont.

What were you smoking? It's hard to say if the experience you describe is common—we've heard of it before, but not that much has been written about it. You've got to remember that, until recently, most people made love with the lights out. The best explanation is the one you've already arrived at—the remembrance of things past can be triggered by current stimuli. (The smell of oranges reminds some people of Christmas, when the fruit was used to stuff stockings.) We wouldn't worry about it—as long as one of the faces you see is not that of your mother, you're normal.

The Old Friend Fantasy

I have a problem that is causing me significant anguish. The only way I can achieve orgasm during intercourse with my husband is to fantasize about a certain man (it is always the same man—the one who claimed my virginity some 15 years ago). When I do come while fantasizing, I always end up crying or moaning that man's name. This appears to be something thoroughly out of my control (though can that be?). It has rendered me inorgasmic with my husband, as, naturally, I am afraid to come, knowing that I will "spill the beans" again. I have now resorted to masturbation as my sole means of gaining satisfaction (and I cry out my fantasy's name then, too). My husband just ignored it the first few times he heard me say another man's name, but he made it clear as time went on that this nasty habit of mine was not to be tolerated. The general message was, you can think what you damn well please, but keep his name out of my bed. What do I do? —Mrs. L. D., New York, New York.

Many women report having a favorite fantasy that they rely on to precipitate orgasm. Researchers call such erotic scenarios "old friend" fantasies, even though the subjects may vary. That much is normal. Anything that works is all right sexually. However, when a technique becomes the *only* source of pleasure, or when it stops working, you have a problem. (For example, a person wearing a wet suit and a feather boa seriously cuts down the chances of a fulfilling sex life.) The fantasy and your sexual behavior are very much in your control. Since your habit of crying out your first boyfriend's name decreases your own pleasure and that of your husband, it's obviously time to change. Analyze the fantasy and see what parts of it truly appeal to you. Does your husband share any traits (gentleness, aggressiveness, whatever) with the man you remember? Replace the fantasy with new experiences, the old memories with new ones, the reruns with prime-time specials. You are not a prisoner of your past. As Tom Robbins says, "It's never too late to have a happy childhood."

Aztec Sacrifice

During the final moments of lovemaking with my boyfriend, I drift into a fantasy world composed of fragments from D. H. Lawrence, Wingate Paine and Salvador Dali. For example, I sometimes imagine that I am spread-eagled on a rock altar in a mountain cave. An Aztec priest slowly lifts a knife. Rays of light play across my exposed body and set fire to my breasts and thighs. Always, as the blade begins to descend, I climax and the fantasy disappears like a piece of broken film. In another recurring fantasy, I imagine that I am tied to the rails of a brass bed, helpless, while masked figures caress my body. When I mentally struggle against their advances, I find that my own sensitivity increases dramatically. The subsequent orgasm is overwhelming. These daydreams are sexual dynamite, but how do I handle them? My lover has asked me to describe what I feel during intercourse and I am afraid to confess the existence of these fantasies. I have heard that erotic daydreams are evidence of sexual maladjustment, but I can't accept this theory. I dig my lover, and if the orgasms I experience as a result of my fantasies are a sign of sexual maladjustment, I couldn't survive improvement. What do you say? —Miss V. W., Taos, New Mexico.

Dynamite, sexual or otherwise, is dangerous only when it is contained. Share your fantasies with your lover—confess is the wrong word. Your imagination is normal and healthy. Psychologists have found that most women fantasize during intercourse and that many of them rely on effective fantasies to precipitate orgasm. Ask your lover to reciprocate. Alex Comfort says in *The Joy of Sex* that if you can't communicate your fantasies, you don't deserve to be lovers.

Fantasy or Acid Flashback

Is it possible to have an acid flashback without having taken LSD or mescaline? My girlfriend, who has never taken drugs, seems to have had one. She visited me for a week in the Rockies (she goes to graduate school in the East); we made love in the snow, in a sauna, in front of a fireplace, in the back of an old Dodge van. Our sex seemed to have an acetylene flare and we really got it on. Subsequently, I received a letter from her—she said that on the flight back, she had an uncanny feeling that she was still making love to me. The feel of her blouse against her skin, the slight rush of takeoff—something caused her to relive what we had done together. She said that the memory was incredibly exact. The whole flight was a balancing act between being sexually excited and being sexually satisfied. Was this some kind of temporary organic psychosis? —D. O., Vail, Colorado.

Dr. Helen Singer Kaplan states in *The New Sex Therapy* that "some patients (in my experience women only) report that sometimes the day after they have engaged in a particularly arousing sexual act with an especially loved and desired partner they experience profoundly pleasurable 'flashbacks.' These are triggered by memories of the erotic experience and are accompanied by intense erotic sensations and feelings of euphoria and love." (Possibly a man feels the same thing when he has a day-after hard-on—he just has to work at it a bit.) The mechanics of the phenomenon are still a mystery, but flashbacks of one form or another are part of human nature. Students who have read *Remembrance of Things Past* might say that your girlfriend was coming home to Proust. A vivid recollection can release the emotions that accompanied the original experience—even the bummer rerun of an acid flashback may be an ordinary response to an extraordinary experience. Therapists from Freud to Janov have worked with such memories to cure people, so we wouldn't classify it as a sign of a psychosis. As long as you get to go around only once in life, you might as well recycle the good parts.

Sharing Fantasies

My wife and I enjoy a loving relationship. She is charming and beautiful, with a sharp, inventive wit. My problem is this: When we find ourselves in bed and our sexual interest peaks, she becomes so absorbed in her fantasies that she leaves me out of the picture. Lately, she has asked that I act out certain scenes from late-night movies or that I pretend to be Paul Newman or Cary Grant. I have become preoccupied with these characterizations and I fear that my own identity has become lost in the crowd. She says that her sex life is terrific but it's gotten to where she won't make love unless I comply with her wishes. How can I drop out of this drama school without losing my precious wife? —J. M., Allentown, Pennsylvania.

Sex is a question not of what's right but of what's left. Fantasy is one way to introduce variety in your lovemaking. It is our opinion that a woman who expresses her fantasies to her husband is probably a very secure, open person. You should feel privileged rather than threatened when she invites you to share these intimate dreams and games. Because she wants you to be Paul Newman one night is no indication that she loves you any less or that she is discontent with the marriage. (Robert Redford is another matter.) But your wife should respect your desire for more opportunities to simply be yourself. Consult a TV guide and schedule your lovemaking to preclude both the "Movie of the Week" and "This Is Your Life."

Would the Real Thing Work?

About a year ago, my husband brought home some stag movies given to him by a friend. One of them showed a beautiful, sexy woman making love to two guys at once. She looked as if she were completely blown away by it, and I longed to be in her place: lying in bed, the guy behind her cupping her breasts, kissing her neck and ears, the other man kneeling between her thighs, kissing her stomach, tugging lightly at her pubic hair with his teeth, performing cunnilingus. It seemed such a tender homage to her body, a total support system for her ecstasy. Later, she accepted both of them and I really spaced out. She had them coming and going. My husband realized my excitement and he used himself and a rubber penis on me during sex that night. I pretended that both were real; the feeling was glorious. Since then, our marriage has gone through a radical change. We spend hours talking, playing and making love. Still, I hunger to make love to my husband and another man at the same time. When we pretend, the effects are the same as the first time. My husband doesn't seem to mind—I think he likes the fact that I enjoy sex more than I ever did before. Do you think I'm overreacting to the film? What would my husband say if he knew I wanted the real thing? —Mrs. S. C., Schenectady, New York.

How about, "Funny you should mention it?" We suspect that your husband has already considered the possibility. He seems quite liberated. Ask him what he had in mind when he brought the films home. Maybe he'll bring the friend along next time. (Then again, maybe he enjoyed a scene showing two women and a man and has another suggestion.) Your reaction to the erotic movie was fairly common. Some women get more turned on recalling what they have seen than they do while actually viewing the movie. The visual image becomes a counterpoint to their own activity—it *looks* like what they *feel* like. The fantasy of a ménage à trois has increased your sense of attractiveness and sexual skill; the reality may or may not add to that. Consider the possible consequences; sometimes it does hurt to triangle.

Giving Permission

My old man and I enjoy fantasizing about sex. I tell him detailed stories, true or false, of the sexiest things my evil mind can dream up. The more decadent the better. He loves it. When we were just married, he was as straight with sex as I was crooked. I was his first. In no time, he began loosening up and even started to reveal his desires to me. I wasn't shocked. A little surprised, maybe. His requests were pure porn. Great porn. Now, I tease him with stories about twosomes and other chicks, orgies, cunning ways to seduce others, anything I can dream up. It's great to be mentally free, but he won't allow me actually to try any of these fantasies (with the possible exception of the lesbian tryst). I'd love to do it with an extra guy or two, but I'm afraid to approach the subject. He's a biker, and I don't need to tell you about how a biker feels toward his woman. He owns me. Nobody else gets any. How can I satisfy my fantasy without risking a broken neck? —Miss F. S., Nashville, Tennessee.

Bikers feel the same way about their women as certified public accountants do about theirs. And our guess is that you dig it (oh, for the days when men were men and women were glad of it). Don't be afraid to raise the subject. You confess to having loosened him up, and he might actually go for the idea. (Then again, it's possible that he pulled the old "Virgin Biker" routine on you, and that somewhere in his sordid past, he'd already tried the arrangement.) If not, and if you still want to try a two-on-one tryst, you can always recruit strangers. A person's sex life is his or her own responsibility. You don't need anyone's permission to play out your fantasies.

The Mandatory Ménage

My wife and I have a passionate and uninhibited sex life. Lately it has become enriched by fantasies taken from various X-rated films that we have seen together. We imagine what group sex would be like; specifically, a ménage à trois with another woman present. I am excited by the image of two women caressing and kissing each other, the symmetry of breasts pressing against breasts, the intimacies based on a woman's knowledge of what turns a woman on. My wife favors a scenario in which she is an invisible observer, watching me enjoy myself with the other woman: She jokingly points out that she has never seen how the muscles in my back move when we make love, and thinks she would get off on it. Neither of us would mind having our fantasies become fact, if we could find a cooperative accomplice, but the more we talk about it, the more we feel for each other and the less inclined we are to admit a third party. We can't figure out what the fantasies mean. Do they indicate some underlying compulsion that must be cured by acting out? Are we closet voyeurs who need help? What do you say? —J. U., Columbia, Missouri.

A voyeur is an innocent bystander in a crowd of exhibitionists; to a certain extent, we are all voyeurs. Fantasies often reflect a desire for distance; they allow us to bring things into focus and satisfy a curiosity that lies beyond involvement. Simply because you have imagined the ménage does not make it mandatory. You can create your own crowd: Place a mirror over your bed or rent a video-tape recorder for a weekend. (This may cost you an arm and a leg, but it's your back that interests your wife and, in addition, you can have an instant replay for the parts that turn her on.) Carry on.

Wife in Bed with Someone Else

Business trips take me away from home for extended periods of time. Consequently, I urged my wife to have an affair while I was gone. She has always had a healthy sexual appetite and I did not feel it was fair to keep her inactive during my absences. For a few months, she said that she wasn't interested in anyone else, but then she confessed that she had had an affair with one of my friends. My reaction surprised me; I was aroused by thoughts of her enjoying intercourse, fellatio and cunnilingus with another man. Now I become excited whenever she tells me of the affair. In fact, I am unable to achieve an erection unless she talks about it. My wife has become disgusted with me and finally has told me to have an affair so that we will be even. I love her very much and I don't want to be with someone else. How do I go about getting an erection without her telling me about the affair? —C. H., San Francisco, California.

It's not unusual for a man to become aroused at the thought of his wife in bed with someone else; the idea that she might be desirable to others increases her value to him. If it's the fantasy that interests you, tell your wife. Perhaps she will tape-record a "confession" that you can play occasionally through headphones when you make love. It may cramp your style; don't do it in the bath and take care that you don't choke yourself with the cord. Most people are able to respond to a variety of sexual stimuli; your obsession with the details is probably transitory. One thing puzzles us: If you do not feel compelled to satisfy your own sexual appetite on long trips, why assume that your wife wants to? Occasionally, when a husband feels insecure about his spouse and believes that adultery is inevitable, he will encourage infidelity to maintain an illusion of control. It's not your choice. The golden rule now reads: You're free and nobody belongs to you.

CHAPTER ELEVEN

Different Strokes

Animal Sex

You won't believe this, but my girlfriend and I get incredibly turned on watching animals mate. We've exhausted the neighborhood cats and dogs. The attendants at the zoo are getting suspicious. Can you tell us what other animals are exciting to watch—in terms of size, penetration, et cetera? —S. W., Hartford, Connecticut.

We don't noah for sure, but we think you must be kidding. Have you tried the common but ever-popular flea? It has the largest penis in relation to body size of any creature alive. Pick up one of those stereo microscopes, put it in your collective lap and try not to jiggle the bed. Whales are also a favorite. Their foreplay is fantastic: A male and a female whale will swim toward each other, leap out of the water and collide in mid-air. Their accuracy is astonishing (which is where "having a whale of a time" comes from), although they sometimes miss (therefore the black-and-blue whale). And for added kink: Whales engage in group sex. Two males will sandwich a female (the extra male acts as a backstop so the other can penetrate). Of course, you'll have to move fast to catch the act—whales are an endangered species. For information on saving the sexy cetaceans, write: The National Audubon Society, 950

Third Avenue, New York, New York 10022. (Isn't it amazing how we worked that in?)

Chuckles

I am a single, liberated woman, age thirty, who very much enjoys making love with the opposite sex. However, recently, my partner has made comments about my soft laughing and noisemaking during sessions in bed. I have assured him that the laughter stems from complete enjoyment and pleasure and that I am certainly not laughing at him. It has become a problem, though, and is interfering with my sex life. Please advise—is this common? How should I handle it with old and new lovers? —Miss C. S., Mobile, Alabama.

Sex is a *serious* matter. Just think of all the sex-starved virgins in China doing without. That should cure you of lightheartedness. If not, think of what your parents, relatives, teachers and neighborhood shopkeepers would say if they knew you were enjoying yourself. Actually, this ticklish situation is the result of your partner's inhibitions, not yours. We don't think you should hold your feelings in check during lovemaking. If you can't let go during sex, when can you? If your current lover insists on putting up warning signs (55 chuckles per minute), then it may be time to find someone else.

Ticklish Situation

Not long ago, I picked up a very lovely woman in a bar on New York's East Side. We seemed to get along very well, and it was unusually easy to convince her to leave with me. I was somewhat surprised when she suggested we return to her apartment. This elegant lady had me in bed with her before I knew what had happened, before I had a chance to make advances on my own. In a very sensuous manner, she began asking me to perform various sexual acts that would please her. I eagerly complied, only to have her smile sweetly and whisper that I wasn't doing things to her liking. Suddenly, without my realizing it, she had slipped what seemed to be homemade bonds made of satin around my wrists and ankles. (I thought she was simply nervously twisting the loose bedsheet around me.) Finding myself bound securely, I started to worry. She grinned and said, "You didn't do very well. For punishment, I'm going to torture you by tickling you with my long fingernails." Well, she had very long nails and proceeded to tickle me with them. For at least forty-five minutes. She literally put my squirming body into spasms, and, much to my surprise, I reached an unbelievable orgasm. As a result of that experience, I find any kind of sex without this added deviation boring. Unfortunately, I have been unable to get in touch with the incredible woman who introduced me to the diversion. Is it unusual to have a longing to be tickled by a woman's long fingernails? I actually find myself looking at a woman's hands to see how long her nails are before I look at her face. Is this fetish common? —R. G., New York, New York.

What's the name of that bar? Oh, never mind. We've heard of this fetish. Actually, all things considered, it's fairly effective. Women will probably be charmed when you detour the normal glance at the breast for a close study of their fingernails. If a woman doesn't meet your expectations, you can gallantly offer her some falsies. And if you can't meet anyone to fulfill your dreams, go home and masturbate with a backscratcher.

Dominance Submission

My lover has become my slave. We are both well adjusted to the fact that I am free to use him or abuse him as I see fit. But my sister is coming to visit me this fall. I want very much to share my slave with her—to give her equal rights to strip him, flog him, order him about. On this I need your advice. He must obey me in all matters and there is no question of his obedience if I tell him to submit to my sister. I get goose-pimples just thinking about watching him, stark-naked and in chains, submitting to her punishments. Still, I wonder—could I be abusing my authority by turning him over to another? —Miss C. R., Washington, D.C.

Very interesting. Have you considered auditioning for the "Gong Show?" As we understand the ground rules of your relationship, your pussy-whipped bureaucrat will probably enjoy the exchange. But what will you do if she sets him free?

Pleasure Pain

Having recently returned from a tour of duty in Japan, I find that I have a slight problem. While overseas, I had a special bedmate who brought out a mild form of masochism in me. Just as I would reach ejaculation, she would give my balls a painful squeeze with both hands. At first, the gesture was excruciatingly uncomfortable and I would stop in my tracks. But further relations began to revolve around such brutal attacks; the excruciating pain would intensify my pleasure. Now that I am Stateside, I catch myself requesting partners to practice this baseball grip during lovemaking. I fear that this dependence could branch out into a desire for other masochistic assaults. What can I do to keep things from getting out of control? —W.F.M., Las Vegas, Nevada.

At certain levels, pain is indistinguishable from pleasure, and your practice differs only in degree from the biting and scratching that many people enjoy as a part of loveplay. Your desire to be grabbed by the balls hasn't gotten out of hand as long as it isn't a compulsion. It's true that you may become conditioned to expect the baseball grip—if it happens every time you have an orgasm, you will associate the two—but conditioning is not addiction. When you're in the box you can swing whenever and however you feel. An extra hint: Keep a resin bag by the bedside—it will improve your partner's grip.

My breasts are exceedingly large (38DD) and are rather heavy, though not very sensitive to light or even moderate handling. My husband finds them visually stimulating and likes me to hoist them up in a scarf or nectie tied as a sling from the back of my neck. He really gets off on slapping them to and fro, and I must admit I enjoy it as much as he does. At times, we get very excited and he ends up smacking them around pretty hard. I fell only a pleasant stinging and no actual harsh pain, but usually after these rougher handlings, there are some fairly large bruises that appear, which last a few days and fade soon afterward. (All my life I've had a tendency to bruise easily anywhere on my body.) My question is this: Could the particular bruises that result from lovemaking be a sign of actual damage? —Mrs. S. W., Los Angeles, California.

Check with your doctor; it will be easier for him to check for potential damage in person. You don't need to tell him how you got the bruises, but it might help. Otherwise, your husband could get hauled in for wife beating. But don't worry. Chances are you aren't doing serious damage (at least, no more than the athletes who are battered and bruised on other playing fields). When it comes to sex, our rule is: If it feels good, do it. When it comes to rough sex play, our rule is: If it doesn't hurt that much, do it.

Serious S & M

Alex Comfort's The Joy of Sex *taught people that it was fun to tie up their partners before making love. Bondage and discipline was a fantasy to be explored by every liberated lover. Fine, except my girlfriend and I really enjoy it. We've even bought leather harnesses, whips, et cetera, and that's where the problem arises: We now have the tools to inflict genuine pain on each other. The costume ball has lost a bit of its luster now that we are skirting the reality. We are thinking about using the whip for more than a prop in our lovemaking. But we aren't sure whether or not we can or should cross the border from B/D to outright sadomasochism. Movies like* Story of O *and* Joanna *celebrate pain in the name of love. We doubt the accuracy of those portrayals. We're not sure what to expect. What motivates a serious sadist? —W. E., Teaneck, New Jersey.*

Beats us. We're not sure that S/M qualifies as a form of lovemaking. According to Ernest Becker, author of the essay "Everyman as Pervert," a sadist cannot stand the mystery of another person, her separateness, her uniqueness. "By treating the flesh with violence and causing it great pain, the sadist literally makes of his partner a predominately external organism: There is no room for subtleties of thought, and no way of keeping thought separate from what one feels and expresses, when he is convulsed with pain. The mind 'comes out in the open' in the screams and pleadings of the body. There is no longer anything private or aloof: The victim is reduced to the barest terms of the body." If that sounds heavy, it is. The master and slave roles are devoid of personality: In fact, sadists report that the better they know their victims, the less satisfactory the experience. The two actors in the S/M drama are bound by force, the whip that connects them. Pleasure is uncertain, pain guaranteed. A sadist never asks his partner if she came or, for that matter, if it hurt. We'd advise caution: These situations have been known to blacklash.

Obvious Put-on #1

At a party last month, I met a fellow who had spent five months in a Viet Cong prison camp. He related two incidents that I found very hard to believe. He claimed that he was stripped and bound face up on a bed, at which point a beautiful young woman fellated him to a throbbing erection. Then a leather noose was slipped around his genitals and tightened. In a very short time, he became numb, remained hard and very excited but was unable to climax. Ten to fifteen women then mounted him one after another for over eight hours. Afterward, the noose was released and a male guard gave him a hand job. In the second story, he was stripped and spread-eagled between two vertical poles and three girls set to work on him. The first buried her face between his buttocks and tongued his anus, the second suck/licked his testicles and the third suck/licked his penis. At the hint of orgasm, the squeeze technique was applied, sometimes with the fingers, other times with the mouth, causing him to lose his erection. He endured this torture for a period of ten hours or more. I don't see how either of the incidents could have happened without some form of permanent damage resulting. What do your experts say? —W.A.B., New Orleans, Louisiana.

Actually, it sounds to us like he spent an average weekend at one of those California sensitivity-training clinics. Regardless of the method used to prolong erection, when the limit of sexual responsiveness has been reached, the penis simply cannot achieve erection again. So much for pleasure torture. No doubt, when he had finished these stories, he offered to sell you a Corvette Sting Ray for only $200—you know, the one that was found in a snowbank in perfect condition, except that the driver, who'd had a cardiac arrest, had been dead for months and no matter how hard you scrubbed. . . .

Obvious Put-on #2

Glancing through a magazine recently, I noticed that one of the models had no nipples. I asked my boyfriend what had happened to them. He looked at me in astonishment and said, "You mean you still have both of your nipples?" He told me that a woman's nipples are often removed by a man in the heat of passion and that one person he knows used to have a whole jarful. They looked like dried apricots. I told him that this was ridiculous, but because my experience is limited, I'm not really sure. What do you say? —Miss F. R., Iowa City, Iowa.

The model whose picture you saw may have been the victim of a careless airbrush or an overreaction to a Supreme Court decision. Possibly, she had inverted nipples. Tell your boyfriend that one erogeneous zone is as vulnerable as the next and that you know a girl who has a jar full of what appears to be mushrooms. That should make him bite his tongue-in-cheek.

Public Sex

I don't know if I should brag or complain. My boyfriend, who is very sexy and well hung, enjoys making love in the oddest places. If you have ever been to St. Louis, you are probably familiar with the Gateway Arch. You can take a seven-minute ride up and down the side in a small five-seat capsule. I know it sounds strange, but last summer we made love during one such ride. (There were hardly any tourists.) We enjoyed ourselves immensely. Can you suggest any other sexy sites? —Miss N. M., St. Louis, Missouri.

Are you a brunette, about five foot one, with a mole on your left shoulder? We caught your act. Ahem. Public displays of lust (P.D.L.s) are spreading as more people take the sexual revolution out of the bedroom and onto the boulevards and beaches, where it belongs. Cities have yet to offer obscenic tours but some of the sites that have—to our carnal knowledge—been hit are the transparent elevators in Hyatt Houses, small gondolas at ski resorts and—perhaps in reaction to the movie hit—roller coasters. (If you thought Sensurround was a treat, try centrifugal force.) We advise caution, as your sport is still very risky. Most people's experience with P.D.L.s is confined to the accepted arenas—drive-in movies, theater balconies and golf courses after midnight. Have fun and keep us posted.

Shaved Pubic Hair

The reader who inquired in the January issue about historical roots of shaved pubic hair deserved a better answer than he got from you. Traditionally, both sexes of the people of the Arabian peninsula have shaved all of their body hair. Since the Arabs are not a particularly hairy race, there is not a lot to shave except in the genital and axillary areas. The men also keep the hair on their heads closely cropped beneath their skullcaps and head shawls. The origins of this practice are lost in the myths of antiquity, but it probably began as a method to prevent lice, since, with water in great scarcity, bathing was largely unknown. Once established as part of their native folklore, it became interspersed with religious belief and was spread throughout most of the lands of the Mediterranean and Middle East as the Arabs broadcast the faith of Islam during the Eighth and Ninth centuries. During an eighteen-month residence in a remote area of Saudi Arabia, I was unable to learn of any erotic overtones to this practice. Even a case-hardened old doc such as I must confess some novel fantasies upon first encountering this not unpleasant sight among my patients. The man who wrote to you claimed that the bald look heightened sensations. Like so much of human sexuality, his feelings are occasioned largely by his mental attitudes; there seems to be no end to what can serve as a turn-on. One must remember that in the male, at least, the area of greatest sensitivity is the glans penis, a part that already is hairless in most men. Incidentally, beneath their heavy black veils, many Bedouin women sport bleached tresses, achieved by the use of camels' urine, which has a high content of ammonia. —K. S., Wichita, Kansas.

Gee, thanks.

Dungeons and Dragons

Dungeons, chains, whips—these are the props of my erotic fantasies. An old lover who was into bondage and discipline introduced me to the pleasures of her (mock) displeasure. I've grown tired of normal relationships; like a reader who returns to paperback murder mysteries, I say to hell with meaning. I want entertainment. Call it a caricature, but the pure simplicity of a slave-master relationship is dramatic. I enjoyed learning her lessons of love. Unfortunately, the girl moved to the East Coast, taking with her the implements of instruction. Since then, I've tried to find other ways of whetting my appetite for discipline. Commercial establishments seem to be the best bet. Los Angeles papers are filled with ads for houses of domination that promise humiliation, leatherwear, handcuffs, strait jackets, the works. One lady claims to have a "sensational motorized cross," whatever that is. I've called their numbers, but no one ever answers. What gives? —Q. V., Los Angeles, California.

Perhaps the ladies are tied up and can't come to the phone. Sexual classified ads aren't exactly reliable. Although outright bondage and discipline (as opposed to casual knot tying and mild reproach) have become fashionable with movies such as *Defiance* and *Story of O*, aficionados still have to show restraint. We can't say the odds favor success: English tutors are hard to come by, or beneath, or whatever. Still, keep trying. (Drop us a note if you find out what the sensational motorized cross does.) Have you considered converting your basement to a playroom? You could invite a lady over, tell her that the house was previously owned by a rather strange couple, segue into "I wonder how this works," et cetera. For additional details, watch any made-for-TV movie. For props, contact The Pleasure Chest, 1022 North La Brea, Los Angeles, California. If worst comes to worst, you can always dress up like a Saint Bernard and enroll in animal obedience school.

Dildo

Let me thank you from the depths of my heart (as well as other parts of my body) for the way you answered the letter on sodomy in the August Playboy Advisor. I let my husband enjoy the act of anal sex several times, but I always experienced a lot of pain. No matter how relaxed or lubricated I was, penetration was extremely uncomfortable. Although I had orgasms, the pleasure wasn't worth the pain, so we dropped the act from our sexual repertoire. Now I have a related problem: Whenever we have oral sex, my husband likes to use a dildo on me. The thing is somewhat thicker and longer than his penis and it hurts like hell. However, I still have orgasms. My husband tells me that the pain is all in my head—a vagina will expand to accommodate any size penis. Is he right? Also, am I some kind of masochist? I always have orgasms in spite of the pain. —Mrs. R. C., Chapel Hill, North Carolina.

A masochist enjoys himself because of the pain, not in spite of it. Sexologists have noted that it's a thin line between agony and ecstasy. As you've discovered, the two are not mutually exclusive. Your husband has correctly quoted Masters and Johnson. A vagina will accommodate a penis of any size—but that process depends on relaxation and the absence of anxiety. If the dildo makes you uptight, the tension will contribute to the pain. It shouldn't be hard to talk him out of using the accessory. Oral sex is a feast that should always be catered to the tastes of the recipient. If you can't do it the way your partner likes, why bother doing it?

Spanking

I am a very sexy cheerleader at a high school in Oklahoma. I have been dating a member of the band. We enjoy sex often, especially when it is preceded by an erotic form of foreplay—spanking. We were first introduced to spanking by my parents, when they caught us making love in my bedroom one evening. They told us we could continue to use my bedroom but only if my boyfriend spanked my bottom. I figured that one spanking on my ass wouldn't make that much difference, so I agreed. My mom had me put my dress, bra, crotchless panties and panty hose back on, along with some high-heeled shoes. Then she told me to bend over the bed, to raise my skirt above my waist and hold it there. She hauled my boyfriend a three-foot-long wooden paddle and had him pull down my panty hose and panties. She looked at her watch and told him to start spanking. Thirty minutes later, he stopped. My bottom was cherry red, had welts on it and stung like hell. But it felt good. We now enjoy spanking almost every time we fuck. Before night football games, we meet in his car and he spanks me until I'm about to cry. The sting wears off pretty fast and I can't feel it, so then we get out of the car and again he spanks me—this time with a paddle. We both enjoy it so much, we would like to know how to prolong the sting and the redness. —Miss H. M., Tulsa, Oklahoma.

Our resident English public school alumnus offers the following tips: Drill tiny holes in the surface of the paddle to decrease air resistance. A thick coating of water sprayed on the target also seems to enhance the stinging action. Break up the strokes into irregular patterns (one minute on, two minutes off, etc.), so that the victim can appreciate the stinging sensation during the intervals. Also, your boyfriend may be using a weak grip. A quick visit to the local tennis pro should reveal the right holds. Friction tape on the handle will help prevent twisting of the paddle at crucial moments. Now, about your parents. . . .

I read with interest the letter in the November Playboy Advisor from the sexy cheerleader who wanted to accentuate spanking effects. As an experienced hand, I would like to offer one bit of advice—position can make a remarkable difference. She should lie on her back and raise her legs together, so her companion can both hold her by the knees and also apply the paddle to the target. This will intensify the stinging and should give the upturned cheerleader the pleasure she craves. But to want to be spanked for thirty minutes? Come now. —J. H., Cheney, Washington.

We'll believe your letter if you'll believe hers. Next.

Since I was sixteen years old, I have entertained the fantasy of being spanked barebottomed. I confided this desire to my husband, but he seems reluctant to do it. We have an extremely good sex life—expressive, inventive, loving—and this is the only area in which we disagree. Consequently, I am becoming more and more frustrated. How can I convince my husband to try spanking? —Mrs. R. C., Fort Worth, Texas.

The desire to be spanked is a common sexual idiosyncrasy: an open mind and an open hand combine well with a person who gets turned on when turned over. After all, the buttocks are a legitimate erogenous zone, even if neglected by many lovers. Ask your husband to explain his reservations. He may be afraid that he will hurt you—tell him that you'll be sure to ask him to stop if you become uncomfortable. He may think it is wrong—ask him to let the punishment fit the crime. We think that he can be persuaded to try spanking (at least once). Sexual experimentation is its own reward and you may end up hearing your husband exclaim: "This is going to please me more than it pleases you."

I enjoy spanking women. However, I am inhibited about trying to find partners. I don't know how or where to start. I have spanked several women after conventional relationships have been established. I know that they did not enjoy going along with me and, for that reason, my own pleasure was diminished. I would prefer to find women who genuinely love to be spanked or who are willing to experiment with spanking as a form of foreplay. As long as my partner is comfortable with her participation, I will experiment to any degree. What should I do? —S. H., Scarsdale, New York.

Ever play "What's My Line?" In one sense, your problem is no more or no less complicated than finding a fantastic backgammon player who happens to be a woman. (Care to arrange a trade?) You know exactly what you want and you don't want to spend time on anything else. To avoid pseudomasochists, you'll have to come out of the cloakroom and announce your special interest. It always helps to provide clues and cues to bring the conversation around—perhaps you could wear a lapel pin emblazoned with a scarlet handprint. (If an obvious straight inquires about the pin's meaning, you can tell her that it is the symbol of a secret order of school-crossing guards.) Personal ads in *Screw* or *The New York Review of Books* are also a means to an end. Think kink.

Stockings

A woman wearing stockings really turns me on. I like all types of hosiery on women and I regularly peruse magazines that feature lingerie ads. I am happily married, but my wife thinks I am crazy regarding this hosiery thing. She refuses to wear stockings to bed, though she is "considering" the matter. Certainly, my interest is not that far off base. I've noticed that many of your models wear stockings—in particular Ann Pennington in the March issue is stunningly stockinged. What do I tell my wife to convince her to indulge my fantasy? —I. G., Salem, Massachusetts.

The concept of stockings as erotic apparel is widely accepted by members of both sexes: We know one woman who collects pictures of bank robbers. No one is quite sure of the history of the turn-on. Some claim that a pair of black hose, with a garter and spike heels, recalls the naughtiness of Victorian courtesans, the flippant sexuality of a Roaring Twenties stripper. Since most of us are too young to have known a dapper flapper, it is more likely that stockings simply call attention to a well-formed leg, ascending the thigh like mercury in a thermometer. Perhaps they remind us of Christmas gifts. Tell your wife that a compromise position is possible: If she'll put them on, you'll take them off. Slow undressing is a turn-on in itself. Enjoy.

Voyeurism

At night, while gazing out of my living room window, I can discern what I imagine to be a scrumptious young thing undressing in front of her drapeless window. Needless to say, I want to see if what I imagine is true. Her building is about two-hundred feet away from mine. What do you recommend—binoculars or a telescope? —J. T., New York, New York.

Jeepers, creepers, look at all the peepers. Our resident high-powered-optics expert came up with three guidelines. Binoculars are the best bet. Both eyes are engaged, and the image is bigger than with a telescope. Your primary consideration is the brightness of the image for night viewing. We know of one voyeur who was sure he was looking at a nipple one night but who discovered during daylight hours it was a Frisbee. The key to brightness is a large objective lens. The larger the objective lens, the greater its light-gathering capabilities. There is a formula for determining the relative brightness of binoculars: divide the diameter of the objective lens by the rated power and then square the result. For example, the relative brightness of a 7×35 unit is 25. Our expert suggests that the optimum night-vision unit is a tripod-mounted 12×80 (whose relative brightness is 43.56) with fully coated lenses (to minimize the diffusion of light within the barrels of the binoculars). The tripod keeps your hands free.

Wheels on Fire

I am a motorcycle fanatic. Over the years, I have developed several techniques for having sex while riding my two-wheeled beast. Usually, the female passenger simply reaches around in front, unzips my jeans and holds on for dear life. An erection makes a great granny handle. Sometimes, if the girl is small enough, I put her on the seat in front of me. She leans over the tank, I enter from the rear and the acceleration causes her to settle back against me. Unfortunately, I have yet to discover a way for a passenger to perform fellatio while cruising down the road. Is there a safe way to accomplish my dream? —F. F., Berkeley, California.

Yes. It's called a sidecar. But watch out for those bumps and potholes. You could lose more than your concentration.

After school, I work at a parking lot. Every now and then, I take one of the cars out for a little spin—usually a sports car with four or five on the floor. When I return from these jaunts, I have a full erection. Why? This tends to be embarrassing. —E. Y., Wyncote, Pennsylvania.

It might be called the Grand Prix syndrome. Your experience is a fairly common male response to tension, excitement, stress and such. Or you may be shifting the wrong stick. The owners of the cars you joy-ride would really give you a hard time if they caught you flagrante delicto (which is not an Italian sports car). There are better ways to get your kicks—find one.

CHAPTER TWELVE

Toys and the Great Sex Aids Road Test

Ben Wa Balls

Business trips take me away from home for extended periods of time. I've considered giving my wife a pair of Japanese love balls, or ben-wa, to keep her happy while I'm gone. Supposedly, they can be quite stimulating. Can you tell me how they function? —B.A.W., San Francisco, California.

Ben-wa consist of two small spheres, usually made of ivory, plastic or metal. One sphere is hollow, the other is filled with mercury. A woman places the hollow sphere in her vagina, follows it with the mercury-filled sphere, then goes about her business. Theoretically, the vibrations caused by the balls clacking together are sexually arousing, but don't count on it. The vagina, like most other internal organs, is virtually devoid of nerve endings. Only the outer third is sensitive to sexual stimulation (so much for penetration). Ben-wa do not even touch the clitoris, which is the sexual nerve center for most women. Still, go ahead with the gift idea. If your wife doesn't get off on the Japanese love balls, she can give them to the kids. They make great marbles.

I would like to tell you of my experience with my ben-wa vibrating balls. You've seen them, little vibrating egg-type things with a few feet of wire, a

remote battery and switch. This little gadget is just superterrific! In the morn-
ing, when I'm in the mood or down, or when it's just Monday morning, while
dressing I insert my little vibrating wonder and put on a pair of tight panties to
hold it in place. Then I run the wire up my tummy and insert the small battery
pack and on-off switch into my bra, then continue dressing. While on my way to
work and stuck in the usual traffic jam, I switch on my little vibrator. I just love
it. I turn up the radio and sit back and begin to have my own little private orgy. I
also switch it on when things are slow in the office (I have my own reception area,
where I have privacy as complete as my 'Vette). These little ben-wa vibrators
work well whether you're wearing a dress (I once wore mine to a disco. Wow!) or
slacks or your favorite jeans, as long as you're wearing a full blouse to cover the
wire to the bra. (I thought this might solve a gift problem for some of your
sensuous readers.) —Miss R. A., Pittsburgh, Pennsylvania.

Chastity Belts

I was reading a new issue of Playboy and discovered a replica of a chastity belt
in the February 1974 "Potpourri." I'm curious: How did chastity belts origi-
nate? Were they really used? It's my notion that if they were popular, there
would be more of them around today. I suspect that they were novelty items even
in the Middle Ages—the whoopee cushion of 1600. I can't believe that knights
really locked their ladies up before riding off to the Crusades. Did they? —F. W.,
Richmond, Virginia.

"Can we have the keys to the belt tonight, Dad?" Actually, knights
locked their ladies up after they got back from the East. Historians claim
that Christians who fought in the Crusades were exposed to the Oriental
custom of passing a ring or a set of rings through the labia of a woman to
ensure her continence. (We leave to your imagination exactly how they
were exposed to the custom.) Christians improved the concept: The
chastity belt evolved into a contraption that circled the hips to hold an
iron plate over both the genitals and the rear. According to Eric John
Dingwal, author of *The Girdle of Chastity*, belts were first mentioned in a
manuscript dated 1405. And, yes, they were worn. Dingwal cites the
discovery of a female skeleton interred around 1600 in the area that is
now Austria. Around her waist was an iron hoop holding a plate over
what had been the genital area. Why it was thought the woman would
need the belt in the afterlife is not known. Perhaps Renaissance men had
heard the joke (it's an old one) about sex in the hereafter. (If you're
hereafter what I'm hereafter, then you'll be here long after I'm gone.)
Maybe you can take it with you. Anyway, if you want to see the real
thing, chastity belts are on display in the Cluny Museum in Paris and

the museum in Kalmar, Sweden. They are included as part of the armor exhibit at the Erbach Castle in Germany.

Condoms

Have you ever tried one of those textured condoms? I answered an ad for a contraceptive that boasted its scientifically designed ribs would enhance a woman's pleasure. When I put one of the things on, my penis looks like the louvered fender of a '55 Thunderbird. The ruffles have ridges. I'm curious: Do the things really work? —M. L., Boston, Massachusetts.

We welcome any excuse to return to our test bedrooms. First reports indicate that the radial-ply condoms do accomplish their goal. They prevent babies. In addition, the tread design improves traction and may keep you from falling out of bed on those slippery curves. The patterned ribs do stimulate the clitoris—whether or not the woman notices and appreciates the effect depends on the position and the pressure being used. The inner walls of the vagina are not sensitive to touch, so much of the effect of the extra texture is lost on penetration. The best positions are those that allow you to lightly draw the corncob condom across the clitoris—we won't make a comparison to a violin bow, but your lover might. The items are definitely worth adding to your arsenal, but don't expect drastic results. It's very hard to improve on the basic sexual act. The rule in our test bedrooms is: Anything that doesn't actually detract from sex gets an A-plus rating.

Cock Rings: Take One

At a party recently, I noticed a man wearing an odd sterling silver ring on a chain around his neck. He explained that it was a cock ring. Worn around the penis, it supposedly prolongs intercourse and stimulates the woman's clitoris. He said that a girlfriend had given it to him as a love token. Can you provide further information? —D. M., Cleveland, Ohio.

Cock rings have been in existence for centuries: Ancient erotic paintings from China and Japan show the devices in use. Gold and silver cock rings are de rigueur for today's rig, but the devices have also been made from ivory, leather, plastic or rubber. When placed at the base of the penis, the ring seals off the corpora cavernosa (the areas that fill with blood during erection) and prolongs the period of detumescence that follows ejaculation. Doctors suggest that the device be used only as an ornament. If you leave the ring on too long, it can damage delicate erectile tissues in the penis. As for stimulating the clitoris—the chances are just as great that you'll end up bruising your lover. You say that the guy received the ring as a gift from his girlfriend? What did he give her in return—a vibrator with a bandolier of batteries?

Cock Rings: A Word of Warning

My lover occasionally uses a cock ring to maintain his erection. We are both interested in knowing if there are any adverse effects from the use of such a device. The last time he used it, he had a tremendous orgasm; however, he seems to have busted a blood vessel, as a small bruise developed on his penis after our lovemaking session. What is the official verdict on cock rings? —Miss C. S., Hollywood, California.

One sex expert warns: "Using a constricting device to obtain or maintain erection makes as much sense as using strangulation to assist in holding your breath. Cock rings are based on the incorrect premise that holding blood inside the penis by mechanical means helps maintain erection. Blood circulates in and out of the erect penis, and attempts to stop this circulation can be harmful. Cock rings can reduce outflow and increase back pressure inside the penis. But rather than contribute to erection, cock rings can bruise the delicate tissues inside the penis in which blood collects to cause erection. Cock rings can seriously damage the penis and should be avoided." Enough said?

The Grope Suit

I've been reading about a Scandinavian sex device called a grope suit. Supposedly, it will keep a woman in an almost constant state of orgasm. Would you know anything about it—for instance, where I could purchase the device? —Miss F. D., Melbourne, Florida.

Grope suits came out of the closet after Alex Comfort devoted a paragraph to them in *Joy of Sex.* As near as we can tell, that's the only place you'll find this piece of apparel named. In case your little brother stole your copy, Comfort describes the attire as a "very tight rubber G string with a thick phallic plug which fits in to the vagina and a roughened knob over the clitoris. The bra has small toothed recesses in the cups which grip the nipples and is covered all over inside with soft rubber points. Once it is on, every movement touches a sensitive area." Yee-hah. In spite of publicity, it's almost impossible to find a grope suit in this country. The Sears catalog doesn't mention one. Frederick's of Hollywood and other lingerie houses seem to be sticking to their nylons.

Makes you wonder about capitalism and the law of supply and demand, doesn't it? You might talk the neighborhood tailor into whipping something up out of an old wet suit, recycled soap dish, a soft hairbrush and a burned-out vibrator. Better yet, invent your own erotic wardrobe: bikinis made out of waist chains, leather thongs, feathered boas, inflated balloons—the fittings are a gas. In cool weather, an inside-out fur coat is a reliable turn-on. If you believe that less is more, try going out on a date without wearing underwear. You'll find that clothes can make a woman.

Slime

Here is an interesting suggestion for women who would like to treat their lovers to something new. The toy-store item Slime is excellent for use in massaging a man's penis. It's surprisingly cool, very smooth and not too messy. It never fails to provide instant arousal. Enjoy. —K. B., Redding, California.

If you say so. We always thought the texture of Slime should be the end and not the means of sex.

The Pit and the Linga Pendulum

Recently I read about an amazing device called the linga pendulum that supposedly can increase the length of the penis by as much as 50 percent, while proportionately increasing the diameter. For those of us who could use a little extra up front, is it for real? —J. L., Denton, Texas.

The account we read suggested that the linga pendulum is, quite literally, a put-on. The man who feels underendowed attaches a miniature ball and chain to his penis every morning and the weight causes his organ to stretch. It also does wonders for his footwork.

There is precedent for the linga pendulum. Women of the Ubangi tribe in Africa wore weights that stretched their ears and lips, until they reached down to their shoulders—and made them less attractive to slave traders; later the tribe came to like the look. Sanshiro Miyamoto slept in traction for several months trying to increase his height by two inches to meet the Detroit Police Department minimum. He gained an inch and a half.

The linga pendulum is medically impractical, possibly harmful and certainly unnecessary. (Slave traders are outlawed and the police department isn't interested.) We don't say that less is more, but in most cases it's enough.

Plaster of Paris

About a year ago, a ladyfriend and I enjoyed the evening by making love. After climaxing four times, I was totally spent, but she was just getting started for a long night. From her purse, she took out what appeared to be a jar of cold cream and started rubbing it on my penis. It took just a few seconds for a warmth to spread through my cock and it became rock hard. We made love again, not once but three more times, and I climaxed each time. If that had not actually happened to me, I would have found it hard to believe. The lady has since moved out of town, taking the secret of the miracle cream with her. I recently bought some worthless gel from an adult bookstore, so my question is: What was that magic cream and where can I get more? —W. P., Portland, Oregon.

It sounds to us as if she used plaster of Paris. However, we suspect that the magic of the evening was all in your head and not in the lady's secret snake oil. With a little initiative and imagination, a girl can get the same results with axle grease. There are a variety of so-called erection creams available—some with heating agents or cooling balms—but the outcome is not so impressive when you do it yourself.

Baby Oil

My wife uses different lotions that are intended for use all over the body. Most of the time, she favors a scented baby oil. The baby oil has found its way to places besides her hands, arms and legs. She uses this oil often in bed. It works very well for both masturbation and intercourse and feels great. The question is—is it safe to use? (As far as oral sex goes, we always go down on each other before we apply the oil, so it's not a matter of swallowing the stuff.) Are there any dangers in using such oils on the more delicate parts of the body? —A. D., New York, New York.

A doctor friend and his lady have recently become addicted to a honey-suckle-scented baby oil that is sold in health-food stores. He reports that the only danger is the conditioned reaction. Whenever he sees a bottle of the stuff or smells honeysuckle, he develops an outrageous erection and an insatiable craving for sex. Other than that, oils are perfectly acceptable accessories for lovemaking. You may not have noticed, but the consistency of a woman's natural lubricating fluids changes during her menstrual cycle. It also diminishes between round one and round two of a given night. Oils allow easy going when there's no shortage of sexual energy.

Hot Tubs

My boyfriend and I have access to a cabin in the mountains that comes complete with a hot tub. We've tried making love in the tub, but the results so far have been disastrous. The water washes away the lubrication and eventually his thrusting becomes painful. Any suggestions? —Miss T. W., Sacramento, California.

Most commercial lubricants (K-Y jelly, oils, etc.) are water-soluble. You can try petroleum jelly, which seems to last a bit longer. Or you can try a different approach. Have your boyfriend enter you while you're perched on the side and then roll into the water. Or have him try a little tantric (i.e., nonthrusting) sex. And, finally, why not try oral sex? If the tub is big enough you can take turns floating on your back. It's like bobbing for apples, only better.

Waterbeds

Conned by the copy writer who said "There are two things that are good on a water bed and one of them is sleeping," I purchased a king-size model of the liquid love pad. I am disappointed. Whenever I attempt intercourse, the lack of support causes problems. I go down, the girl goes down, the bed goes down—it's like chasing your shadow. Then I get thrown out of bed by the resulting tidal wave. I've been thinking of re-enacting the scene in Point Blank in which Lee Marvin empties a gun into a bed abandoned by Angie Dickinson; it's gotten that bad. Do you have any suggestions? —L. W., Brunswick, Maine.

Don't believe everything you read, unless you read it here, and then only if it can't be verified anywhere else. For all the copy writer's claim, a water bed could be equally good for pole vaulting, tap dancing or playing marbles. To correct the situation, add some water. A properly filled mattress should be firm, so that a stray elbow or knee can't touch the floor or the bottom of the bed. A frame will help contain the wave action, and also will increase the life of the mattress. A pillow placed beneath your partner's hips will add some support. We suggest that you alter your approach: The irresistible-force-meets-immovable-object style of lovemaking is fine if one is into or onto the missionary position. On a water bed, the woman is not impaled; rather, you share each other's genitals. They become a focal point for a free-fall frolic that resembles aerial ballet. If all this tossing and turning, slipping and sliding is still a bother, grasp the frame for leverage. A pull-up motion can duplicate the powerful thrusting of the old-fashioned push-up/collapse tactic. Adjust your rhythm to the ripples and you'll have a swell time.

Water Weight

One of my girlfriends told me that making love on a water bed is like having a third person in bed who knows more about pleasure than the two of us put together. I want to get one for my apartment, but my landlord says no. There's nothing in the lease about it, but I would rather convince him of the safety than resort to legal measures. Can you help? —L. D., Ann Arbor, Michigan.

Water-bed leaks are infrequent—a frame and safety liner will prevent flooding, should one occur. Your big worry is weight: A six-by-seven-foot water bed tips the scales at 1600 pounds when full and slightly more than that when occupied. Check your city's building code to find the minimum floor-load capacity for apartments; in most cities it's from 40 to 65 pounds per square foot. You'll be safe unless your aquatic erotics include orgies. Also, for a few dollars, you can obtain tenant-liability insurance, so that the reparation of possible damage would not diminish your landlord's bank account. That should convince him.

Satin Sheets

My husband and I have enjoyed our king-size water bed for almost five years. Recently, spurred by an advertisement in Playboy, *we purchased satin sheets. We love the sensuous feel, but we have encountered a problem. The surfaces are almost friction-free; we are forever searching for pillows that slither off the bed during the night. Any suggestions? —Mrs. A. M., Baltimore, Maryland.*

One of our editors had the same problem with satin sheets, only worse. He claims that he spent half of one night trying to pin down his date, who kept slipping out from under him. (As we recall, the same thing used to happen when he used percale sheets.) He subsequently installed eyebolts in the frame of his water bed, along with safety straps, and developed a reputation as a bondage freak. To take care of the disappearing pillows, he had snaps sewn onto the bottom sheet and one side of the pillowcases. Strips of Velcro (the zipperless zipper material) would also work.

Shower Massage

I may be dumb, but it seems to me that the television ads for shower-massage units imply a sexual use for the pulsing water. The instructions that came with my unit are somewhat obscure and I have yet to turn on the water to have the water turn me on. How are the damned things used? —L. D., Los Angeles, California.

Women have discovered that shower-massage units (also called French shower heads) are great for masturbation. Rather than let their fingers do the walking, they've found that a well-aimed water jet can do wonders. It doesn't work as well for solo men (let the E.R.A. tend to *that* inequality). In fact, one of our editors compares the effect to being mugged in close quarters. However, couples who shower together can double their pleasure. The tub is not the safest place for slipping and sliding in a standing position. The best bet is to remain motionless while letting the water play on target. As we see it, there's only one drawback to the thing: drought. Word has it that the water shortage and subsequent rationing in Northern California have created legions of sexually frustrated women. A few conservationists claim these women are getting their just desserts. What do you think caused the water shortage in the first place?

Soft Bondage

Variety is more than the spice of life; it is an essential ingredient. My wife and I have explored with pleasure and exhausted the geometrical positions of lovemaking—now we would like to experiment with other forms of lovemaking. Specifically, those that fulfill fantasy needs as well as physical needs. We would like to try bondage, but there are few, if any, intelligent guides to the subject. I browsed through some catalogs at an adult bookstore—they seemed to be a cross between Mickey Mouse and the Marquis de Sade. What do you suggest? —*T.G.H., New Orleans, Louisiana.*

Alex Comfort's *Joy of Sex* has a remarkable chapter on bondage; it should be read by anyone who contemplates an erotic caper with a captive audience. However, if you want to strengthen the nuptial knots before you buy the book, consider the following: Bondage is based on the theory that orgasm is a release from tension; the greater the tension, the greater the release. Old-time moviemakers used bondage as a vehicle for suspense: Witness the heroine tied to the tracks helplessly awaiting rescue from an oncoming train. Most bedrooms won't accommodate Amtrak, so you'll have to create an equivalent. If you are successful, the results can be spectacular—one woman reported that when she was tied to a bed, her orgasms hit her with the force of the aforementioned train and left her forever confused as to what it was she wanted to be rescued from. You won't need the accessories shown in the catalogs; most homes contain all that is required. Use soft materials—bathrobe cords, stockings, leather shoelaces, pieces of clothesline, old school ties. Tie your knots well—your partner should be able to struggle without escaping—but do not cut off circulation. (The Scout Handbook is still the best manual on knot tying, and it does add a dimension.) For starters, spread-eagle your partner across a pile of pillows. If you do not have a brass bed or a fourposter (favorites among bondage aficionados), run cords under the bed. Secure her ankles and wrists, but don't overlook other sites. A well-placed cord can be as exciting as an extra pair of hands. Criss-cross two cords over her breasts or throw a half hitch around each thigh. (Comfort suggests, as an alternative, binding your partner thumb and toe in addition to hand and foot.) Remember that suspense and helplessness are the keys; proceed slowly and savor your handiwork: Tease your partner, stroke and kiss her breasts and genitals, then withdraw. Slow genital manipulation can be sublime. Arouse her to several orgasms before penetration. Some words of warning—agree beforehand on a distress signal (to indicate discomfort or pain) and untie her as soon as you are done. And then it's your turn: In a somewhat different context, Abraham Lincoln said, "Familiarize yourself with the chains of bondage and you prepare your own limbs to wear them."

Bondage Accessories

My lover and I are into bondage. We both get really turned on when he handcuffs me. With my arms behind me, the handcuffs cut into my wrists and hurt. We have tried leaving my arms in front, but that is not as much of a turn-on for me. There are times when he has me wear them on my legs all night. That leaves marks on my ankles that take hours to disappear. Any suggestions? —Miss S. H., Hitchcock, Texas.

The November 1979 *Sex News* features some soft restraints (velvet-lined wrist cuffs) that might do the trick. You might also try some old school ties, nylon stockings or silk scarves. They are easier to sneak through airport security, for those trips away from home. For more information, write to The Pleasure Chest (20 West 20th Street, New York, New York 10011) for a catalog of other B&D regalia. Then tie one on.

My girlfriend and I have sexual relations frequently. Every time we start to make love, she insists that I tear off her clothes, tie her to the bed in a spread-eagle position, and then rub Ben-Gay all over her body. She says this makes her hot with desire. She then demands that I flay her with a feather boa and tease her with my tongue until she is breathing heavily. Finally, she encourages me to enter her and make love as violently as possible. When we try to make love in the usual way (without any extravagances), she cannot climax and finds no enjoyment. I am afraid that if I continue to satisfy her whims and fetishes, our sex life will become ritualistic, boring and less pleasing. What can I do to rid her of this weirdness? —V. G., Philadelphia, Pennsylvania.

What weirdness? You've probably heard that special-interest lovers (flagellants, leather freaks, et al.) are somehow limited, that their pursuit of pleasure doesn't possess as much variety as normal lovemaking. Nonsense. Do you know how many knots there are in the Boy Scout Handbook? Do you know what it's like for a shoe fetishist to walk into a Thom McAn's? Some persons seek and enjoy a high level of activity (your girlfriend, for example); others consider sex more of a spectator sport. Everything else being equal, we think you should continue to satisfy her. Imagine the state of your head if nothing turned her on. If you're afraid the Ben-Gay will rub off, wear a wet suit to bed.

Goat's Eyelid

Have you heard of something called a goat's eyelid? It's supposed to be very sexy, whatever it is. The best I can come up with is what might be a variation on the old butterfly flick (where the male rests his testicles on a woman's eyes and she flutters her eyelashes). But doing that with a goat would be perverted, if not downright dangerous. They eat anything, right? As a master of sexual information, can you enlighten me? —D. P., Nashville, Tennessee.

Close, but no inflatable doll with three operating orifices. According to G. L. Simons (of *Simons' Book of World Sexual Records*), the goat's eyelid, or happy ring, was a Tibetan version of the French tickler: "After a goat was killed, its eyelids were removed together with the eyelashes. First they were put in quick-lime to dry; then they were steamed in a bamboo basket for not less than twelve hours—this procedure was repeated several times. Once completed, the process yielded a sex aid that could be tied around the penis (jade stem) prior to coitus. The goat's eyelashes were supposed to give the woman a pleasant tickling sensation." That is, if she didn't run from the bedroom screaming after her lover described the origins of his new toy. Maybe this was the source of the Old Testament adage, "An eyelid for an eyelid." Fortunately, to the great relief of goats, modern French ticklers are made of plastic or rubber. You can pick one up at your friendly neighborhood marital-aids shop.

Vibrators

Over the past few years, masturbation has become an accepted practice: It's fun, healthy and psychologically normal, as long as you don't get kinky about it and tie yourself up first. But now I think we've made too much of a good thing. The ubiquitous vibrator has created a nation of sexual isolationists. Remember the old ethical question: If you could connect yourself to an infinite pleasure machine, would you ever unplug? My girlfriend has acquired one of those vibrators with various attachments. It produces an instant, powerful, never-ending orgasm that is awesome to behold. The climax she gets from her new toy is obviously better than the one she gets from me. I'm afraid that she's becoming addicted to the ecstasy. She says comparisons are out of the question. Her orgasms are her business and her responsibility, not mine. She then quotes the Gospel according to Betty Dodson that a woman who gets in touch with her own sexual response will learn what she likes and will thus be in a better position to tell someone else what turns her on. So what do you do when she learns that she doesn't need any "someone else"? Swallow a couple of batteries and hum? My girlfriend defends her new friend, saying that at least a vibrator doesn't roll over and go to sleep afterward. —M. F., Los Angeles, California.

The Mad Dog Art and Ordnance Works of Evanston, Illinois, has plans for a vibrator that will do just that. It will also smoke a cigarette and when the girl pulls on a string, a recorded voice will say things like "I love you," or "Take that, you bitch," or "Your insight into the phenomenological implications of the silverware-and-madeleine imagery in the first volume of Proust's *A la Recherche du Temps Perdu* is unparalleled in the history of Western Civilization." Seriously, now, although it may be hard to accept, the women's lib belief in "to each his or her own" makes a lot of sense. If you allow her orgasm to become the only definition of your adequacy as a male, then you'll be in big trouble. You feel good when she has them, guilty when she doesn't and worse when she has them with someone or something else. There's more to sex than climaxes. What happens between humans is a softer, more varied relationship involving things like trust, surprise, communication and sharing. Have her use her toy while you are making love and you'll get off on the good vibrations, too. If you still can't cope with the damn thing, find a vibrator virgin and move to the country where there's no electricity and they don't sell batteries.

Shortly after my boyfriend and I started living together, he bought me one of those bullet-shaped vibrators. He said that he wanted me to enjoy myself and to learn more about my responses. Well, I really got into it, or vice versa. I began to use the vibrator whenever he wasn't home. He asked me once which was better— the vibrator or him—and I told him the truth: that I preferred him. Okay. But when he discovered that I sometimes masturbated while looking at pictures of nude men, he freaked out. He tore up the pictures and left a nasty note on our bed saying that I really knew how to get to him. I don't understand. I feel that he introduced me to a very beautiful experience, then pulled the rug out from under me. Can you explain his behavior? —Miss O. N., Virginia Beach, Virginia.

It's a new twist to the old double standard. We've received a surprising number of letters suggesting that vibrators invoke the old insecurities that lead to vows of chastity, the quest for the virgin bride, et cetera. Your boyfriend's fear of comparison may be deep-seated and unreasonable, but it is nonetheless real—even when the object of comparison is a permanently erect penis-shaped piece of plastic or a two-dimensional photograph of another man. He may be intimidated by your ability to have multiple orgasms—"How can you keep them from having fun, after they've had ecstasy?" The situation is absurd but not hopeless. Perhaps someone will invent a vibrator that becomes soft and inoperable after five minutes' use. Or maybe your boyfriend would agree to pose in the nude, so that your masturbatory props would not threaten his ego. Liberation requires patience. You might invite him to join you in a session with the vibrator, so at least he can have a hand in your pleasure. Give it a try.

Vibrators are this girl's best friend. Any time, anywhere. I've carried the little buzz bombs on buses, airplanes and trains. (The engines drown out the drone.) But when it comes to turning on guys with the device, it's another story. My roommate is willing, but what turns me on turns him off. He says that the instrument is too intense and he winds up feeling pain or, worse, nothing at all. Why the inequality of the sexes? I'd like to share something nice with a friend. Any suggestions? —Miss K. H., Chicago, Illinois.

Good Vibrations. Take Two: Men who try Orgasmatrons and other earth-shaking devices often find that direct contact with the penis is painful. The most common solution: Wrap the vibrator, or your boyfriend's penis, in a warm towel. (Think of a bottle of champagne wrapped in white. Watch out for the cork.) The soft material will act as insulation to absorb the general shock. Some men find that a vibrator does not work as well when the target is dry—the friction produces numbness. A thick layer of lubrication (i.e., a peanut-butter-and-petroleum-jelly sandwich) will ensure a fine experience.

Tradition gives us sex in the shower; technology gives us the battery-powered vibrator. Will a combination of the two shock my girlfriend? —T. E., Washington, D.C.

Shock her? Probably not. Excite her? Perhaps. It is unlikely that a battery-powered vibrator could harm your girlfriend in the shower or elsewhere, but the water might harm the vibrator by shorting out the batteries or by corroding the metal fittings. Until the vibrator folks market a waterproof product, you'll have to improvise. A tightly sealed plastic bag or a condom placed over the vibrator should protect the vital parts without spoiling the party. Electrical devices that plug into wall sockets should never be used near water.

The Great Sex Aids Road Test

We decided it was time for an official investigation of sex aids. Dildos. Vibrators. Inflatable Dolls with Three Operating Orifices. Clitoral Stimulators. Being of the opinion that the best sex aid is a woman, we had never really gotten acquainted with erotic technology, let alone tried one. We wanted to know: Do they work? Are they worth buying? Would you take one home to your mother?

We thought of hiring Ralph Nader, consumer advocate, to test the devices. He wasn't available. So we did the next-best thing: We recruited three couples. Sexual adventurers who had long since given their dog-eared copies of *The Joy of Sex* to the Salvation Army. Lovers who had seen *In The Realm of the Senses* four times. People who owed us money. We turned them loose with a toy chest of sex accessories, collected their comments on three-by-five index cards and tabulated the results. No matter what you may think of marital aids, one thing is clear—they make great conversation pieces. Most of the comments were witty. For example, when faced with a dozen French ticklers, one of our test pilots remarked, "They are great, if you want to make love to an extraterrestrial." Another researcher, gazing upon an oversized spiked dildo that would crawl across the floor at the flick of a switch, knocking over furniture and terrorizing the natives, commented, "You could tame a country with that thing. It's the perfect marital aid. You put it on your mantel and threaten your wife with it. 'Cook dinner or else.' Who says sex is the most fun you can have without laughing? This is how the items stacked up.

Vibrators: The cordless vibrator is the Model A of sexual accessories, the magic bullet guaranteed to cure sexual ills. Sizes range from 5 inches to a monster 16 inches in length. Our test couples reported that size did not increase pleasure, since penetration is not the goal of vibrator-assisted masturbation. The comments: "We noticed that the larger models lasted longer. The little buggers tended to shake loose their connections. Also, the larger models are quieter. Noise is the major drawback of battery-powered vibrators. There's something about a raucous buzz that is not conducive to astonishing sex." Texture is a problem. The hard-plastic vibrators seem impersonal. Our favorite of the bunch was a soft, flexible 7-inch vibrator called the Stim-Vib. "It didn't intrude on our fantasies. It was warm, almost skinlike." "The main advantage to cordless vibrators seems to be their portability—the perfect companion for long trips. I can see my girlfriend walking through airport security with a bandolier filled with them."

The manufacturers of vibrators seem to realize that noise and hardness are problems. In the past few years, they've introduced attachment kits, with sleeves that deaden the sound and change the sensations. The leader in the field is Marché Manufacturing (11933 Vose Street, North Hollywood, California 91605). One test couple rates the Sensual Encounter Kit ($19.95) as follows: "One of the sleeves looked like a cucumber with spikes. Another looked like a naked palm tree. A major revelation of the road test was that looks are deceiving. The cucumber softened the vibrations and produced waves of sensation. The palm tree felt like a feather duster. My partner said she felt like she was walking stark-naked through a beaded curtain."

The second generation of vibrators includes remote-controlled variable-speed ben-wa eggs and cock rings. A thin wire connects the operating mechanism to a battery pack. The comments: "You can tuck one of the eggs into your jeans, put the control unit in your pocket and have a very interesting ride on the bus." "The cock ring was hard plastic and the prongs tended to bite into your flesh. If you feel comfortable with your dick in a lobster claw, this is the device for you. However, it will produce an erection in spite of itself." "These small guys are even noisier than the bullet-shaped vibrators. It sounded like we were making love on a construction site."

Two vibrators emerged as genuine class acts. The Sex Charmer—a pink plastic figure of a turbanned snake charmer, complete with snake—from United Sales, 4731 W. Jefferson Boulevard, Los Angeles, California 90016, was a delight. The girls loved it: "He's cute." "It belongs on the dashboard of your car." "It's a nice gift for someone who might be nervous about sex gifts. It defuses the bad image of the vibrator." Of course, if you want to get serious about automated sex, buy the Prelude 3, the state-of-the-art vibrator. One touch produces instant orgasm: "You can get lost in your pleasure. It helps to have someone else in the room, just to chaperone. It is the one vibrator that is coeducational. If you are trying out a position—say, when the man enters from the rear—where the clitoris doesn't receive stimulation, just plug in the Prelude. You'll both get off."

French ticklers: These things make you wonder where Frenchmen got their reputation for being great lovers. With names like Porcupine, Fuzzball, Satan and Little Devil, they produce more laughter than pleasure. As a sex aid, they are useless. The discomfort factor is high: "Would you put a sea urchin in your vagina?" Still, they make great finger puppets with which to entertain the kids in your neighborhood.

Clitoral stimulators: The major surprise of the road test was the reaction to the Magico and the Excello clitoral stimulators: "They look tacky, they feel tacky when the man slips one over the shaft of his penis. But during intercourse, the tiny rubber prongs separate the folds of the labia and expose the clitoris. The gentle massaging action truly excites a woman.

And this is one of the few sex aids that don't intrude on the man's pleasure."

Lubricants: Every bedside table should have a bottle or two of oil. There is nothing like a massage to lead into a gentle, relaxed session of sex. The products that are marketed specifically as erotic oils (Orgy Gel, Emotion Lotion, Crease Grease) tend to be more expensive than the same products in mass-market form. You may find it cheaper to buy baby oil. You have a variety of flavors and scents to choose from; however, our couples thought the manufacturers used chemical overkill: "It smelled like we were making love in a candy store. The odor and taste were too strong." The most interesting lubricants use a glycerin base: "You rub the oil in, then breathe on it and the surface of your skin heats up. Very interesting."

Lingerie: Included in the road-test toy chest were several small bits of nylon mesh that, on further examination, proved to be bikini underwear and cutout bras. The holes are strategically placed to grant access to erogenous zones. One couple describes its experience: "At first, we thought this stuff was too tacky to try. All things considered, we'd rather go naked. But then we got into the fantasy trip behind the lingerie. If lingerie didn't turn some of the people on some of the time, it wouldn't be around anymore. The cutout bra acted like a golf tee. The little fringed circles supported the nipples and held them up like an offering. Anything that focuses attention is a good sex aid. Those nipples became my partner's entire universe. Her skin was very sensitive. Not bad."

Shackles and chains: Ever since Alex Comfort suggested tying up your loved one in *The Joy of Sex*, mild bondage has been an accepted part of the bedroom repertoire. The Pleasure Chest, a chain of sex boutiques based in New York, has a large mail-order business in custom-designed leatherwear. The quality of the craftsmanship was far beyond that of any of the other items we tested. These people are *serious*. The road test: "We had the same reaction to the shackles and chains that we had to the lingerie. Learning to get into a different erotic trip can be very exciting. The key to this scenario is helplessness. The woman is exposed, waiting, arched like a bow, rising toward a single point of stimulation. Be it a kiss on the nipple, a tonguing of the clitoris, or the slow penetration of an erect penis, she is afraid that you will leave her, so she focuses all of her energy and attention on the moment of contact. This is a fantasy we've all grown up with—the damsel in distress, the virgin in the castle dungeon. A spread-eagled woman is a sight to behold."

Rejects: During the course of the road test, our couples came across some products that were counterproductive. Heading the list are the numbing agents (Mr. Prolong, Stud 100, Endure) that purport to increase the male's endurance. They utilize benzocaine to deaden sensation: "They work as an anesthetic, but who needs it? You might as well be in the next room as in bed with your girlfriend." "The products are touted as a cure for premature ejaculation, but since they end up numbing your girlfriend as well as you, it just defeats the problem. The whole point of sex is learning to recognize what is happening to you at any given moment. The numbing agents make you feel like you're playing blindman's buff."

Other candidates for the trash bin include penis extenders (condom-like sheaths with rubber plugs that increase the size of a man's erection). They cut sensation and are generally uncomfortable. They are also totally irrelevant. Most of a woman's nerve endings are in the outer third of her vagina—to go beyond that does not contribute to her pleasure.

And, by unanimous decision, the tackiest sex aid we tested was the inflatable Sweet Sixteen doll, with natural hair and three operating orifices. The inside of the mouth was razor sharp. If someone tried mock fellatio, the Sweet Sixteen doll would bite it off. We have enough trouble with real women. Still, the thing is a great conversation piece. If you hit a dead spot in the middle of the week, you can always inflate her and take her to a fancy French restaurant.

Conclusion: Our researchers all survived the road test in good spirits. And reasonably good health. (One or two complained of exhaustion.) They were in agreement on one crucial point—no matter what their opinion of individual products, the road test had been a sexual adventure. They had been curious, and they satisfied their curiosity as well as their sex drives. Said one: "With most of these products, my interest lasted as long as the first set of batteries. I doubt if I will incorporate many of them into my sex life—maybe the Prelude 3, maybe the oils. But the rest are disposable. They're great for one date, but you wouldn't want to live with them. My suggestion: Conduct your own road test."

Notes From The Sexual Frontier

Perhaps the most common misconception about *Playboy* is that it is a magazine for single men. Perhaps the most common misconception about singles, about our culture, is that singles are the true beneficiaries of the sexual revolution. Judging from the letters we get, the most interesting sexual developments happen within relationships. At least half of the letters we receive are from married people. The sexual frontier is not a line that exists in space. It is the barrier between the two partners of a relationship, where expectation meets experience, where exploration meets inhibition, where the way it might be runs head on into "that's the way I heard it should be."

This section charts how the widely publicized advances of the sexual revolution actually happen to people. The etiquette of dating has been changed by women's lib. Apartment politics, the art of living together in glory, is an art that didn't exist two decades ago. Threesomes, foursomes, et cetera are coming out of the closets.

What follows, then, is a collection of war stories, straight from the survivors. Enjoy.

CHAPTER THIRTEEN

Dating

Why? Because We Love You

My girlfriend accused me of having a one-track mind. She claims that sex doesn't have any meaning if that's all I think about when I'm with her. Unfortunately, when I'm with her, that is all I think about. If you saw her, you'd know why. Even when I'm alone, I think about her. I'm wondering if it's some kind of obsession. Has anyone done research to discover how often a man thinks about sex? —S. K., Arlington, Virginia.

Ah, Romance. A few years ago, Dr. Paul Cameron at the University of Louisville tested about 3100 subjects and determined that the idea of sex crosses the healthy young mind every ten minutes. Hmm. Our watch is a little slow today. Where were we? Oh, yes. As for the meaning of lovemaking: Socrates once said something to the effect that the unexamined sex life is not worth living. Tell your girlfriend that she should be proud to be part of such focused contemplation. Better her navel than your own.

The High Cost of Dating

A couple of my friends were talking about dating and how expensive it is to maintain a relationship these days. It is no longer merely acceptable for a girl to share the cost of an evening—in our circle, it has become mandatory. Is it my imagination, or does inflation hit singles harder than the rest of the people? —S. W., New York, New York.

The old marriage proposal that two can live as cheaply as one is based on the notion that married people don't have to date. Singles are an endangered species. Ray DeVoe, a New York investment strategist, recently compared the cost of loving with the cost of living. As quoted in the *Chicago Tribune*, he found that the average price of an evening on the town has increased 310 percent over the past twenty-five years, while the consumer price index rose only 172 percent during the same period. Some of the grand gestures have gone up astronomically—the cost of flowers has increased some 740 percent in twenty-five years, a gold necklace some 1000 percent. Diamonds are a girl's best friend—they've increased in cost by 1630 percent. The basic candlelight dinner has escalated by 464 percent. Dom Perignon bubbled up a mere 317 percent. Even a low-rent date (pizza to go) has risen 180 percent over the past twenty-five years. Maybe the Government should establish a rebate system for singles. Take a girl to the movies and get a check. Take a girl to dinner and get a check. Take a girl to Plato's Retreat and get a check and a checkup. No one said that being single was easy.

Dutch Treat

A few years ago, it was considered fashionable to let your date pick up her share of the dinner tab—if not the whole check. That was at the height of women's lib. Recently, I've noticed a swing in the other direction. My dates head for the powder room when the waiter shows up with the check. Is there a new generation or a new etiquette? —J. P., New York, New York.

Dutch treating may have been considered fashionable, but it was never widespread. A recent Gallup Poll revealed that only 38 percent of the men surveyed had ever had a check picked up by their date. Only 36 percent of the women surveyed said they had taken a man to lunch or dinner. (We assume the 36 percent date the 38 percent; the remaining 2 percent probably need glasses.) Our rule: Play it by ear. If she doesn't move for the check, pick it up. If you can't pay the full tab, volunteer to wash dishes for fifteen minutes. Then ask for the employee discount.

The Bottom Line

A couple of guys at the office came up with a question that we think is a natural for the Advisor. Simply stated: If you were on your way home from work with only $15 and were planning to spend that money on a date, how would you spend it for maximum effect? —T. H., Grand Rapids, Michigan.

We discussed a similar question at a recent articles meeting. If you were given $5000 and told to furnish an apartment, what would you do? Does the guy who spends $5000 on a stereo and sleeps on a straw mattress have better luck with women than the guy who spends the money on an antique brass bed, mirrors, whips and chains? We decided that the guy who bought the stereo had the better deal—at least if he wasn't getting laid, he could still enjoy the stereo. The same thing applies to the economics of dating. Spend the money on items that say something about yourself: Buy a bottle of wine and two copies of a James Clavell paperback. Take along the latest Bruce Springsteen album. Or convert your cash into quarters and head for the nearest Space Invaders machine. Try for the double bill at the Bijou. A person is always more interesting when he is having fun. Of course, the next step is spending your money wisely—on the things you've learned interest your date. Special gifts: the collected works of her favorite poet. Batteries for her vibrator. Like that.

How to Pick Up Girls

I am a nineteen-year-old, easygoing, polite, college sophomore. I smile a lot. I'm not fat. I don't swear in front of girls and I like to comfort them when they are feeling bad. I enjoy bodily contact—holding hands, slow dancing, making out to a point. I don't force anything on a girl that she doesn't want, especially sex. That's my hang-up. I want to have intercourse. Bad, but not bad enough to go to a whorehouse. Because I'm a nice, polite guy, I attract or end up with the nice, polite girls who don't know the first thing about sex and/or have no intentions of getting it on. The girls who want a little sexual fun out of life think that because I am a nice, polite guy I don't want to ball, which I do, or that I don't know the first thing about sex, which is true. I feel lost and left out. How can I make it with a girl? —N. B., Ormond Beach, Florida.

There are as many theories on how to make it with women as there are women in the world. One often advanced claim is that for every mild-mannered Clark Kent with superdesires smoldering under his nice-guy exterior, there is a Diana Prince whose prim and proper exterior conceals a wow of a Wonder Woman. According to this theory, you simply invite your girl to a quiet, private place—it can be as small as a telephone booth—throw off your disguises and you'll find yourself streaking across the sky together. Shazam! This theory assumes that your mild-mannered exterior is a disguise. You may find yourself under arrest for indecent exposure when you discover that your Superman costume is still at the tailor's. As an alternative, you might consider the Static Quest, a tactic based on the classic advice on what to do when you feel lost: "Stay in one place. Get to know yourself. If someone is looking for you (or it), her path of search will cross your point of rest. If you both go wandering around, there is no guarantee that your paths will ever cross." The Static Quest also builds character and contributes to an implacable calm that is itself attractive to girls. However, we have found that sex seldom occurs because of anything you do; it occurs in spite of what you do. Therefore, don't worry about your inexperience. Sex is one human endeavor in which both those who can and those who can't teach and learn from each other.

The Girl Next Door

Maybe Playboy *can help me. I'm twenty-one and single. Hopelessly single, from the looks of it. Every month, I look at the girls in your magazine and wonder where I can find one of my own. But I don't know where to begin to look. Any suggestions? —E. S., Rochester, New York.*

Try the girl next door. It has worked for us for twenty-five years. And, from what we've read, it works for other people. In *A New Look at Love*, Elaine Walster and G. William Walster point out that proximity is a critical prerequisite for love. "One sociologist interviewed 431 couples at the time they applied for marriage licenses. He found that at the time of their first date together, 37 percent of the couples were living within eight blocks of each other and 51 percent lived within sixteen blocks of each other." No, the study was not conducted in a sixteen-block city. Makes sense to us. After all, most traffic accidents happen near home, and some good must come from those random collisions.

A Few Words About Anxiety

My social life is a disaster; I can't seem to meet an attractive woman who shares my interests or who is compatible with my personality. I've tried special-activity clubs, but I don't know what to say to other members: "Excuse me, miss, are you here because you like to collect snakes, or are you here because you want to meet someone looking for someone who collects snakes?" I've tried singles' clubs, on the assumption that everyone there shares an interest in meeting other people, but they are governed by a law of unnatural selection: the arrival and immediate departure of the fastest. By the time I find the girl I'm looking for, she's already gone, if she was there to begin with. And then, on top of all of this, I recently saw Play Misty for Me *on TV—the movie wherein Clint Eastwood picks up Jessica Walter, who turns out to be a homicidal maniac. Now I'm afraid to approach any of the girls I see in bars. Are there more efficient alternatives? —R. S., Chicago, Illinois.*

Actually, the anxiety and/or paranoia of singles' clubs are perfectly suited to romance. In a *Psychology Today* article titled "Adrendaline Makes the Heart Grow Fonder," by Elain Walster and Ellen Berscheid, H. T. Finck is quoted as saying: "Love can only be excited by strong and vivid emotion, and it is almost immaterial whether these emotions are agreeable or disagreeable. The Cid wooed the proud heart of Diana Ximene, whose father he had slain, by shooting one after another, her pet pigeons." Here's looking at you, Cid. It seems that two conditions are necessary to inspire passionate love: (1) physiological arousal and (2) a reasonable interpretation of same ("This must be love, because it's not indigestion."). Anything that stirs up emotions will do; the more intense the stimulus, the more powerful the attraction. In one of our favorite experiments, researchers told subjects that they were going to give them electric shocks, let them worry about it for a few minutes, then introduced them to an attractive lab assistant. Most of the subjects expressed a significant interest in the girl. (We hear Vincent Price is negotiating for the film rights.) Perhaps you can use your fear as a springboard for an affair: The process, by the way, is reversible. Gestures that intrigue, nauseate, anger or terrify are apparently more effective than manners. Your victim will ask herself, "Why is this happening to me?" and, in the absence of conflicting evidence, may assume that it is love. If you're lucky, you'll win the heart of a woman who hasn't showered since she saw the murder scene in *Psycho*.

Early to Bed

How's this for a dating dilemma? One of the girls who work in my building is a real knockout. I've asked her out for dates a couple of times but to no avail. She is taking night courses in accounting, so dinner dates are out. I also get the sense that she doesn't like the pressure of a weekend date—the notion that the sheets get turned down when the sun goes down. She seems to like me, but I just can't find a way to fit into her schedule. Any hints? —A. A., New York, New York.

We have found that the early-to-rise, early-to-bed system works. A 7:30 A.M. session of racquetball or a jog around the park (followed by a shower) is a simple low-pressure way of getting to know someone. If you want something less athletic, try a breakfast date at one of the swankier hotels in your city. (No, we are not suggesting a morning-after room-service rendezvous—that comes later.) A breakfast can be just as elegant as a candlelight dinner and, in most cases, a hell of a lot less expensive. The atmosphere is unhurried—it is less noticeable if you go in late for work than if you take a long lunch. You can become better acquainted and eventually break into prime time.

Age

Over the past few months, I've noticed that a lot of my old girlfriends and female co-workers are beginning to date younger men. One of them explained that this is a trend, that women are interested in finding "unscarred companions." Another said that young guys grew up in a liberated era and are more inclined toward an egalitarian relationship, free of male-chauvinist hassles. In other words, they help with the dishes. Another woman said that she is keeping a twenty-three-year-old at her house in the Hamptons, just for the fun of it. If that keeps up, I'm going to have trouble finding dates my own age. Not that that's important. I'm currently going out with a girl five years my junior. But I'm interested in your reaction to this trend. Is this sudden interest in younger men widespread? —E. R., New York, New York.

We don't know if the phenomenon has reached the proportions of a national trend, but it has prompted at least one book *The Age Factor*, by Jack LaPatra. The author points out that chronological age is an invisible taboo. We are called upon to act our age, to date people our age— without details on what age really means. In a study of age-different relationships, LaPatra found a pattern that he describes as a natural, instinctive union: "Two people are attracted to each other, in a romantic or friendly way, by a sense of liking bolstered by the perception that each has things to offer that the other wants. The attraction begins the relationship, but the exchange of needs sustains it. The quality of the mutual gratification depends on the development of the individuals involved." And that development has little to do with age. Actress Jeanne Moreau is even more eloquent on the subject: "There's a magic about numbers. Thirty, forty, fifty . . . it's been imposed by the culture. All those rules about who you can love and who you can't love and how. Since I was a little girl, I've been violently opposed to rules. Why should I deprive myself of my adventure, which is my life, of going through something for the first time because perhaps I am not twenty anymore? Why should I defer to society in that way?" With older ladies like her, we're happy to be younger men.

And Now for Something Completely Tacky

I'm a frequenter of singles bars and disco dens, so I'm always on the lookout for techniques that attract women. As you probably know, one of the stickier moments in an evening comes when you exchange phone numbers. Napkins, black books and the like seem so gauche, and I think I've come up with a better solution—having matchbooks printed with my name and telephone number on them. Please give me your opinion of this trick. —J. R., Chicago, Illinois.

Tacky but effective. They might mistake you for a restaurant. To prevent that, you could print testimonials from former girlfriends on the inside cover: "Loads of fun." "Couldn't get enough." "Hubba-hubba." "Great conversationalist." "I nearly fainted when I saw it."

A Few Words About Hotels

Suds. Nothing turns me on like lots of suds in a bathtub big enough for two. I first experienced this treat in a massage parlor—since then, I've made use of king-size bathtubs in the houses of rich friends. In a pinch, I will settle for an outdoor Jacuzzi, but when it gets right down to it, I prefer bathtubs. The problem is finding one. I'd like to introduce my latest girlfriend to lovemaking dans la lavatory. How can I find a hotel with a giant-sized tub? —F. J., New York, New York.

Would you believe bridal magazines? Many honeymoon suites come equipped with the accessories necessary for a weekend of kinky sex—mirrored ceiling and walls, giant tubs, vibrating mattresses, round beds, video-tape equipment, et cetera. It's a shame to waste such goodies on beginners. Check out the ads, and then check in. As long as your latest doesn't get the wrong idea, it could be a great (though expensive) weekend.

Why is it that a change of scenery can escalate a sexual relationship? I am currently dating a woman who lives in another city. When she visits my place, the sex seems to go one way. When I visit her place, it seems to go a different way. When we meet on neutral ground, such as a hotel room, the sex can go right through the roof. We spent a night at the UN Plaza Hotel in New York that was not to be believed. Chrome, glass, air conditioning and kinky sex. There's something very erotic about room service and a view of the city. It's a style I could become accustomed to—but I don't know if I can afford it on a long-term basis. Is this usual? —J. P., Chicago, Illinois.

Luxury is one of the few FDA-approved aphrodisiacs. A weekend in a local hotel can be romantic. The sex is usually better for a variety of reasons. A hotel room is remarkabley free of distractions. There are no dishes to be done, no income-tax forms piling up on your desk. There are fewer ghosts: If she finds some lace underwear under the bed that doesn't belong to her, it speaks poorly for the maid, not for your past. You won't be interrupted with a call from an old flame. A hotel rendezvous sidesteps the power struggle/invasion-of-privacy hassles that always seem to accompany the old question Your place or mine? Finally, there's nothing new about the idea—in fact, it's becoming something of a trend. Many of the hotels in major cities offer weekend rates for couples who want to get away from it all but not too far away. It seems to work.

After fifteen years of marriage and a recent divorce, I am back in the ball game. I suspect that in my years in the dugout, the rules may have changed. How does an unmarried couple check into a hotel or motel these days? As I recall from many years ago, you carried in two bags, you had rings that looked like wedding bands and you signed the register Mr. and Mrs. Is this still the case? —R. B., Philadelphia, Pennsylvania.

The rules of our national sport have not really changed in fifteen years. Innkeepers are still concerned about the reputation of their establishment and do not condone openly any activity that violates law, custom or the other guests' ideas about propriety. Most hotels and motels insist on a Mr.-and-Mrs. signature; if you're willing to falsify the register, they'll look the other way. Confrontations are rare—desk clerks seem to be blessed with the kind of indifference that English teachers would call a suspension of disbelief. There are few laws that specifically prohibit the use of an assumed name or fictional relationship when registering in a hotel or motel, unless it's done with the intent to defraud. (Delaware, Indiana, Maine, Massachusetts, Michigan, Minnesota, New Hampshire, North Dakota, Ohio, Virginia and New Jersey do prohibit the use of ficticious names; Arkanasas, Georgia, North Carolina and Mississippi also have laws against misrepresenting relationships.) In most cases, you can avoid problems by paying the double occupancy rate in advance. Bear in mind that state laws against adultry, fornication or sodomy still apply, although prosecution for conduct of this type *in private* is rare. Be sure to double-lock your door and keep your blinds drawn, and do not admit anyone who is uninvited. The risks of this kind of behavior increase or decrease according to the community and its standard of morality. Be sure you're familiar with both.

The First Time

As a freshman coed, I had an affair with an older man who initiated me in the wonders of sex. I learned many ways of giving and receiving pleasure and consider myself fortunate to have had such a kind instructor. However, now, two years later, I am dating someone my own age and it seems inevitable that we will end up in bed. My question is this: What should I do the first time we make love? I am afraid that if I make use of any of the things I learned from my first lover, my partner will think that I am too experienced and will be turned off instead of

turned on. I want to please him, but how forward should I be the first time?
—Miss H. O., Northfield, Massachusetts.

A sage once revealed the secret of the perfect handshake: A person's grip should be only as firm as the one he (or she) receives. Too strong and you intimidate the other person. Too limp and you embarrass your new acquaintance. The same principle applies to sex. Relax; it's not a one-shot audition. First nights are always tentative, exploratory. Try to make it something else and you may not make it at all. Besides, you like your friend enough so that there will be other nights. If you ever feel that a given technique needs a footnote, use the line from *Three Days of the Condor* when someone tried to explain Robert Redford's surprising effectiveness as an operator by saying, "He reads a lot." Since you've written to us, you are no doubt familiar with the contents of this column. We are perfectly willing to be used as an excuse for introducing weirdness into a relationship, though we much prefer honest communication between partners (your boyfriend may also be a reader, so watch out). One more piece of advice: We recently read a study that indicated some 60 percent of college students making love for the first time neglect to use any contraceptive measure—usually because they have not expected to end up in bed. Since you are the one who will choose the time and the place, make sure you are protected. Birth control is one indication of experience that your boyfriend will fully appreciate.

The First Time: Take Two

Some of the guys at work were talking the other day about the peculiarities of making love to a woman for the first time. We discovered that, almost against our will, we tend to revert to a high school approach—"measuring" our progress from first base to second base to third base (where, on the advice of the base coach, we stop for some cunnilingus), then on to home. My first-night feeling is, "I can do better than this. Hell, I have done better than this." I can't figure out why we repeat that amateur mating dance. What do you do on first dates? —M. V., Tallahassee, Florida.

It depends on how our companions react when they see our collection of whips, chains, leathers, grope suits, ben-wa balls, vibrators, French postcards, Jacuzzi baths, overhead mirrors and video-tape cameras. Or, if we're at their place, how we react when we see their equipment. We are not always the one to initiate sex and we almost never insist on control of the event. Other than that, we tend to proceed from left to right, from the outside in, and so forth. These are individual quirks and should not be viewed as strict guidelines. The high school approach works as well as any other—if you're troubled by its being amateur (it's not), simple reverse the sequence. After all, what you learn about each other is more important than what you know about sex. And no matter how you begin, it's bound to get better.

Discretion—What Not to Say After a First Date

As you probably know, college dorms are bullshit city. Every guy I know brags in great detail about his sexual conquests. For the past two years, I've listened. As a virgin, I didn't have anything to contribute. However, a few months ago, I met a dynamite chick who changed that situation. We've made love several times. The problem is this: The guys in the dorm are pressuring me to kiss and tell. I'm reluctant to do so. It strikes me that publicity is an act of disrespect. Am I being too conservative? With more experience, will it become easier to talk about sex? —M. C., Madison, Wisconsin.

Discretion is the better part of ardor. And your reluctance to talk is completely normal. Sociologist D. E. Carns conducted a study to find out how talkative people had been about their first sexual experiences. He found that if the event had occurred with a casual date or a pickup, 61 percent of the males said they had immediately told others about their conquests. In contrast, only 13 percent of the males who felt some romantic involvement with their partners were moved to broadcast the news. Only 8 percent of the casual Casanovas practiced complete discretion, compared with 35 percent of the romantics. What you create in private with your lover is the best defense against peer-group pressure. Keep it to yourself. And the twenty million readers of this column promise to keep it secret, too.

Who Initiates Sex on a Date

I found myself in an unsual situation a few weeks ago. A female friend from high school paid a visit to my college. Before the night was over, she tried to initiate a sexual encounter. Since I am deeply involved in another relationship, I was not too interested. However, since I didn't know how to refuse, I said what the hell and tried to go through with it. The evening was a disaster. How does a guy say no without hurting a woman's feelings? —R. X., Dallas, Texas.

We can understand your confusion. Our culture teaches us that man initiates sex, while woman sets the limits. The stereotypes are pretty deep. Three researchers asked students to rate a list of strategies for having sex and avoiding sex as masculine or feminine. Without fail, the strategies for initiating sex (touching, wandering hands, direct requests, etc.) were all labeled masculine. Those for avoiding sex (body language, moralizing, logic, etc.) were all labeled feminine. However, the sexual scripts were not mutually exclusive—some 84 percent of the men reported that they had been approached by a date to have sex, but did not necessarily have it, on at least one occasion. If your sexual script won't let you say no, your body will resort to mime—and loss of erection is one way of saying you'd rather not. That trauma goes well beyond hurting someone's feelings. Say no. Now that women are taking the initiative, they will have to learn to take an occasional rejection. We assume that you have been turned down on occasion. Why not recall the most graceful technique and make it your own? If you've never been turned down, you have no business writing to us.

My girlfriend and I recently got into a discussion of sex roles. I claim that man is still the initiator of sex in a relationship, that for all of women's liberation and such, we still have to do most of the work. She claims that in most ongoing relationships, a woman is just as likely as a man to want and initiate sex. Are there any studies that shed light on this subject? —J. L., Houston, Texas.

Dr. Clinton J. Jesser, a professor of sociology at Northern Illinois University, recently reported that sex in a relationship in which the partners are already intimate is just as likely to take place subsequent to a direct or indirect invitation from the woman as from the man. *But here's the rub.* Dr. Jesser found that (1) although women say they ask directly for sex as often as men do, men report that women take the initiative much less frequently than women claim; (2) women tend more frequently than men to use indirect sexual cues such as eye contact, change of appearance or clothing and change of tone of voice; (3) most of the people interviewed but especially the women believe that men would be turned off if women were too aggressive. Too bad. We can't settle the debate: but you shouldn't drop the topic. Next time you talk to your girlfriend, why not catalog all of the techniques you use to signal sexual invitation—from the ever-popular "Bend over and spread" to the more romantic candlelight dinner to the classic "Think I'll slip into something more comfortable" to the simple clicking off of "The Tonight Show" halfway through Johnny's monolog. Not all sexual invitations have to be engraved.

How to Say No, or Maybe

This is not the sort of problem you usually deal with, but I've decided to write to you about it, anyway. Over the past few years, I've found a disheartening pattern in my social relationships. I've gone to bed with more women than I've wanted to—for the simple reason that I couldn't think of anything better to do with them at the time. We go out to a movie or dinner and the next thing I know, we're at my place. I live in a one-bedroom apartment and there's not much to do there except get it on. The problem is, sometimes I find myself with a woman and don't really want her. It's a bummer to have sex with a woman I'm not really interested in, but sometimes the opportunity for sex arrives before I've made up my mind. I go through the motions. The next morning, I feel horrible. Am I being too sensitive? —E. G., Madison, Wisconsin.

We should all be so unfortunate. Seriously, sex therapists have reported that more and more men complain about being pressured by circumstances into having sex before they are really ready for it. Bernie Zilbergeld, author of *Male Sexuality*, points out that "even in these days of instant sex and instant intimacy, sex still means something special to most people; it's not something you do with just anyone. In sex, you allow a unique access to yourself—to your nudity, to the feel and smell of your body and its fluids. And it can go even further. You may allow access to your emotions, at least to your interest and excitement. In doing so, you run the risk that this may be the start of real contact with the other person, a kind of intimacy, with all the possibilities and dangers that intimacy implies." In short, you discover that you are not an easy lay. Zilbergeld suggests that people with this attitude try minimal contact on first encounters—coffee dates, short walks, a movie, dinner, then dropping her off. One of the benefits of this approach is that you get to know each other. In addition, you can discuss sexual preferences before you get into bed—that way, if and when you do, it's likely to go well.

Your Place or Mine?

As a single woman, I've grown tired of the inevitable late-evening wrestling match on a first date—especially the question "Your place or mine?" Is there an advantage to home court? Is there a nice way to tell a guy that you'd like to see him again, but that you are not interested in doing it that night? —Miss M. T., New York, New York.

According to our sources, the question most frequently asked in singles bars is "Your *face* or mine?" As for home courts, we took a survey of the office and discovered that most women have an easier time dealing with dates on their own ground than effecting an exit from someone else's lair. Most guys view their apartments as extensions of their bedrooms. If it's a studio apartment, it *is* his bedroom. If you enter a man's private quarters, then you have already crossed a threshold. On the other hand, if you invite someone over for coffee, you can always ask him to leave (or sleep on the couch). But the best strategy is to announce your intention early in the evening. You don't have to be overly aggressive. Something this side of Jill Clayburgh in *Starting Over* ("Get the fuck away. I've got a knife. I'll cut your balls off.") should do.

How to Say "Later"

I am sick and tired of having previous sex life questioned by nearly total strangers on a first or second date when I don't respond to a sexual come-on. For the record, I make love only to men I know and it takes a lot longer than one drink, or one hour, or one date for me to achieve a comfortable state of knowing. It has been my unfortunate experience to have this attitude interpreted as un-liberated, hung up or sick. My conservative behavior has nothing to do with my libido or my sexual skills. In fact, I've thought of taking along a letter of recommendation from previous lovers that I could give to potential ones. Something like: "I have known Miss K. for several years. My personal experience with her has been socially, emotionally, intellectually, spiritually and sexually grati-fying (not necessarily in that order). She displays no hesitation regarding sexual expression once an appropriate rapport has been established. Her tastes are varied and she gives superb head—with or without Cool Whip. She has a delightful repertoire of carnal interests that includes a variety of positions, costumes, erotic material and sound effects. She encourages the use of visual aids and all devices that heighten pleasure. She has read and mastered many of the principles set forth in The Sensuous Woman, The Joy of Sex, *the* Tao of Love & Sex *and the* Kama Sutra. *She is orgasmic. She is not hung up. She does like sex. She is not gay nor is she a virgin. Because she is discriminating in her choice of sexual partners, she is at low risk of catching and spreading venereal and assorted other communicable diseases. I have found Miss K. to be an unusually versatile, verbal, witty, sensitive, sensual, sensuous, affectionate, loving and absolutely delicious partner. I recommend her for any alliance that is being considered." Et cetera. What do you say to that? —Miss G. K., New York, New York.*

We are impressed by your credentials. We don't have any openings now, but we'll definitely keep your note on file. As for the other guys you've been running into—maybe you should change markets. If you hang out in places where strangers go to meet strangers for casual sex, you get what you deserve. If you date friends of friends, they may already know enough about you to accept your pace. If you meet a person in a place where you have gone to enjoy yourself—skiing, reading, music clubs—the pressure to perform is less, simply because there is something else to do.

Adrenalin Makes the Heart Grow Fonder: Take Two

My roommate and I are planning a vacation for the Christmas break. After a semester of hitting the books, we want to boogie. Our dilemma: Do we hit the beaches or the slopes? We conducted an informal poll of the guys in the frat house to see which locale was the luckier and came up with a draw. Who meets more girls—sun bathers or skiers? And what are our chances of scoring? —D. B., Minneapolis, Minnesota.

We searched our files and could not find a study that related directly to your question. However, we did uncover an interesting experiment, described in *A New Look at Love*, by Elaine Walster and G. William Walster, that might help. Researchers investigated the notion that fear and excitement increase sexual attraction and contribute to passionate love. It seems that in North Vancouver, there are two bridges that span Capilano Canyon. One is a 5-foot-wide suspension bridge that "tilts, sways and wobbles over a 230-foot drop to the rocks and shallows below." The other bridge, a few hundred yards upstream, is a solid, safe structure. Psychologists placed an attractive young college girl at the end of each bridge. Whenever a young man would cross, she would meet him, give him a questionnaire and ask him to fill it out. She would also give the man her telephone number and offer to explain the project later, if he wanted to call. Who followed up on this opening? The men who had taken the risky bridge. (Nine of 33 men who crossed the suspension bridge called the coed. Only 2 of the men on the solid bridge called.) What does this mean? Try taking a vacation in North Vancouver. At first glance, it would seem that adrenalin makes the heart grow fonder. The excitement that surrounds a ski vacation should increase the sexual tension, especially in comparison with a beach vacation, which is seldom if ever described as a high risk. However, a shrewd observer will note that there is less competition in the low-risk atmosphere. (Two as opposed to 9 callers.) You'll have to make up your own mind. Since we are going skiing in a few weeks and would like to have the mountains to ourself, we recommend the beach vacation.

Body Language

While I was taking a photography course at a local college, I met a foxy, fun lady. We dated a few times, then we just drifted apart. She started dating a guy she met while she was in high school and has been going with him for about a year. Not long ago, however, she came over to my house (I asked her to come over) to pick up some pictures that I had taken of her. All I can say is that in the past year, she has turned into a fantastic-looking chick. Now for the dilemma. I recently read that if a woman lightly caresses her groin line, from the hip to the pubic area, she is giving you a signal. Well, this girl did just that while she and I were chatting. I care for her very much and I guess I would like to win her over. What I want to know: Should I let her know how I really feel about her? —M. T., Mobile, Alabama.

When it comes to body language, every couple needs a simultaneous translator. Unfortunately, such a body linguist would probably cost a bundle and isn't likely to be listed in the Yellow Pages. The next-best thing is to ask your friend what she means by a given gesture. (Remember Mae West's famous line: "Is that a gun in your pocket or are you just pleased to see me?") Maybe she read the same thing you read and *was* consciously trying to give you a signal. Maybe it was unconscious; in which case, mentioning it to her casually may make her suspect that she really was giving you a signal. She'll probably vote in your favor (Who knows a person's mind better than someone else?). Of course, there's always the chance that she has crabs. . . .

How can you tell when a woman is sexually excited? I've been cruising singles bars and discos for several years and I have never been able to tell when someone is responding to my come-on. I recall reading in a book by Desmond Morris that blushing and sweating are sure signs of sexual arousal. Is there any truth to that claim? —W. C., New York, New York.

Some, but not enough to help you make it through the night. There are four stages to sexual arousal—excitement, plateau, orgasm and resolution. The physiological signs of excitement are not exactly neon. The more common signs are the erection of the man and, in the woman, vaginal lubrication, nipple erection and a slight increase in the size of her breasts. On occasion, a woman may experience a sex-tension flush (a reddening of the skin on the breasts, shoulders and abdomen) near the end of the excitement stage. The full-tilt blush doesn't occur until later stages, so unless she's having an orgasm right there, chances are it's something you said. Mark Cook and Robert McHenry, two English sex researchers, have suggested that by the time a man is in the position to see a woman's sex-tension flush or observe vaginal lubrication, he already knows that she is sexually excited. Obviously, they've never been to Studio 54. Spontaneous sweating does occur in one out of three women—but only after orgasm. Then again, maybe the air conditioning just quit or her roll-on stopped working. There are many studies that claim body language is a good indicator of interest, if not arousal. Psychologist Elaine Walster notes that people who like each other tend to stand close together, and actually lean together, as though shutting off competitors. (Great, unless you're on a subway.) Other sociologists have pointed out that eye contact is a good sign—in an average conversation, people look at each other only 30 to 60 percent of the time. The more you like someone, the more you look at her. (You don't want to let her get away do you?) In any case, the best sign is verbal: a simple yes.

The Morning After

This may sound weird to you, but I have a major hang-up about the morning after. If I've spent the night with a girl—or, rather, if she's spent the night at my place—I can't wait to see her leave, preferably at the crack of dawn. I'm grumpy in the morning, not the best company, and I like my privacy. I prefer to shower alone, shave without an audience and generally get my head together. My question is this: Are there any subtle ways to ask a date to leave? —B. V., Chicago, Illinois.

If it's a weekday, tell her you have to be at the office by 7:30. If it's a weekend, and you are hung over and realize that the girl you brought home was an error in judgment precipitated by the same thing that caused your hangover, ask for a medical leave of absence and explain that you have to run down to the corner for some aspirin. Or take her out for breakfast. Actually, she's probably just as eager to abandon *your* company and get her own chores done. Maybe she wants to go home and change her clothes. (Old adage: If a secretary wears the same clothes two days in a row, she is having an affair. Or she is underpaid.) Be civil. Hell, you can even be honest. Just explain that you need a few hours of privacy to reflect on the glory of the preceding night. She'll understand.

Small Talk

I've been dating my latest girlfriend for about a month. We met while I was working at a bar. At first, it was fairly easy to converse—I suppose because there was a counter between us, and whenever I got stuck for something to say, I could tend to some small task behind the bar and thus conceal my shyness. However, when she and I are alone, I seem constantly to be searching for a subject to talk about. I become so self-conscious trying to impress her that what I end up saying is not enjoyable for either of us. I keep trying to live up to the image of a witty man about town; the result is frustration. Any suggestions? —A. M., Saginaw, Michigan.

It's not your job to do all of the talking, or even half of it. (We thought bartenders were professional listeners.) The wisecracking bon vivant,

with a pocketful of *mots justes*, is a Hollywood invention: If you're paying scriptwriters, you expect to hear something for your money. The
same standard does not apply to dates. Most women can do without
that kind of manic monolog (cf. Joni Mitchell's line: "The times you
impress me most are the times when you don't try"). For the time being,
schedule activities that don't demand conversation or that, at least, supply a topic—concerts, sports, sex. A famous wag once wrote, "Love
means never having to say a goddamn thing." When asked to clarify his
remark, he replied: "It is impolite, if not impossible, to talk with your
mouth full."

The Long Distance Love Affair

*Please help me. Through some very dear friends, I recently met a man whom I
find witty, articulate, charming and comfortable to be around, as well as a
sensitive and remarkably compatible lover. However, he lives in Chicago and I
live in New York. Although we both have careers in our respective cities, neither
of us can afford to commute regularly. Can you offer any suggestions on keeping
the flame burning? —Miss M. C., New York, New York.*

You should do the same thing you'd do if someone local had to leave
town for a month or two. Write letters. Send Mailgrams. Try telephone
sex. We don't mean listening to each other's heavy breathing, though
that's a start. Try talking, in clinical detail, about the times you spent
together. It's not what you do in bed, or how often, but how you
remember what you do. Tell him what you liked, what you didn't. (That
kind of critique can have disastrous results when you're in bed, but over
the phone you can discover what turns you on without feeling threatened.) You may feel awkward at first—most people have a major inhibition about talking about sex. Get over that and you can start providing
each other with scripts for future activites. Believe us—it works. We
have the telephone bills to prove it.

Should You Take a Date to a Porn Movie?

*For the past few months, I've been dating a girl who must have been raised in a
time capsule—right out of the Fifties. At least, that's the only way I can explain
her rather capricious conservative streak. She enjoys garden-variety fucking, but
she's still into basics—i.e., having fun with the fundamentals. At her rate, we'll
be getting to fellatio around the turn of the century. I'd like to speed up her
progress and have considered taking her to a porn movie. Do you think she would
be turned off by seeing X-rated exercises? —H. H., Kansas City, Kansas.*

First of all, we thought fellatio *was* one of the fundamentals. Oh, well. We can't say for sure what your girl's reaction to a porn movie would be, but based on recent research, we suspect you would be pleasantly surprised. Two scientists at Purdue University showed a ten-minute X-rated film to a group of students. They found that the females were more likely than the males to indicate a belief that the actors in the film were enjoying themselves. The group's physical responses were strikingly similar—the females were no less aroused than the males. So buy some popcorn and take your date to the flick. A good erotic film may open her eyes, if not other parts of her anatomy.

A Modern Pandora's Box

For several months, I have been struggling with something that I just don't know how to handle. My girlfriend and I have always respected each other's privacy, but in a weak moment, I let curiosity get the better of me. She has a small metal box that she keeps locked. She told me that it held some personal mementos. I'd always wondered what was in the box, and one night while she was away, I found the key and opened it. Inside were a stack of 35mm slides and a reel of film. I cannot tell you the sinking feeling I had when I saw what was on the transparencies. Her old boyfriend had been a photographer and had obviously taken the pictures—there were shots of my girlfriend without her clothes on. The first few frames of the movie showed her face as she engaged in an act of oral sex. I put everything back where it had been and tried to pretend that nothing had happened, but that hasn't worked. I haven't felt like making love to her since. I can't even kiss her without thinking of what her lips were doing in that movie. She's never done that with me. She'd always acted so innocent about sex—I thought she was a virgin when we first made love. She never seemed to be interested enough in sex to keep pictures of a guy without clothes. I am afraid of what she will say if I tell her what I did. I'm afraid of what more I might find out. What should I do? —B. M., Syracuse, New York.

Respect for privacy is often used as a front for lack of confidence. One cure is to trade the insecure suspicions of "What we don't know about each other can't hurt us" for the trusting curiosity of "What we find out together is a measure of our strength." It's said that people who keep Pandora's boxes expect them to be opened. We're not sure that's true, but people who want to talk do tend to leave clues—diaries left unlocked or astrological charts circled in the morning papers. (If you can't read my mind, read my horoscope.) Obviously, what you thought about your girlfriend was wrong—that's no excuse for not finding out what she is really like. It won't do to suffer in silence: Confess your actions or ask her to go over the contents of the box with you. If you want to put things in perspective, borrow a trick from Sherlock Holmes: Place a smoke bomb under your bed and see what she tries to save—you or the box.

How to Say "I've Had Better"

Okay. Here's the scenario. You meet a terrific-looking woman who makes smart, funny conversation. Things progress as they do and you take her to bed. You can't believe it, but she's absolutely terrible in bed and she doesn't seem to know it. What do you do? Try to fix it? Tell her you won't be seeing her again? Tell her why? Help! I have found myself in this predicament and it's killing me. —J. R., Los Angeles, California.

First, we suggest that she be securely bound and gagged in a padded cell and that you have a supply of tranquilizer darts handy, in case she gets violent. Seriously, the simple fact is that when it comes down to just two, she ain't no better or worse than you are in bed. If you want things to change, don't criticize the way it was. Suggest the way you would like it to be. And don't necessarily start the conversation in bed—where you are most vulnerable to a swift kick or a cutting line. Start it at midday ("Hey, have you ever tried a wet suit and a feather boa?"). That way, the excitement and anticipation can build for a whole day. Or, in the event of a turndown, you have the rest of the day to look for a new date.

How to Ask for More

Sex is, without doubt, my favorite activity. I could do it all night, every night. However, I find that when I ask a man to continue making love, to try for a second or a third round, the results are less than satisfactory. Most of my partners feel threatened or anxious. They shrug and roll over to go to sleep. Is there a polite way to say that once is not enough? —Miss D. L., New York, New York.

Yes, but it means talking with your mouth full. A command performance is not the best way to produce an encore. Words can create an atmosphere that renews desires, but it's chancy. For example, "If you don't get it up again, I'll make you the laughingstock of Manhattan" is not likely to produce the desired result. The best way is without words. Don't break up sex into rounds or make your pleasure dependent upon his having another erection. Just continue doing what you were doing— touching, stroking or mumbling. A little oral communication can work wonders.

Breaking Up is Hard to Do

I've read with interest the surveys that indicate coeds are as sexually active these days as male students. I am a junior in college and can attest to the truth of those reports. The girls are free to initiate sex and seem to be on equal footing with men. I may be paranoid, but they also seem to be the ones who terminate sex. Looking back over my own affairs of the past three years, it seems to me that, in almost all cases, my companions were the ones who broke up with me. What gives? —E. J., Cambridge, Massachusetts.

Maybe it was something you said. Don't worry. Your experience is common. A two-year study of dating relationships at Bradeis University revealed that coeds are usually the ones to break the bad news. Women terminated affairs in 51 percent of the couples studied, compared with 42 percent of the men (in 7 percent of the cases, the parties were in mutual disagreement). It seems that men are more romantic to begin with and are more likely to feel depressed, lonely, unhappy or guilty at the end of an affair. (So much for macho.) Women are generally more aware of problems in a relationship or set higher standards for partners. The study put an end to the old hell-hath-no-fury image of scorned womanhood. If you break up with a girl, she won't be waiting in the rhododendron with a switchblade. In fact, the study revealed that when a man calls it quits, the couple tends to stay on friendly terms. Moral: If you like a girl, get the affair over with quickly, so that you can really get to know each other.

CHAPTER FOURTEEN

Long-term Relationships and Live-Togethers

Communication

The other night, my girlfriend of five years accused me of lack of interest. She asked me why I no longer talk to her and said she fears that the romance has gone out of our relationship. I replied that I express my love for her in bed, sexually. The rest of the night was spent in silence, both sexually and verbally. How do we get out of this impasse? —K. L., Detroit, Michigan.

Cynics and irate lovers like to say that the only things communicated by sex are disease and/or the genetic code. If you're interested, our Unabashed Dictionary defines a sex object as a conversation piece. Anthropologist Ray L. Birdwhistell conducted a study of 100 couples who had lived together happily for more than fifteen years and found they spend a median of 27½ minutes per week talking to each other. The topic of conversation usually involved directions to parties or other social events. One interesting side light of the Birdwhistell study—couples apparently have their most intense dialogs on the third date and then again in the year before they get a divorce. Birdwhistell concluded that human communication is essentially nonverbal. We agree. You seem to equate sex with the nonverbal, while your ladyfriend equates interest with the verbal. It's not that simple. We tend to view relationships in terms of investment potential. The initial exchange of words is a principal sum that compounds interest daily. Obviously, the interest will never be as large or as romantic as the original sum, but it is still something to look forward to.

I am a twenty-eight-year-old single female and I've been living with my lover for the past year. (He moved into my place.) We get along very well, share chores and have many common interests—as well as a good sex life. We split expenses straight down the middle, even though he makes between two and three times what I do. This arrangement has resulted in his having quite a hefty savings account, while I often have to borrow from him to get through the week until payday. He claims that we are equals and thus share equally in expenses. He also says that he doesn't want to feel that he supports me and that he shouldn't be penalized for making more than I do. Obviously, my dissatisfaction hasn't been so much that I've asked him to leave—but when I think about it, I wonder if it shows something about his feelings for me. Am I being petty or is this a major obstacle in a relationship? —Miss A. J., New York, New York.

Welcome to the wonderful world of cohabitation politics. Just when things are going nicely, money rears its ugly head. Or is that tail? You've turned the budget into an emotional equation: You have to give everything to support your half of the relationship, while he gives only a third of himself. Look at this logically: A living-together relationship is a small business. Roommates—regardless of sex—generally split everything down the middle. If your boyfriend were a she, you wouldn't expect her to pay two thirds of the expenses, right? Also, since he was the one who moved in, we conclude that you were once able to support yourself in the same apartment. You've apparently just discovered that two can live three times as expensively as one. We recommend that you draw up a contract and keep a log of the items you purchase for the apartment. There are some expenses you will want to keep separate (for his weights, the batteries for your vibrator). On major items, such as stereos, you could buy shares. If you separated, you would determine a fair price for the object and one could buy out the other person's share. It obviously matters a great deal to you. You should bring the subject up with your boyfriend. He may take into account your feelings as well as your finances.

A Touch of Class

I need a little help. I know it's fashionable these days to hear women complain about the lack of quality attention from their men. Well, I'm a man living with one of those "new" women who is busy juggling a career, other relationships and me, and I'm not getting enough attention. How do I get it without whining? —F. H., New York, New York.

Traditional roles have taken such a beating in the past few years, it's hard to figure out who's on first, let alone who's on top. A lot of what women have been complaining about in their relationships with men—the need for more and better communication—goes both ways. Point out that since you are both busy people, you've got to make room for some quality time. Our suggestions: (1) Sunday-morning specials. Unplug the phone Saturday night. Devote Sunday morning to a terrific breakfast, the papers, good talk and slow sex. (2) Go away overnight once a month. Lots of hotels have great weekend deals. (3) Have a weekly activity—karate lessons, jogging, subscription symphony or theater tickets—and do it together like a "date." (4) Meet her for lunch once a week—if Jimmy and Rosalynn can make the time, so can you. Trust us. Whatever you pick, she'll be delighted to find out that you'd like to see more of her. It's exactly what women have been asking for all along. Men, too.

How Much Is Too Much?

My man and I seem to disagree on two important points concerning our sex life, frequency and quality. I maintain that twice a day, every day, for the past two weeks is too much. Can this continue indefinitely? Are there others out there like him, or is he one of a kind? Second, he recently told me that while he is making love to me, he is fantasizing about other women he knows. I can't believe that there is nothing wrong in this (at least for our relationship) and that everybody does it but doesn't confess it. My guy says that he is the way all men would be if they just followed their natural instincts. These questions are really becoming bothersome, since both of us are studying for the bar and he likes to take frequent sex breaks from studying. —Miss R. G., Fort Lauderdale, Florida.

If things haven't changed for you between the time you wrote to us and the time you receive this answer, you may be completely exhausted by now. There is no such thing as a "normal" frequency for sexual encounters, but twice a day for two weeks isn't necessarily excessive. However, it's strictly a matter of opinion and personal preference—be it once a day, once a week, even once a month. The pressure of studying for his exam may have driven your boyfriend to seek a sexual release from tension. Other men might actually suffer from temporary impotence under identical circumstances. As for fantasizing about other women, that is not unusual—almost everyone fantasizes about a different partner at one time or another. But if your boyfriend is dreaming about someone else *every* time you make love, the two of you may have a serious problem. It sounds to us as though both of you need to communicate better and compromise more often.

Getting Your Way in Bed

My roommate and I have a very satisfying sex life. However, there is one aspect that you may be able to help me with. She prefers the traditional missionary position, while I find the rear-entry position the most satisfying. It seems to me that when I enter her from the rear, I feel as if I am going into her more deeply. On the other hand, she tells me that face to face provides greater intimacy: i.e., kissing and hugging. My question: Is there any position or variation that will satisfy both our needs? —B. L.

A change in attitude might help. Sam Keen, in his book *What To Do When You're Bored and Blue*, notes: "In erotic friendships, sex is an expression of a union, a celebration of a meeting that has already taken place. . . . In making love, the trick is to begin at the end. Start when compassion has already been established." In other words, if your girlfriend is depending on mere position to establish the intimacy, you're in trouble. Next time you are in bed with her, you might examine the full imagery of each position: If you can tell her in more detail what it feels like when your enter from the rear—the heart-stopping view, the genital sensation—the sharing of that knowledge will make the pleasure as intimate as a hug.

She Wants to Date Around

After having a very close relationship with me for precisely two years, my girlfriend has suddenly announced that she'd like to date other guys. She feels that, since I was her first real date, she should be able to date some other guys to see if I really am the guy she'd like to remain with for a while. I hate it. We really do love each other, and I can see her point, but I can't stand seeing her with other guys. I don't see her even half as much as I used to, due to the fact that she doesn't think that we should see as much of each other while she "plays the field," as it were. (A) Do you think that she might just be trying to get rid of me? (She's still friendly when we're together, but that's not too often.) (B) Is there a way that I can get her back? (C) Should I be excessively nice to her, or should I let her know I'm furious? (D) Should I join the French Foreign Legion? —D. H., San Francisco, California.

She just might be trying to get rid of you. Vague dissatisfactions felt by one member of a relationship can wreak havoc on the other. Since you were the first person with whom your girlfriend had a serious affair, it seems to us natural that she might want to see what other guys might be like. That doesn't make it any easier, mind you. On the other hand, if it's the kind of intimacy you've shared for two years that she's having problems with, it could spell trouble. Nobody likes to be compared with other guys. Everything seems to be on the line. Consequently, when you do see her, the impulse is to be exceptionally attentive and solic-itous—i.e., you become a simpering wimp. Hang loose. We suspect that your girlfriend is just going through a maturation process. If she finds someone she likes more than you, let her go. If she wants to come back, fine. Just tell her that once is enough. If that's not the case, hang on to your memories and break new ground. You shouldn't join the Foreign Legion unless you kill her. If it comes to that, you can apply to: French Foreign Legion, 13400, Aubagne, France.

The Desire for More Experience

I am a nineteen-year-old male, presently living with my girlfriend, who is also nineteen. My problem is this: I get very jealous when I think of her past lovers. I tell myself that it's stupid and useless to feel like that, but it doesn't help. Part of the problem is that she started having sex fairly early (at 14) and has had at least ten sexual partners since then. On the other hand, I lost my virginity at eighteen and had intercourse only three times (with the same girl) before I started going out with my present girlfriend. I was very shy and never had much luck with girls. It has always bothered me that I started having sex so late and have had such little experience. I guess I'm very insecure about how I am as a lover, though my girlfriend has never said anything to make me believe that I'm not satisfying her. I love her and don't want to hurt her, but I want to experience sex with other women. I don't know what to do. I guess I'm jealous because she has had so much more experience than I have. —G. G., Pittsboro, North Carolina.

Experience means different things to different people. A friend of ours recently had a woman tell him, "You must have had a lot of lovers to get this good." His reply: "No, I merely loved one woman well." All you can learn from a one-night stand is what you can learn from a one-night stand. Quality comes from collaboration. The age at which you lost your virginity doesn't mean anything—though this is a matter most Amer-ican men are very concerned about (they tend to lie a lot about it). Before you go off on a quest to experience other women, learn what you can from the present relationship. If you have her undivided attention, you have everything.

Jealousy

Alas, I find myself involved with an extremely jealous lover and it's driving me nuts. I mean, I like this girl and spend most of my time with her. I don't fool around, except on the rare occasion when someone makes me an offer I can't refuse. The problem is, she is jealous even when there is no reason to be. I can't talk about past affairs or even mention another woman's name in her presence. I find that attitude restrictive. If I could do something to make her feel better, I would, but it seems to be a no-win situation. Any suggestions? —E. C., Santa Fe, New Mexico.

Psychologists who have studied jealousy have come up with some not too surprising findings. It seems that the emotion is closely tied to feelings of insecurity and/or an unflattering self-image. Your girlfriend may feel inadequate in some way; consequently, she invests a great deal of herself in the relationship. It becomes her major vital sign. If you give any indication that you are not as involved as she is, that the relationship does not mean as much to you as it does to her, then you'd best be wearing a steel jockstrap. There are two ways to cope with a jealous lover: The first is positive. Make sure you articulate what it is you like about her. For example, compliment her on her perfume. That is surefire—even when she's not wearing any, she'll be pleased. The second approach is to avoid threatening situations. One study found that there was a common agreement on what makes a person green—a sort of Geneva convention on jealousy. The five most effective tactics were (in descending order) discussing and exaggerating the appeal of some third person, flirting, dating others, fabricating attachments and talking about previous partners. If you find that you can't get through life without engaging in those activities, you may have to find a new partner—one who is totally self-assured. And then you'd better hope your self-image is intact.

This may sound old-fashioned, but I am completely faithful to my man. We have a satisfying relationship and plan to be married. However, outside interference is breaking us up. He is very jealous about me, which I love, as it only proves to me how much he loves me. Lately, he has been getting daily phone calls telling him what I've been doing while he's at work and/or away for the night. Nothing they say is true, but since he can't know for sure, it's putting him under a great strain. He worries constantly about me and is on the verge of nervous collapse. I have offered to wear a chastity belt, if we can find out where to buy one or how to make one. Do you have an answer? —Miss F. W., Portland, Oregon.

They? It sounds to us like inside interference is causing the trouble. Whether or not the crank calls take place (they may be an invention to cover up his own doubts), it is obvious that your boyfriend is excessively jealous. He'll listen to strangers but not to reason. (Have you considered making your own daily phone calls?) Forget the chastity belt: Possessiveness is nine tenths of the flaw. We recall the story of the insecure man who dreamed that he was given a ruby ring that, for as long as it was worn, guaranteed the fidelity of his lover. He awoke and found his finger buried to the hilt in the ruby-red ring of his girlfriend's private parts. Anything less won't do. We suggest that you take Bertrand Russell's counsel: Jealousy must not be regarded as a justifiable insistence upon rights but as a misfortune to the one who feels it and a wrong toward its object. Those who shut love in a cage destroy the beauty and joy that it can display only while it is free and spontaneous. He who fears to lose what makes the happiness of his life has already lost it.

Breaking Up

Finally, after two years of fighting, I broke up with my girlfriend. Apparently, she has taken the split quite hard, missing work for several days, et cetera. I am worried and have considered suggesting that she see a psychiatrist, possibly at my expense. Would this be appropriate? —C. M., Hartford, Connecticut.

You might find wisdom in the following anecdote on the need for professional help in everyday crises: The owner of a cat was distressed to find his pet in a tree. He called the fire department and asked them to send a hook and ladder around to fetch the cat. The fireman told the man to wait an hour, that the cat would come down on its own accord. The man called back fifteen minutes later, convinced that the cat would never come down. "Excuse me, sir," said the fireman, "but have you ever seen a cat skeleton in a tree?" If you want to see a psychiatrist to work out your own feelings of guilt and responsibility, fine, but don't patronize your ex-girlfriend. Emotional Marshall Plans are seldom appropriate and are never appreciated.

Help. I'm caught between a rock and a hard place. I need your advice. A while back, I began dating a very beautiful waitress. She spent lots of time with me. One Sunday night while we were together, my ex-girlfriend suddenly waltzed into my apartment, using her own key. I was shocked, confused and not at my best. I let my date leave and spent the next half hour fighting with my ex. I realized my mistake almost immediately. After she left, I called the waitress and was politely told to get lost. I want her back. What should I do? —B. L., Los Angeles, California.

Rule number one: Never give out keys to your apartment. Rule number two: Always give the one you're with your total attention. If the phone rings, don't answer it. Better yet, disconnect the damn thing. Cancel all of your magazine subscriptions. A bird in the hand. . . . We don't understand why you tolerated the invasion by your ex-girlfriend or why you let her stay. Unless, perhaps, you get off on fighting and miss the discord. As for rebuilding your relationship with the waitress—be patient. Persevere.

How do you tell someone you're living with to get lost? About a year ago, I met this guy—we liked each other, dated, made love. The only friction came from playing "your place or mine?"—the insecurity of being away from our respective creature comforts for a night (his music, my macrame), the sense of wasting a space by leaving it unoccupied—all seemed to detract from what was going down between us. We tossed a coin; he sublet his apartment and my place became our place. It was a mistake. I feel like my whole life has been invaded. I'm under a constant pressure to relate, to be domestic. There's no time left for my creative pursuits and that's a capital offense. More and more, I find myself taking it out on him. I want to go back to the old arrangement, or maybe to see him out of my life entirely, but the trouble involved is frightening. How can I broach the subject? —Miss P. B., Hartford, Connecticut.

Breaking up is hard to do. That's why you feel so good when it stops. You can drop subtle hints: Walk around the house singing "I shall be released." Short sheet his side of the bed. Leave a U.S. Post Office change-of-address card with his name nailed to the door. Or you can take drastic measures: Ask him to deposit a check for you. On the back of the check, write "This is a holdup" and hope that they aren't too hard on him. However, we're not sure that revenge is in order. It seems to us that the situation is to blame. A sense of invasion often occurs when you subdivide an old territory. In your next incarnation, find a larger apartment. If there's not enough space for you to live alone together, then you won't live together for long. State your case soon and make it clear to your roommate that moving out is not the same as moving on.

CHAPTER FIFTEEN

The
Married
Life

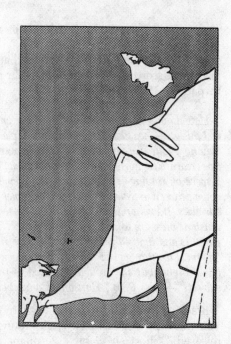

Boredom

My husband and I share great lovemaking but only in one position. Originally, we tried various positions, but I seldom reached orgasm, which frustrated my husband completely. Now he makes love in only the one position that suits me best (the little sweetheart), while at the same time he tells me that I'm not normal, not like all the other women in the world. Having been raised in a sexually conservative family, my family does not believe in dirty talk or marital aids. So what do I do to get him to try other positions and try to make them work? —Mrs. T. W., Macon, Georgia.

A recent survey of psychiatrists asked the question: "Why do some married couples stick to unvaried sexual routines even though these are found wanting?" Almost half of the group cited two reasons: fear of being rejected and considered abnormal, while just over half of the group claimed to have deep-seated inhibitions. Thirteen percent cited lack of imagination as the fault. We think it's simpler than that. Some people are comfortable with sex only when it works. The orgasm becomes critical. It is the only way to establish that sex is good for both of you. Consider your own reactions—you call your husband a sweetheart for catering to your specific needs for orgasm. That kind of subtle reinforcement can lead to boring routine. It calls to mind the sign on the muddy road in Tennessee: CHOOSE YOUR RUT CAREFULLY—YOU'RE GOING

TO BE IN IT FOR THE NEXT TEN MILES. There is no reason to expect every sexual position to produce an orgasm; indeed, most women are reliably orgasmic in only one or two. How do you change? Switch to a my-turn, your-turn style of lovemaking. Try it standing up, hanging from the chandelier, sitting on his lap in front of the TV—for the fun of it. Show enthusiasm. Then switch to old faithful for the final round.

Is That All There Is?

I have been married for a year to a very exciting man—both intellectually and sexually. The problem is, after a year of everything from bondage to bubble baths, I think he has become bored sexually. I desperately want to get the excitement back into our sex life but don't seem to have any creative ideas. Any suggestions? —Mrs. N. M., Atlantic City, New Jersey.

Sure. Try the missionary position with the lights out. It never hurts to return to basics. Or try doing it in different places at different hours of the day. Actually, you may just be experiencing the "newlywed" effect. Carol Tavris and Susan Sadd, authors of *The Redbook Report on Female Sexuality*, found that 80 percent of newlyweds rated their sex lives as good or very good, but that the figure drops to 68 percent of those married one to four years. The frequency of sex also diminishes somewhat after a year. It doesn't change much after that: Partners resolve themselves to "Is that all there is?" And what you have doesn't sound so bad. You might ask your husband what he likes; if it turns out that he's turned on by the Dallas Cheerleaders . . . well, as a poet once said, "Man's reach must exceed his grasp . . . that's what masturbation's for."

When the Thrill Is Gone

How do you go about restoring sexual interest in a relationship? My husband and I seem to have reached an impasse. We still make love once or twice a week, but there is no spark. He doesn't seem to be open to changing the routine. I gave him a copy of The Joy of Sex for Christmas. He told me that he didn't have time to read it but that I should read it and give him a summary. Is our situation hopeless? —Mrs. D. K., Los Angeles, California.

If you can figure out a way to summarize *The Joy of Sex*, you might have the ultimate quickie. As for the situation you describe: It may not be hopeless, but it's certainly fucked up. Many men are reluctant to discuss sex with their wives, and vice versa. They may feel that their fantasies are too bizarre to be realized in their own homes, so they retreat into silence and apathy. If you try to disregard the heat of your own fantasies, you will soon find yourself trapped in routine, dutiful sex. And that is no sex at all. Sex therapists have spent the past decade trying to find ways to break down the communication barrier between partners. Michael Castleman describes one exercise in his book *Sexual Solutions.* Each person makes a list of all the things he or she wishes the other person would do in bed, then ranks the list in terms of "least difficult for your partner" to "most difficult." Start with the easiest (and you may be surprised at just how simple some of the suggstions can be—kissing, hugging, snuggling, etc.) Don't try to rush through the list in one night. It can take months before you are at ease with the give-and-take of lovemaking. Of course, if the list starts with spiked heels, whips or chains, or a complicated maneuver involving the Dallas Cowboys Cheerleaders, you may have a problem.

Newlywed Blues

About a month ago, I married a wonderful girl whom I had dated for two years. Now I find myself in a dilemma: Her sex drive isn't nearly what mine is and it's driving me up a wall. For the many months we dated, she insisted on a hands-off policy, which I assumed was due to a series of unsuccessful affairs in her past. In the month we've been married, we've had intercourse only twice. The rest of the time she insists that I stay on my side of the bed, and she politely but firmly resists any affectionate approaches. She stays up watching late movies or reading murder mysteries until two or three in the morning in what I think is her way of avoiding intercourse. Ironically, when the subject of newlyweds comes up in conversation with friends, you'd swear she was a slave to my sexual desires. I might mention that when we do have intercourse, there is no problem—she seems to enjoy it as much as I do. I deliberately have not subjected her to unusual positions or unique sexual methods. I performed oral sex on her once and she obviously enjoyed it, but since that time she has resisted my advances. Is there anything I can do to improve the situation? —F. R., Fort Wayne, Indiana.

The other night we heard a character in that old movie *Lady Luck* tell a troubled friend: "Son, you just broke the eleventh commandment—never accuse a woman of your own imagination." Or lack of one. Your letter is a catalog of things you assume about your wife. Get her side of the story and you'll probably have company on your side of the bed.

Afterplay

Can you tell me what to do with a husband who has to get up and wash himself as soon as he climaxes? For five years, I have asked him to stay in bed after making love. The afterglow is as nice as the foreplay for me. But he simply laughs and says, "Later." When he comes back to bed, he is dressed in pajamas and ready for sleep. He won't even let me touch him. I realize that he is not a romantic man, but I could live without the words if he would just hold on to me once in a while. Any suggestions? —Mrs. G. R., Kansas City, Kansas.

In part, it's the nature of the beast. Masters and Johnson filmed couples who fell asleep after intercourse and discovered an interesting pattern. The men tended to remain in a stationary position, while the women tended to try to cuddle up to their mates, apparently seeking to sustain the feeling generated by lovemaking. However, it also seems clear that your husband (and possibly you yourself) views sex as a self-contained event. When it's over, it's over. Have you considered following him into the bathroom—a site whose erotic possibilities are often overlooked? Hot water, soap on skin, the feel of rough towels add up to a textural treat that should not be missed. A second round (in a clean setting) might arouse your husband's interest and break him of a bad habit. Our guess is that his foreplay is as abrupt as his afterplay. Often, couples fall into a routine in which the only time they touch each other is when they're in the bedroom. One way to recapture romance is to display affection at other times of day—with touches that are not directly connected with sex. Do it often enough and he may get the point.

More on Boredom

After ten years of an exciting, satisfying marriage, I seem to be turning into one of those frigid women you read about. My husband is tall and good-looking, but over the past six months, he has fallen into the habit of asking for sex instead of just taking it. My stock answer seems to be, "Maybe later" or "I'm tired" or "I'm just not in the mood." He shrugs and leaves me alone for the rest of the night. The worst thing of all is that I don't mind being left alone. A few months ago, I broke off a two-year affair. It had been reasonably satisfying, but I was afraid of getting caught. My lover was not as sexually talented as my husband, yet I regretted leaving him. On the occasions my husband and I have sex, I enjoy it—not with my previous gusto, but my climaxes are still very powerful. Recently I told him that perhaps I did not like being asked, that perhaps I just wanted to be taken. I have been neither asked nor taken since. How can I reverse this trend? —Mrs. F. D., Kansas City, Kansas.

Frigidity, when it exists, involves having sex and not having orgasms. Your problem is not having sex. We suspect that you are bored with a ten-year pattern of being the available wife. Passive acceptance of sex often leads to a brief but effective period of passive resistance. A country-and-western song we heard last year described this declaration of independence as: "If you don't leave me alone, I'll find someone who will." You didn't have far to look; now, you'll have to rekindle your husband's desire as well as your own. Initiate sex for a change. The love you make should equal the love he takes.

How to Find a Sex Counselor

A friend confessed to me that he and his wife have serious sexual problems. Of course, I told him to write to The Playboy Advisor, but he felt that the problems were too serious to be worked out in a letter. He wondered if you could recommend a sex therapist? Any ideas? —B. A., New York, New York.

The field of sex counseling is overrun with quacks and turkeys who are perfectly willing to take your money for the benefit of watching you and your wife (or is it your friend and his wife?) take off your clothes and cop a feel or two. We do not think that someone who prescribes two dry-cell batteries and a vibrator four times a day is what is needed in most cases. The American Association of Sex Educators, Counselors and Therapists offers a consumer's guide listing qualified educators and therapists throughout the country. Those included in the directory adhere to a code that bans nudity and erotic body contact between therapist and patient. The book is yours for three dollars from AASECT, Suite 301, 5010 Wisconsin Avenue, NW, Washington, D.C. 20016. Tell 'em The Playboy Advisor sent you.

What Is Normal

My husband and I have been married for eight years. During that entire time, he has been addicted to bondage. At first it wasn't so bad, but over the past few years, it has gotten steadily worse. Now sex is no longer merely unpleasant, it is actually painful. It seems that it doesn't matter to my husband whether or not I get anything out of intercourse. All I feel is thoughts of degradation and humiliation. Lately, to go along with the tying-up and gagging routines, he has installed a series of hooks in the ceiling. He hoists me up in the air to hang by my arms and legs. It hurts. He gets disgusted and angry when I complain. He says that normal intercourse doesn't satisfy him. We have tried it once or twice, but it is obvious from his subsequent behavior that he is less than pleased with the results. I have suggested that we try counseling. He says it probably wouldn't work. He's had this hang-up all of his life and simply refused to believe that anyone can help. He's afraid that if he tells anyone about it, word will get out and he will lose his job. What do you suggest? —Mrs. E. H., Mobile, Alabama.

The new sexual morality holds that everything is permitted—until it becomes boring. Fetishes are considered abnormal and pathological when the given behavior is the only way the person can enjoy sex. Your husband's obsession with bondage seems to fall within that category. When mutuality disappears from a relationship, and one person enjoys himself at the expense of his partner, it's time to call for help. Sex therapists keep their work completely confidential, so your husband's fear of exposure is groundless. (Incidentally, how does he explain the hoist when you have guests over?)

Does She Need a Counselor?

I've been married seven years to a woman who's almost frigid. When I can convince her to have sex (it has to be a Saturday or Sunday afternoon before six P.M.), she has the following stipulations: The dishes must be done, the house cleaned and our son out of the house. I must wash my genitals. She takes a shower, brushes her hair and then drinks a glass of brandy to get loose. After all that, she is ready. We seldom have intercourse. She never orgasms when I'm inside her. Usually, she puts my cock in her mouth. When I come, she runs to the bathroom and spits out my sperm. I get her off by manual stimulation of her clitoris. She's not really into that, either. As a result, we have sex only about once a month. I'm totally frustrated, constantly horny. I don't want to get divorced, because of my son. Can you help? —L. S., Cleveland, Ohio.

Your wife makes sex sound like a human sacrifice. The situation is not healthy—for you or for her. No sexual relationship can succeed if the two people involved don't communicate. You aren't going to be able to arouse your wife's interest in sex until you find out why she goes to such extremes to avoid it. She's the only one who can tell you what the problem is. If she can't put her feelings into words, professional counseling may be necessary. If she refuses to talk or to seek outside guidance, there are several alternatives. Hire a maid to do the house cleaning. If your wife still isn't interested, make it with the maid.

Affairs

What is Playboy's position on extramarital sex? My girlfriend and I are thinking about posting the bans. Our one difference of opinion concerns fooling around. I have enjoyed a healthy series of relationships with other women and I don't want to give up that option. I'm not sure that I could, even if I wanted to. My girlfriend thinks that marriage should be exclusive. She thinks that she should be able to satisfy all of my needs. I say that her view is old-fashioned and next to impossible to maintain. What do you think? —D. W., San Francisco, California.

A recent study of Lewis Yablonsky, author of *The Extra-Sex Factor*, may shed some light on your debate. Yablonsky found that over half of America's married men have sex outside marriage. The secret to success appears to be secrecy: 80 percent of the men who play around do not tell their wives and feel that their affairs do not affect their marriage. The 20 percent who practice kiss-and-tell romance find that extra sex, or the confession of it, does tend to destroy the main relationship. Yablonsky tried to find out why men crave extramarital sex. The single largest response (48 percent of the men) was: "I enjoy relationships with other women, and sex is only part of that." The rest of the top five: "I like variety" (40 percent), "I was away from my wife for a time and it was available" (34 percent), "I wanted a little adventure and excitement in my life" (31 percent), and "my sex life with my wife is fine, but I need more" (31 percent). Most of those reasons do not reflect negatively on the wife: It seems that some men have a need for the company of more than one woman. If you get married, then fool around, what will it feel like? Half of the men had positive feelings, while the rest were divided between negative and mixed feelings. Probably the one experiencee shared by most men is enjoyment of variety: 72 percent said that sex is *different* with other women, and some cited oral and anal sex specifically as things they can do with a mistress that they can't do at home. Our final verdict: We haven't met your girlfriend. She may very well be able to satisfy all of your needs. After all, almost half of the married men in America don't fool around. It's your choice.

Why We Fool Around

What do you do when you discover that your partner is having an affair? Or that he has had affairs in the past? It recently came to my attention that my husband had cheated on our marriage. I was very hurt. Our sex life has been incredible, and there shouldn't have been cause for him to wander. He says the same thing—that the sex was great—but that there were other reasons. Can you shed any light on this? —Mrs. D. K., Boston, Massachusetts.

First, we would ask you to change your vocabulary. We're not sure that cheating was what he had in mind. Several studies—ranging from Alfred Kinsey's to Morton Hunt's—have shown that approximately 50 percent of married men have extramarital affairs. It is rare that such affairs are discovered (only 3 percent of all affairs are accidentally uncovered). According to pollster Lewis Yablonsky, 80 percent of the men who fool around do not tell their wives. The 20 percent who kiss and tell do so to get rid of guilt, to cause pain or to challenge the status quo of the marriage. Contrary to soap-opera wisdom, sex isn't the only cause of extramarital affairs. Dr. Avodah K. Offit, author of *Night Thoughts, Reflections of a Sex Therapist*, suggests that there are at least fourteen predictable times for sexual infidelity to occur: "All have to do with loss or stress, either transient or permanent, and represent attempts to cope or adapt. These include any point when a man or woman is (1) deciding on or beginning a career; (2) heavily involved in expansion or success; (3) changing jobs; (4) traveling extensively alone; (5) depressed by failure; (6) bored by monotony or fatigued by dull overwork; and (7) retiring." In addition, she states the following: "Family crises and events that are often related to extramarital adventures include: (1) pregnancy and childbirth; (2) the period during which small children receive a great deal of attention at home; (3) times of bereavement, such as the death of a parent; (4) periods of other emotional crisis—a child's accident or a mate's illness; (5) the 'empty nest' syndrome when children leave for school or college; (6) any time in a person's life when she or he confronts the process of physical aging, an awareness that occurs at least in every decade of life; and (7) any time of stress, such as moving, buying a home or any major change in style of life." So our first advice is this: Don't look at the affair but, rather, at everything else that is going on in your life.

The Coolidge Effect or Why Variety is the Spice of Life

Is there a biological explanation for adultery? My husband recently read an article that claimed promiscuity seems to be built into the nervous system—at least into the male nervous system. The authors suggested that "when the nervous system gets the same stimulation repeatedly and predictably over a long period, it is not so aroused as when it was new." I can go along with that, but I'm not sure that it's a reason to fool around. Isn't the theory a lot of hogwash? —Mrs. I. I., Detroit, Michigan.

We telephoned Scot Morris, our expert on sociobiology—the hot, new theory that tries to explain certain similarities between animal and human behavior in terms of genetic imperatives. He says that experiments with animals clearly show that even a sexually exhausted male can be rearoused by a new female. The phenomenon has been called the Coolidge Effect, to commemorate a widely repeated anecdote about Calvin Coolidge. Seems the President and Mrs. Coolidge were visiting a Government farm. They were taken on separate tours. Upon arriving at the chicken pens, Mrs. Coolidge paused to ask if the rooster copulated more than once a day. "Dozens of times," the caretaker replied. "Please tell that to the President," Mrs. Coolidge requested. When the President passed the same pens and was told of the rooster's virile record, he inquired, "Same hen every time?" No, said the caretaker, a different hen every time. The President nodded, then said, "Please tell that to Mrs. Coolidge." The effect has been noticed in other animals. Apparently, when a vigorous young ram is placed in a cage with a receptive ewe, he might copulate with her about seven times in the first hour. However, if the ewe is removed after every ejaculation and a fresh female is substituted, the ram might copulate eleven times in the first half hour. (We recently decided to repeat this experiment ourself. We placed an editor in a cage with a receptive ewe, and we are happy to report that absolutely nothing happened, even though he is from Texas.) So the theory is definitely not hogwash. Sheepdip maybe, but not hogwash.

Open Marriage

About a year ago, my wife and I began to discuss books such as Open Marriage *and the possibility of having sex with other persons. (We were both virgins when we married ten years ago.) Shortly after these talks, she got a job as a secretary—mainly to get away from the house and the kids. The winter passed and then, one day, she told me that she'd had a brief affair with a man at work. I was shocked. I asked her to tell me every detail of the affair, since I felt this would help me understand. Our marriage went through a radical change. We spent hours talking as we had never before. We made love constantly. In spite of these changes for the good, I brood about the inequality—my wife has had an extramarital affair and I have not. I feel left out. I would like the experience of getting to know a married woman well enough to become intimate. My wife says that now that she has found out what sex is like with another person, she won't repeat the incident. She also says that since our marriage has improved, there is no reason that I should ever want another woman. Even if some gorgeous creature throws herself at me, I should refuse. I feel that she has lost her right to ask for a pledge of faithfulness. I don't want to change my lifestyle and go to bars looking for available women; but I also feel that if I just go to work and do my daily errands, I will never have an affair like hers. That is a bitter pill to swallow. Is there anything I can do to balance accounts? —M. F., Los Angeles, California.*

The reprisal theory of open marriage (don't get angry, get even) seldom works, and it may lead to open warfare. For one thing, the third person in a revenge relationship often winds up a bitter victim. An affair of your own would probably threaten the delicate balance of your marriage, but not for the reasons your wife cites. She wants you to learn from her mistake (which seems not to have been a mistake); what you both fail to realize is that any affair you undertake is likely to be different from hers. She said yes to an opportunity that presented itself; it appears that you would have to create the opportunity. If you want to get to know a married woman, try your wife.

After sixteen months, my marriage has become a nightmare. I love my husband and he loves me, but he says he prefers a marriage "dating style." He encourages me to go out with other men and to sleep with whomever I want. He demands that he do the same, with no questions asked except "Did you have a good time?" He says he cares for me and wants me to have his children. His whole concept of marriage sickens me, but I would do anything for his love. Do you think he is right? —Mrs. G. J., Detroit, Michigan.

He's right only if *you* think he's right. If you don't, and you want another kind of marriage, it may be necessary to find another kind of marriage partner. His encouraging you to ball other guys—when he knows that it's contrary to your lifestyle and offensive to you—could be a cheap cover-up for the guilt he feels at balling other women. Tell him if he's got to do it, you'd rather he did so without your knowledge and that you prefer not to be an accomplice in his extramarital amours.

Leaving Marks

A few weeks ago, I was invited to have an affair with the wife of a neighbor. We met in a hotel room for lunch and fucked our eyeballs out. Later, as we were dressing, she noticed that I had given her a slight hickey on the breast. With some scorn, she looked at me and said, "It was nice, but you're kind of new at this, aren't you?" I asked her what she meant. She said that partners who were experienced at illicit get-togethers didn't leave clues, that the hickey was not the mark of a man, that it was very high school. I'd never heard that before. Is leaving no clues common etiquette? —D. K., New York, New York.

Part of the excitement of illicit love is keeping the secret. Men should leave their bullwhips and brass knuckles at home. Women should trim their fingernails, go without lipstick and take off their spiked heels before climbing into bed. But discretion should not be allowed to get in the way of vigor. Hell, if she's going to take all the fun out of having an affair, it's almost not worth having one to begin with, is it?

The Other Woman or the Next Wife

My wife and I have been together for three years. Our marriage, which at first seemed to have been made in heaven, has broken down completely. I've tried to get her to discuss our problems, but to no avail. She refuses to admit that we have any, and she will not go with me to see a counselor. Divorce seems to be the only answer and, frankly, I want it. My problem is this: Recently, I ran into my best friend's sister. It had been ten years since I'd last seen her and I found her very appealing. She knows I'm married, but she doesn't know my marriage is on the rocks. How do I declare my interest in her? She comes from a good family and is a nice girl. I don't want her to get the wrong idea—that I am just a dissatisfied husband seeking solace or that she would be the other woman. Believe me, I don't want to let her out of my life. —*N. J., Burlington, Vermont.*

Marriages made in heaven have the same troubles that plague other imported jobs—it's hard to get spare parts and the repair charges are outrageous. We suggest that you keep these affairs separate. Do what is necessary to resolve your marriage—one way or another. Explain the situation to your friend's sister as honestly as possible. When you do talk to her, don't force yourself into a category such as "ex-husband-to-be" or her into one such as "nice girl." Stories tend to come out the way you write them. You might want to ask her brother to act as a go-between—what are best friends for, anyway? Of course, he may punch you out: "Not with my sister, you don't." Take care.

The Wandering Spouse

I'm a happily married man, and my wife and I share a beautiful sex life. We've been married for one year now and I've found out that she is oversexed. This worries me very much, because my company is sending me on an eight-month business trip out of the country and I'm afraid that she will have relations with other men while I'm away. I know it sounds funny, but is there any way I can find out if she has had relations with other men? I think eight months is a long time for my wife to go without sex! —*J. M., Los Angeles, California.*

First of all, there's no such thing as an oversexed person. Sexual drives vary and there's no way you can measure the difference between normal and above-normal sexuality. Except for a few deviates whose names appear on the masthead of this magazine, everyone is basically normal. No, there's no way you can find out whether or not your wife has had sex with other men. If you're the happily married man you say you are, shouldn't her word be good enough? Often, fear of a spouse's infidelity stems from a person's own desires for promiscuity. A man figures he might have sex with another woman and immediately assumes his wife feels the same way. Eight months isn't so long a time. Besides, you can always save your money and send her a plane ticket for a romantic weekend.

The Danger of Illicit Sex

My wife and I have been happily married for years. Up to this time, our relationship has been monogamous, but we've been talking about extramarital affairs recently. She said that she did not object to them in principle but that she had read somewhere that fooling around was bad for your health. She is not referring to crimes of passion or jealous lovers but, rather, to the chance of having a heart attack while making love to a mistress. It sounds like an old wives' tale to me. Is there any truth to the story? —J. R., New York, New York.

Uh, we hate to be the bearer of bad news, but your wife is on to something. The chances of having a heart attack while making love are infinitesimal, but if you do have one, the chances are that you will have it with your mistress and not with your wife. A study of thirty-four cardiac patients who died during intercourse revealed that twenty-nine of the thirty-four were having an extramarital affair. We don't know what this means; we're not sure we want to.

Friend or Lover

My husband and I have been married for six years and our relationship is very satisfactory. We love each other, but of course in a different and more enjoyable way than at first. A short while ago, I saw an old boyfriend. We spoke on the phone a few times and met twice. It was all quite innocent, but we decided to call it quits before something happened. Now I find I think about him more than ever before. I value his friendship and would like very much to get together occasionally—when we're down and need someone other than our daily friends or family to talk to. People say one thing leads to another, but I believe that we are capable of handling ourselves: we aren't children anymore and we would not jeopardize our families with any foolish moves. I have thought about my husband's finding out, but he still talks to old girlfriends on a casual basis and this doesn't bother me. Do you think there is something wrong with continuing my friendship with this man? —Mrs. W. F., Atlanta, Georgia.

Marriage should never spoil a beautiful friendship, or vice versa. We suspect that your sudden interest in this man is neither casual nor innocent (if it were, you would not feel the need to write to us, nor would you worry about your husband finding out). When you called it quits before something happened, you implied a strong desire for something to happen. The conditions you set for your future meetings—being down or in need of escape from your immediate situation—suggest that you are already discontent and that you anticipate trouble with your marriage. One thing does, indeed, lead to another, but these domestic dominoes may fall the wrong way if you continue to deceive your husband—and yourself.

Why Men Will Always Girl-Watch

Would you settle a debate I'm having with my wife? She gets upset whenever I girl-watch. I say that is man's nature, that we are turned on by visual eroticism. When I ask her if she gets turned on by erotic movies, or looking at Playboy, *or watching men in the street, she says no, that women usually respond to touches, not glances. This can sometimes become a source of friction: For instance, I can be turned on just watching her read a book. When I approach her, she gets upset, not seeming to realize that what she is doing could be considered sexy by an observer. For her, it's just reading. She seems to respond only to close-quarter cuddling. Is there a reason for this difference? Is it permanent?* —E. C., Boston, Massachusetts.

Kinsey found that twice as many men as women were likely to become aroused by seeing members of the opposite sex. There were often physiological responses—up to and including erection. In contrast, the few women who reported being turned on did not have a marked physiological response. Richard Hagen, author of *The Bio-Sexual Factor*, offers this explanation: "The male is the sexual aggressor, fertilizing as many eggs as he can. And it stands to reason that the male who is most often aroused and most often in pursuit of females will have a selection advantage. . . . Three males are swapping yarns on a grassy hillside. One becomes aroused only when a female is at arm's length, another becomes aroused at ten yards; and the third becomes aroused at fifty yards. If a female walks by—at any distance—which male is most likely to get up and go after her? Obviously, the one whose sensitivity for arousal extends the greatest distance." Of the various sexual signals— touch, scent, taste, voice quality, vision—the visual has the greatest range in ordinary humans. Sociobiologists like Hagen argue that we are descended from generations of males whose roving eyes found what they were looking for—at least once. Thanks, Dad.

Basic Disagreements

Prior to our marriage, and for about three years after, my wife dressed sexy. While I was overseas in Vietnam, she dressed sexy and had an affair. She continued to dress sexy when I came back from Nam. No underwear or bras or anything. She is very beautiful and built like crazy. Here is the problem: A year ago, we had a child. Now she claims that she is too old to dress sexy and that as a mother, she should be more conservative. How can I persuade her to dress super-sexy again? —L. E., Atlanta, Georgia.

If your wife is more at ease in conservative clothes, it's her right to dress accordingly. We suggest a compromise: Drop the issue as far as streetwear is concerned and ask that she look "supersexy" for you when you are at home. Dressing sexy is great, but it's underdressing sexy that really knocks your socks off.

Over the past few years, my husband and I seem to have lost the ability to have meaningful verbal and physical communication, but I have hoped that our marriage could get back to its earlier, more promising footing. While my husband was out of town, I found in his study a large and costly collection of the most farout pornography imaginable, which led to a heated discussion on his return. I held that this sort of material should not be in our home, where our children might run across it, and added that I found it personally degrading. He seemed to understand, but later, when I asked him if he had gotten rid of the literature, he said no, that he wasn't going to and that we were not to discuss it again. I don't want the marriage to blow up over this, but I feel that it will unless I can get him to see and respect my point of view. How do you suggest I handle this very serious issue? —Mrs. H. B., Glenview, Illinois.

Unless your husband has abandoned experience and embraced fantasy, you do not necessarily have a valid complaint and you are not necessarily degraded. He has a right to enjoy pornography privately is he wants to; you have a right to demand that he respect your views. The collection should be kept from the children, if *that* is your wish. However, we think you should concentrate on the verbal and sexual breakdown in your marriage. You might begin by asking yourself what prompted you to rummage in your husband's study while he was out of town.

Different Levels of Desire

My husband seems to think that you'll agree with him that my sex drive is well above the average (whatever that means) for a woman of my age. The facts are that I'm twenty-nine years old and have been married for nine years. I immensely enjoy all facets of sexuality: I accept pleasure for what it is. I feel the itch about twice a day, when I get up in the morning and when I go to bed at night. Ideally, I would like to have intercourse (or a mutually acceptable alternative) with my husband in the morning and then masturbate before I go to sleep at night. Please note that my interest in masturbation is no reflection on my husband's expertise or on the scope of our activities—I just enjoy it. My husband is adamant that few women, statistically, desire sexual activity as much as I do. I find it hard to believe that I'm the least bit unusual. Are there any figures to back up my contention that my level of activity is probably not unusual? —Mrs. L. D., Chicago, Illinois.

Your appetite is not unusual. We found one study that indicates some 19 percent of the women surveyed wanted sex at least once a day, while another 10 percent felt like getting it on more often that. Amen. The author concluded that desire was variable. For the majority of women, it fluctuated according to their feelings for their partner. Your husband should regard your hunger as a compliment. There is no such thing as too much desire. The numbers are nonsense and are not the real source of your problem. Your husband probably views your appetite as a source of pressure. Your morning and evening routine has become a series of command performances. We suspect that if you varied your schedule—or abandoned it—you would both be free to experience sex spontaneously. Waylay him when he comes home from work; or do it in the car on the way to a movie.

Should She Try a Woman?

I'm twenty years old and love my husband very much, but I can't seem to get any kind of sexual satisfaction. I've never had an orgasm. Instead, I put on a good act in bed while we're making love, and my husband thinks I'm satisfied. I feel like I'm missing out on something in life. Having never masturbated, I'm not even sure what I'm missing. A couple of friends who are bisexual have often invited me over to get better acquainted. I don't want to seem overeager, but they are women and they know what women need for sexual satisfaction. I've mentioned the invitations to my husband, and he thinks it's a great idea. It would fulfill his fantasies of being in bed with two women. I kind of like the idea, but not with my friends. Should I find some other women on my own? Or, if that fails, should I go out with other men? Does this situation justify an extramarital affair? —Mrs. T. R., Madison, Wisconsin.

Faking orgasm is a felony offense that carries with it its own punishment: You get the sex you deserve. We don't think it's a good idea to experiment with bisexuality or to have affairs with other men simply because you've been unable to get sexual satisfaction from your husband. Why do you think a bisexual friend would help? You are a woman, and you haven't figured out what is sexually satisfying for yourself. Strangers probably won't do any better. Why don't you try to get to know your own body before letting others attempt to do so, especially since you are uncomfortable with the idea of being in bed with your friends? You might pick up a copy of *Homosexuality in Perspective*, by Masters and Johnson. They found that when women make love to women, they are gentler, take more time and generally devote themselves to the other person's pleasure. None of those tactics are beyond the grasp of heterosexuals. Do some homework and compare notes with your husband. When you've gotten your act together—then you can think about taking it on the road.

Two-Career Couple

My husband and I have a sexual problem that is sabotaging an otherwise loving marriage. We both work, and what with my job, preparing dinner, doing some housework and tending to our pets, I am so exhausted that I sometimes just like to go to sleep when we finally get to bed. I enjoy sex immensely, find my husband attractive and sexy—and tell him so—but find it difficult to hop into the sack and feel any great enthusiasm for lovemaking. When I show my reluctance, however, my husband gets irritable and unfriendly. What do you recommend? —Mrs. R. A., Altoona, Pennsylvania.

If the problem is simply one of fatigue, as you state, then try varying the time of your lovemaking—before dinner or in the morning or all day Sunday, for example. Or, since both of you are working, eat out more often. Or let the housework go occasionally or ask your husband to share it with you. It's possible, though, that the problem is deeper than you realize. If a change in your daily routine doesn't enhance your sexual turn-on, then you should consider the possibility that there is something amiss in the marriage. Hopefully, the easy solution will work—but if it doesn't, be prepared for some soul-searching and penetratingly honest conversation with your husband.

Sex and Pregnancy

My wife just gave birth to our first child. Needless to say, for the past months, our sex life has been in disarray. I was looking forward to taking up where we left off, but now, for some reason, my wife experiences discomfort during inter-

course. She does not lubricate (which, as I understand it, indicates a lack of excitement). Is it psychological? What gives? —*J. W., Chicago, Illinois.*

Congratulations on becoming a father. And welcome to the world of once-and-future lovers. Pregnancy can be a trying experience for husband and wife. A woman's body plays odd tricks on her following childbirth, tricks that can confuse and interfere with a reawakening sex drive. In an article in *Medical Aspects of Human Sexuality*, James P. Semmens and F. Jane Semmens point out that for some time after birth, a woman's sex organs are slower and less active. It will take longer for lubrication to occur and the over-all quantity will be reduced. Also, a nursing mother has a lower estrogen level, which further restricts her capacity to lubricate. She may suffer vaginal dryness (a probable cause for her discomfort) for as long as she nurses. Use a commercial lubricant such as K-Y jelly in the interum. If the problem persists, your wife may be experiencing complications following her episiotomy (the incision made to facilitate delivery). Have her check with her gynecologist.

CHAPTER SIXTEEN

Beyond the Fringe

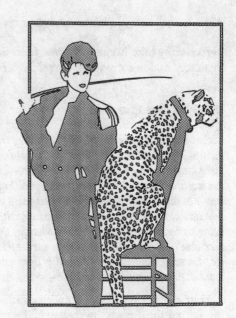

Couples on the Prowl

Have you ever heard of couples trying to pick up single women to complete a ménage à trois? The other day, I was lying in the park sunbathing when this tiny dog started bringing twigs and sticks and laying them at my feet. I looked up and noticed that a couple were handing twigs to the dog. They smiled and asked me out to lunch. I declined the invitation, because I wanted to stay in the sun for a few more hours. Later, a friend told me that the same couple had picked her up a few weekends earlier with the same trick. Apparently, the dog is trained to fetch young girls. My girlfriend went home with them and had a lovely day in bed. Most of the action happened between my friend and the other young woman— she claims that couples who are on the prowl almost always do so because the man can't satisfy the woman alone, that the arrangement is a cover for lesbian encounters. Is this true? —Miss M. R., Chicago, Illinois.

Hardly. Couples on the prowl are essentially looking for a safe way to introduce variety into their sex lives. In some cases, a woman may be interested in exploring lesbian fantasies and feels less threatened if her mate is along. (These same women would never engage in a one-on-one encounter.) In return, the male is often titillated by seeing his wife with another woman. If he were left out, he would feel threatened. There are also couples who pick up unattached young men for much the same reason. The phenomenon is not rare: The surprising thing about couples on the prowl is their success quotient. More often than not, the single person they take home has some fantasies that need exploring, too; for instance, making it with a Yorkshire terrier.

One Plus One Plus One

Can you give me your opinion on a very troubling matter? For the past three months, I have dated one man exclusively. Every time we see each other, we make love. During that time, I have not been able to attain an orgasm, in spite of the fact that he claims to have tried everything. The only solution to this problem—to his way of thinking—is to include another girl in our sessions. I find this ridiculous. I have been very orgasmic with other men. I believe that he is not being patient enough. He, in turn, charges that I am the first woman he has not been able to satisfy and that he deos not see why I should be different from others. (By the way, he has not included a third party in his previous relationships.) How do we resolve this impasse? —Miss A. R., Providence, Rhode Island.

Your partner has come up with a rather novel excuse for experimenting with a third party (necessity is the pimp of invention or the mother of deviation), but we doubt that a ménage à trois would be the answer to your problem. While a triangle might show him by direct comparison that all women are different, it might also double his failure rather than his fun. Since you are more familiar with your response than he is, do what you can to increase your pleasure. Patience is not something that can be measured or corrected with a stop watch: By making orgasm the goal of your lovemaking, you may have changed the event into an endurance contest with no winners. Love for the moment, not the finish. Sex is a mystery, but when it works, it reminds us of what Raymond Chandler said: The ideal mystery is one you would read if the end was missing.

She Wants Another, He Wants Another Man

My husband and I have a very open and secure sexual relationship. Over the past year, he has really gotten off on the fantasy of two women making love in his presence. I'm all for trying whatever turns him on—but my problem is this: I'm hopelessly heterosexual. I can't recall ever being the tiniest bit attracted to another female—not even when I was in an all-girl's school. I don't think I'd be physically stimulated in a bed situation with a woman. Now, if my husband wanted me to have a ménage à trois with another man, I'd have no problem. We've done threesomes with two males on me and I've liked it fine. I've tried to psych myself into getting turned on by another woman, but the idea still leaves me cold. I'd like to find some way to endure the experience and let my husband enjoy his fantasy. Any suggestions? —Mrs. T. W., Austin, Texas.

"Hopelessly heterosexual?" It sounds like a terminal disease. As nearly as we can tell, you sound healthy enough. Your viewpoint does not exclude the possibility of satisfying your husband's fantasy. How about a foursome with two other women? You could watch them in action and, who knows, once you see that there's nothing to fear, you might want to join in. Another alternative: Plan a ménage in which two females concentrate on the male, not on each other. It may not be quite what your husband wanted, but we're sure he won't complain.

Why?

Has anyone ever come up with an explanation of why normal heterosexual males would enjoy watching two females make love? Most porno flicks contain at least one lesbian scene, and I must admit that after we get over our initial shock, my friends and I are quite turned on by the activity. For the life of me, I can't figure out why. —C. N., Coral Gables, Florida.

Why not? You don't have to be sexually rigid to be upright. Some psychologists treat the fantasy of two women making love as a sexual Rorschach. They suggest that the male viewer fantasizes that he will rescue the females from themselves (cf. the hero sandwich). Others feel that the viewer finds the scene less threatening than a heterosexual encounter—he can imagine himself involved in the action without the obstruction of a member of his own sex. Real-life swingers report that when the women get together, the men view the activity as a prelude or an interlude. The sex will not be complete until a man steps in. (Never mind what the ladies think.) We have our own theory: Any image that expresses affection, intimacy, the classic interaction of yin and yang, or yin and yin and yang, is a potential turn-on. (Then again, our editors have been known to get off on everything this side of an Army training film.) If you are aroused by one attractive woman, adding a second should double your pleasure, if not your fun. And consider the bargain: You're getting two for the price of one, which these days is something to get excited about.

What to Do in a Triangle

I have an unusual dilemma. Two female acquaintances (a beautiful blonde and a well-built brunette) have recently invited me to join them in bed. This is the sexual fantasy of most men in America, but it has me stumped. I have never been in a ménage à trois, and I don't have the foggiest idea of how one manages two women at once. Any tips would be appreciated. —S. F., Raleigh, North Carolina.

It's simple. First you huddle. Then you tell the blonde to go long on the count of three, while the brunette goes out five yards and button-hooks. We suspect that things will work out. When the two women in a triangle initiate a get-together, they usually have something in mind. They may double-team you, in which case you should just sit back and enjoy. One of them may lend a helping hand, i.e., while you are making love to one, the other will stroke, kiss or nibble whatever comes in view. Or they may spend the evening pleasuring each other, in which case you should take along a good book to read.

Two Into One Doesn't Go

For the past few months, my husband and I have been living together with one of my girlfriends. We've come to the point where the three of us are sleeping and loving together. My girlfriend is, for all intents and purposes, my husband's second wife. There have been plenty of hassles. My question is this: Can a triad marriage survive? I love my husband and my girlfriend very much. At night, I often wake up wondering if they are sneakily enjoying sex. I also wonder why my husband keeps his back toward me when he sleeps—which he does whether I alone am sleeping with him or whether my girlfriend is in bed with us. This is all so new to me. I'm afraid of spoiling our love for each other, and yet I feel so confused. Can you help? —Mrs. I. A., Boston, Massachusetts.

Experimental relationships should be conducted along the lines of a bomb defusing. Perhaps you know the scenario: The squad leader sits there turning nuts and bolts, radioing each move back to headquarters. Thus, if the situation blows up, those who follow won't make the same mistake. In your case, it is time for a face-to-face-to-face conversation. Call your moves. Some of your suspicions may be groundless (for example, in what direction did your husband curl before you started sleeping in triplicate?). If properly aired, your other doubts will become less dangerous. You need to establish guidelines—will it continue to bother you if they make love in your absence, et cetera? Negotiate, if you expect to make your peace.

Group Fiasco

After two months of careful research, I found four couples who seemed to be interested in mate swapping. My partner and I had agreed beforehand that at least three of the couples had to be married, and it turned out that we were the only unwed couple in the group. The weekend before our first official gathering, my best friend, his wife, my girlfriend and I dined out. (We were all charter members of our proposed swap group.) The evening was warm and relaxed; so we decided to start our activities a week early at my place. I retired to one bedroom with my friend's wife. To my surprise, I found that I could not build an effective erection, no matter what techniques we employed. I did not have time to find out if this was a serious or lasting condition; one hour after we started, my best friend kicked down the bedroom door and began to strike his wife violently. I restrained him and when he quieted down, we discussed the situation. He had not touched my girlfriend and he claimed that he had entered the mate-swapping scheme to test his wife. He also accused me of having nothing to lose, since I was not married. Is he right? I would like to avoid a repeat of this fiasco, and I wonder what I did wrong. —A. R., New Brunswick, New Jersey.

Everything. You and your friends apparently are sexual conservatives who feel your erotic encounters should follow *Robert's Rules or Order.* Sex stops being fun when it becomes official. Your friend was wrong when he said you had nothing to lose—you did, your friendship with him. We suspect that you were somewhat concerned about losing your girlfriend, or you would not have sought the safety of married couples. Finally, your temporary impotence and your friend's violence indicate that you have strong subconscious objections to mate swapping. As Aristotle said, "The impulses of an incontinent man carry him in the opposite direction from that toward which he was aiming." You have no business in the swap business.

My wife and I met another couple and after only three visits, we were playing strip checkers. When we were all naked, we changed partners and started making out like newlyweds right in front of each other. I was really getting it on with the other girl and I looked over at my wife and her partner and it looked like they hadn't lost any time, either. I asked the other girl if she would like to go to the bedroom and she answered yes. To my surprise, her husband entered the bedroom after we had been balling about five minutes and blew his stack. My wife and I got dressed and left, knowing that we would never see them again. Two days later, they came over to our house and we sat around drinking all afternoon. All four of us just sat there like bumps on a log, making conversation. The subject of what happened that night hasn't come up again. It was the first time my wife and I ever did anything like that so we don't know why the other couple still sees us. Do they want to start the relationship again? How can we bring this out into the open? We're not sure what they want. —B. R., Lake Jackson, Texas.

It sounds like they aren't sure what they want, either. Maybe it was their first time and they wanted to kiss and make out. Invite them over to talk about it. Maybe it would work out if you took it a bit slower. Try strip chess. Or blindman's bluff. What he can't see won't bother him.

The Friendly Persuasion

During my first marriage, my wife and I pursued a swinger's life. We both allowed ourselves to become too involved with one couple and eventually were divorced. When my second wife learned of my past activities, she simply said that group sex was not her style, that she would never participate in any orgy or a swap. Other than that, we clicked on everything. She is extremely attractive, sexy, well educated, her own person in every respect. I wouldn't be writing to you if all were perfect, however. In the past few months, we've become quite close to a neighboring couple. We've been to nudist camps together, played strip poker together and, on several occasions, made love in the same room. I am totally turned on by watching another couple going at it. Now I'm becoming obsessed with the idea of group sex. I need the variety of more than one person, of women other than my wife. It's an almost uncontrollable urge, but I haven't given in to it because of my wife. If anything, she's becoming more conservative, giving up miniskirts and low-cut necklines for a little-girl look. She will go to a nudist camp, but she won't wear a string bikini to a public beach. She will screw in front of other people, but she displays a real turn-on only when it's just the two of us. Should I approach her to see if she would go along with the group-sex thing or should I keep my mouth shut, maintain my happy marriage and take advantage of whatever comes along? I never knew frustration could cause such daily mental pressure. —B. H., Prescott, Arizona.

Before you try to persuade your wife to try group sex, you must realize that she *is* her own person. You seem reluctant to accept the fact that she is happiest with just you. (Your divorce indicates that you were unable to accept the fact that your first wife could be happy with someone other than you.) Perhaps it would be better if your wife were not actively involved in your quest for variety—it is your problem, not hers. We're not suggesting that you keep your desire for extramarital experience a secret. A marriage should be based on mutual consent, if not mutual confession. She may agree to yield her exclusive rights to you without asking for further details. Finally, you should put your obsession into perspective: What you are looking for won't be better than what you have, only different. And what you have is pretty good.

Girls Will Be Girls in Groups

For several years, my girlfriend and I shared a house and our bed with another couple in a postgraduate group marriage. Sexual borders were fluid: casual nudity, daisy chains, cluster fucking or just sipping wine and enjoying a good book while the three others got it on. We were close, intimate. Then our friends were offered a job overseas and the household broke up. Seeking to fill the void, my companion and I started checking out swingers' magazines. It has been a disappointment. A lot of the ads picture just the woman (20 pounds lighter and five years younger). Sound somewhat chauvinist? At a club catering to swingers, I ran into a single man who looked at my companion and said, "I like her. My wife doesn't swing, but I know several girls who do. Take your pick." Then he pulled out his wallet and showed me pictures of possible accomplices. These incidents are the opposite of what we want: Women are not collateral, to be exchanged like hostages for a safe passage. We are looking for emotional involvement. Have we just run into the wrong people? —S. K., Cambridge, Massachusetts.

We'll trade you one dog-eared Yogi Berra for a Mickey Mantle. Dr. Gilberg D. Bartell painted a similar picture (vivid, but still 2-D) of the American way of swinging in *Group Sex*. Often, a man who is interested in crowds will use his wife or girlfriend as a ticket (in some cases, a man like the one you described never even sleeps with the girl he brings). The women have their revenge: Dr. Bartell found that fewer than 25 percent of male swingers are able to get it on regularly at open, large-scale parties. With nothing but time on their hands, women tend to end up with one another: 75 percent of the women in foursomes engage in homosexual activities. Our guess is that you'll have trouble finding what you want through magazines or clubs. Widowers and divorced men almost never resort to mail-order brides; you'd do best to re-create the conditions that resulted in your original success. Or join the Peace Corps and get assigned to your friends' new home.

My mate and I have been together for almost two years, and after a previously unhappy marriage for each of us, we feel very lucky to have a second chance with someone so compatible. Our relationship is based on mutual respect and honesty. And speaking honestly, my man needs "a little strange" now and then. We had a threesome with a friend of mine (female) about a year ago, and it was wonderful for us. We have not heard from her since. We would like to have another experience of that nature with someone willing. My mate would rather I participated also, though I do not object to his having a one-night stand if he needs to. (I am very secure in our relationship, because I'm all that he needs in all important ways.) If that sounds contradictory, let me say that our sex life, though great, was at its peak for a month after our "orgy." I must admit that I get a lot of enjoyment from being a voyeur as well as a participant. While I am heterosexual, I am not opposed to performing with another female for the enjoyment of my mate. Our problem—where do we find willing ladies, or couples, who would enjoy this as much as we do? You can't just approach a stranger. —Mrs. R. S., Indianapolis, Indiana.

Why not? This column receives a lot of letters from people who have engaged in a ménage à quatre once—and who seem unable to make it happen a second time. Maybe it's the shock of all that astonishing sex. What did you say to your friend in the first place? Try the same approach on other friends or strangers. In a sense, trying to find a third requires the same etiquette as regular dating. You don't proceed immediately to the proposition. Rather, get to know the person in a neutral setting. Suggest a get-together, with no strings attached. It is very easy to sound out a person's feeling on this subject without committing yourself to scandal or fiasco.

Labels

A few months ago, the Playboy Advisor mentioned that about 75 percent of the women who participated in foursomes engaged in some form of homosexual activity. I wonder about the opposite—male-to-male interaction in such encounters. My wife and I have been happily married for a little over five years. We have enjoyed sexual escapades with other couples. On several occasions, while the women embraced, the other male and I also petted and even performed oral stimulation on each other. I may sound nuts, but it seems to me that the experiences involving male-male activity were the most fulfilling—everyone was into everyone else. My wife thinks the whole idea of two guys demonstrating appreciation for each other is magnificent and very mature; however, because of prior conditioning, I still have doubts and some guilt feelings. My question: Am I bisexual? —W. D., Atlanta, Georgia.

No; you're a registered Democrat. The problem with any label is that it includes people with whom you wouldn't be caught in the same room. Bisexual is an adequate word to describe a person who is as turned on by a person of the same sex as by a person of the opposite sex. Tres chic, but in certain parts of the country, that could get you well hung. Since all of your activity has taken place in crowds, rather than in one-on-one encounters, you might be more comfortable with a word that makes your bias clear. Try octopedaphile—someone who gets off on sex in a room where there are eight legs. Of course, you may be confused with the guy who likes to watch his wife make it with a Shetland pony, but that's life.

Boys Will Be Boys

One of my friends and I double-date every Saturday night—no one girl yet. Each Saturday date is about the same: dinner or a movie, then drinks. And, always, we get a double room at the Holiday Inn and the four of us bang away until early morn. For nearly two years, that is how it has been. As I say, that is how it has been—until one Saturday a month ago, and that night started the same as always. After we had dinner and a few drinks, we got ready for the sexual games. My friend told my date that one thing that really turned him on was seeing two girls make it. My date blushed a little, but she told him (and me) that the thing that really got her was seeing two guys make it. And so, after some discussion and a lot of uncertainty, it was agreed that my friend and I would have sex together while the girls watched, and then we would watch while the girls got it on. Since I had never gone down on another man, I was really at a loss as to technique, et cetera. But, to make a long story short, we did each other for about ten minutes (neither ejaculated) and then watched the girls go to it. We finally finished up with our dates. Sex had never before been as urgent. Since that night, I haven't seen my friend and neither of us called the other. I think that I am a little embarrassed and perhaps he is also. I am sure that I can rationalize our behavior that night, but having thought about it for a month, I think that I really enjoyed having sex with him. And this new experience has brought about a new thinking in my attitudes about men having sex together. Until that night, I probably would have fought anyone who suggested such a thing and I'm sure that had it not been for the moment and the friend, I probably never would have experienced sex with another man. Right now, I'm a little mixed up. I have strong feelings toward my friend—I don't think sexual ones—and new attitudes toward straight guys having sex with other guys. I know that it doesn't make any sense saying straight guys having sex with other straight guys, but neither of us is gay. Please shed a little light on the subject. —G. D., Raleigh, North Carolina.

There are *always* surprises in sex, especially when you live at the edge, double-teaming dates at a weekend orgy. (If it will ease your mind, what you did probably falls more under the category of group sex than of gay sex.) It was an experience and you learned something about yourself. We think you should call your friend. This is certainly nothing that should break up a good relationship. As you said, he probably has the same feelings you do and we think you'll both rest a lot easier if you discuss them over a couple of beers.

Second Thoughts

I've been happily married for two years. My husband and I have always had an open sex life, and until lately, he has had no desire for any other woman. Recently, however, while we were visiting my girlfriend, I went to the store for beer and was gone for about ten minutes and left them alone. I knew my husband wanted to have sex with her, but he had told me he wanted me there to have a threesome. I really didn't want to share him with anyone else, but I figured that would get it out of his system. I got back from the store to find them in bed together. They said they were sorry and I said it was all right. In the meantime, her brother came over, and we were all kind of excited by then, so clothes started flying and we all jumped into bed together. I wanted to enjoy myself but was kind of jealous. I spent most of the evening watching my husband. They were really enjoying themselves, but I could tell it was only lust; there was no feeling involved. When it was all over, my husband and I went home; we talked, cried and made love. Since then, we've been closer than ever. Our sex life is better, too. He's the best man I've ever had in bed—my friend thought so, too. I know he's always been straight with me, so I'm happy. I think he's got it out of his system. What do you think? —Mrs. J. W., Richmond, Virginia.

If you were completely happy, you wouldn't be writing to us. On one hand, you were a willing accomplice to the encounter. Your trip to the store gave your husband the "permission" he needed to fool around. On the other hand, you were upset; you feel cheated, because you did not enjoy yourself as much as the other participants. We suggest that you rethink some of your basic attitudes toward sex. You are not your husband's keeper (the mother-may-I? approach to sex can be a drag for both partners). And sex is not a scarce commodity or a limited natural resource to be hoarded and conserved. You may be right to separate lust from feeling, but not at the expense of either. (What's so bad about lust?) We think that your marriage can survive this. Don't dwell on it.

How to Pick Up Girls—For Girls

I am a twenty-six-year-old single woman with a sexual appetite that rivals most of your readers'. I am ravenous. Lately, I have become obsessed with a desire to make love to another woman at least once in my life. How does a woman who is considered straight (and rightfully so) go about finding someone of the same sex who is willing to experiment with a lesbian affair? Do I run an ad? Wear a sign? —Miss K. C., Tucson, Arizona.

Essentially, you are asking, How do you pick up girls? Well, it's not easy. The same rules apply to your predicament as apply to heterosexual encounters. Anyone who sets out to find a one-night stand probably won't. Sex is usually more fulfilling when it is a consequence of everything else that goes on between two people. As a rule, making love is easier with friends. That way, if it doesn't work out, you're still friends. Talk to the women around you. You'll be surprised at how many share your curiosity. Most of them are afraid of approaching strangers, of being seduced or of being used by a professional—someone who is familiar with the game. At an opportune moment, ask your companion if she would like to satisfy her fantasy with an amateur. If she refuses, don't take it personally. Her hesitation originates with the same upbringing that made you shy in the first place.

Labels: Take Two

Until the age of twenty-one, I waited for the right person to come along. I always expected that it would be a man, but last summer I found myself in love with another woman. I have never had such a great friend, at least not one to whom I wanted to be so close or to give so much of myself. I have slept with this woman and touched her intimately but never to the extent of performing cunnilingus or doing whatever else lesbians do. That may happen. I feel that I want all of her, but I have reservations about taking an active role. That's part of my confusion. It was enough of a shock to find that I could love another woman; I may be gay, but I'm not a dyke. I still prefer a man sexually. I cannot restrain myself from looking at a man's beautiful body not repress the excitement I get from a man's touch. I do not look at my friend's body as a source of sexual pleasure: I see her as someone I can compare myself to. A few weeks ago, I talked to a counselor at school about the future of my sex life. He used phrases like "whichever way you decide to go" and "It's a decision you'll have to make," implying that I would become either straight or gay. Since my love for my friend did not result from a decision, I'm not sure that it's a matter of choice. Do the options have to be exclusive? —Miss M. S., Boulder, Colorado.

Categories are the stock in trade of psychologists, but they are too often the stocks of a puritan culture. It used to be thought that if your were not exclusively heterosexual, you were exclusively homosexual. Stray once and you were gay. The anxiety was everywhere. We knew one counselor at an Ivy League who could attract a year's worth of clients by leading his students through the following syllogism: A person who responds to contact with a member of his own sex is homosexual. If you are a man who masturbates, you receive pleasure from contact with a member of your own sex: therefore, you are homosexual. The sexual revolution side-stepped the old categories, which may be why more people walk funny these days. It is a not uncommon experience for the right person to be the wrong gender. Individuals have become free to pursue identities that are not defined by anatomy or by rigid social roles. Bisexuals are double agents in the battle of the sexes, but there are no traitors. The model of a gay relationship in which one partner is aggressive and masculine, the other passive and feminine is a relic of the past. You don't have to become a dyke in order to consummate the bond with your friend. This single experience will not brand you for life, nor will it prevent a healthy involvement with a man at some point in the future. As long as you love the one you're with, you're doing well.

Changing Sides in the Sexual Revolution

I am a reasonably attractive male, twenty years old. I recently went through what was for me a very emotional ordeal. About a year ago, I met a very attractive Oriental girl. We went out a couple of times. Eventually, we went to bed. I really enjoyed myself with her. After going with her for a while, I moved in with her. Everything was going great. I was really interested in marrying her. One day, while she was at work, I had the day off. I was bored. So I got snoopy and started to go through some old pictures of hers that she had stuffed into a box in the back of the closet. I ran across an envelope, on the cover of which was the name of a major reconstructive-surgery clinic. I opened it and found documents of name changes Social Security–number changes, work records and birth certificates. What it came down to was: The girl I had fallen in love with had had a sex-change operation. It was a tremendous emotional blow to me. I didn't know what to do. I didn't let her know that I knew about it. Gradually, I enjoyed sex less and less with her. I left her, needless to say. Since then, I haven't been to bed with any girl. I almost find it hard to even talk with one. Is it wrong for me to think so badly of her? I just don't understand. I'm afraid it has left an emotional scar for life. Is there any way for me to get over this? —C. H., Denver, Colorado.

Life, as the man says, can be a bitch. And silence can be a breeding ground for pain and confusion. Maybe you should at least talk this over with your friend. Maybe not. Although the facts of this situation border on the bizarre, the basic problem is the same with any breakup. It used to be said that the only cure for a woman was another woman. We're not sure that applies here, but it's the best show we've got. When a relationship disintegrates, you should go out and have an affair or four or five. You need to liberate your own sexuality from the details of the immediate past, to assure yourself that your arousal is not dependent on your former partner. As the years pass, you'll look back on this as a great war story for those times when your children ask you, "And what did you do in the sexual revolution, Daddy?"

Take Two

Being a twenty-five-year-old single male, I lead an active sex life. I thought that I had seen and done everything—however, something happened not long ago that has me totally freaked. One sunny Saturday afternoon, I was checking out the action at the local beach, when my eyes came across a beautiful blonde who was as foxy as the girls who grace your magazine. After about fifteen minutes of small talk, it was obvious that she wanted to get it on. My little sex kitten turned out to be one of the greatest partners I have ever had. She not only wanted to make love all day—in every position—she also was a master of oral sex. She gave the best head I've ever had. Later that night, the lady let it slip that she used to be a he named Bill and had undergone a sex-change operation. Imagine my surprise. I don't know what to think. What should I do now? —B. R., Miami Beach, Florida.

It's a rare phenomenon, but one that has to be faced: In the sexual revolution, there are some persons who want to change sides. At first glance, a whole new set of problems arises: Should a gentleman offer a transsexual a Tiparillo? Perhaps the simplest way to end the confusion is to take your new friend at face value. If you can't tell the difference, there isn't any. In one sense, you've had the best of both worlds. Maybe it's time to retire.

Transsexual Surgery

One of the local newscasts featured an item on the U.S. Army's attempt to discharge a WAC because she had married a transsexual—i.e., a woman who had become a man. I must admit, I can't figure out how they perform that operation. What are the details? —J. J., Swansea, Massachusetts.

A series of operations is required to transform a female into a male. After a program of hormone therapy, the patient undergoes a double mastectomy and a radical hysterectomy. The final stage—the creation of a penis—is the most difficult. Skin from the hip, abdomen and thigh is used to construct an artificial organ. So far, surgeons have been unable to build a penis that functions normally. The patient must decide whether he wants to use the organ for urination or for sex. Most transsexuals opt for the latter. The improvised penis is the size of an erection. To copulate, the transsexual inserts a rod. (He has to urinate sitting down.) All of this may sound like more trouble than it's worth, but to a female who feels trapped in the wrong body, the operation offers an opportunity for a life with some semblance of normalcy.

TV Guide

My boyfriend recently told me that he likes to dress in women's clothes. He has been trying to explain this to me for a long time, but he's so full of guilt that he could never really talk about it. I would like to marry him but not until I can understand more about his problem. I'm getting an ulcer trying to guess what's on his mind. I don't know whether I should feel threatened or not. What should I do? —Miss T. D., New Orleans, Louisiana.

Your boyfriend is a transvestite—a man who derives pleasure from playing musical wardrobes. It's a common fetish and the fashion exchange is about as far as it goes. Clothes do not unmake the man. Almost all transvestites are completely heterosexual; most are married and their marriages are generally as successful as anyone else's. Although no one knows the exact origin of fetishes, it is believed that they are the result of what psychologists cal imprinting. If a young person has an intense sexual experience in, around or because of a certain object, it is possible that this object will always be a symbol of sex to him. For example, a transvestite might have first masturbated in a bathroom where his mother's lingerie was hanging to dry. (Washer-dryers may put an end to the phenomenon.) If you'd like more information, write to: Transvestia, P.O. Box 36091, Los Angeles, California 90036. This organization is devoted to transvestites and has volunteer counselors in many areas of the country. So go ahead with your marriage plans—just think of the money you'll save on clothes.

Sex at the Office: It's the Same Story

I currently work for a large, well-known insurance company in a department that has a female supervisor. She is a thirty-year-old divorcée; I am in my early twenties. A few weeks ago, I was told to report to her office just before the end of the day (a Friday). No sooner had the other employees left than she politely informed me that she wanted me and that it could benefit my future with the company. Since she is very attractive, and I was not getting any at the moment, I figured, "Why not?" We ended up at her place and had a very fulfilling weekend. We spent most of the day and night in the sack—performing intercourse, oral sex, anal sex—all done in varied positions. On Sunday, I got a real surprise. She told me she was having a friend over and that she wanted me to watch and take pictures. By then, I was game for anything. When the doorbell rang, I climbed into the closet as ordered and got the cameras ready. The guest turned out to be a girl from work, who had started about the same time I did. They spent considerable time making gay love and even went as far as to use a strap-on dildo on each other. I enjoyed watching this act and had a fantastic ball after the girl left. Today at work, the supervisor told me that she wanted me to move in with her and share in her sexual happiness. She spelled out what she wanted from me, which included joining her and others in threesomes. Naturally, I am moving in. Do you think I'm making a mistake? —T. N., Hartford, Connecticut.

Sounds to us like you lifted this plot from some X-rated *Up the Organization* that you bought at Weird Harold's adult bookstore. If so, you left out the "redeeming social value" twist that usually mars pornographic fantasies of this sort—the hero finds that he really loves the other girl, but when he declares his true love to the supervisor, she pulls out pictures that she had taken of him, threatens blackmail and everyone lives unhappiliy ever after. Moral: It's okay to have a skeleton in the closet as long as it doesn't own a camera. If you're serious, then you do have a problem. Don't give up your apartment. Insurance companies are notoriously conservative—some don't issue policies to unwed couples living together or charge higher premiums if they do. They are probably less lenient with employees. Office affairs require a great deal of discretion, a quality you obviously don't possess, since you wrote us this letter and now some thirty million readers know about your exploits.

Recently, I began having an affair with my boss—a woman in her early thirties. I have been the assistant director in her department for about five years (with salary increases but no promotion). At first, the affair was "the usual old stuff"—sneaking off to motel rooms at noon and knocking off a quickie and a few intimate moments in the office. Then she started demanding more. One evening, she insisted on wearing a pair of leather boots to bed, then she began wearing a leather girdle much like the ones the Roman soldiers wore. At first, I found this behavior rather exciting—even when she decided to strap on a dildo and screw my anus. Now, though, it's gotten to the point where I can't take it anymore. She has taken to insisting that I let her tie me up with leather straps, and even once put a dog collar around my neck and tied the leash to the bedpost. Before she'll let me screw her, she always wants to do her little thing with the dildo— now she even refuses to grease it up with a lubricant. I find all this demeaning and humiliating, but I'm afraid that if I break it off, she'll have my job. How can I get her to settle down and quit demeaning me without putting my professional relationship with her in jeopardy? I'm afraid she might blackball me in the industry if I get on her bad side. Besides, except for her kinky habits, she's a beautiful person and a tremendous lay. —K. L., Green Bay, Wisconsin.

What we have here is the basic, all-American employer-employee relationship; i.e., the worker gets it up the ass. Obviously, she has read *Winning Through Intimidation* and you haven't. It's time to take the reins yourself: You seem to be in a bit of a dead end in your current position (even without the unprofessional relationship with your supervisor).

Start looking for another job in the industry or for another department in the same firm. Your fears of retribution are exaggerated—she can't tell anyone about your extracurricular performance without endangering her own position. Your on-the-job performance should speak for itself. Next time, don't fish in the office pool, especially when it's stocked with piranha.

Desire

*It has surprised me recently to find almost no professional litera-
ture discussing why a person becomes sexually excited. There are, of
course, innumerable studies that have to do with that tantalizing
vague word "sexuality": . . . Statistical studies of the external genitals, foreplay, afterplay, accompanying activity, duration, size,
speed, distance, metric weight and nautical miles. Venereal disease,
apertures, pregnancy, berdaches, morals, marriage customs, subinci-
sion, medical ethics, sexism, racism, feminism, communism and
priapism. Sikkism, Sweden, Polynesia, Melanesia, Micronesia, Indo-
nesia and all the tribes of Africa and Araby. Buttocks, balls, breasts,
blood supplies, nervous nipples, hypothalamic supplies, gross national product, pheromones, implants, plateaus, biting, squeezing,
rubbing, swinging. Nude and clothed, here and there, outlets and
inlets, large and small, up and down, in and out. But not sexual
excitement. Strange.*

—Robert Stoller, Sexual Excitement

As you know, I am a veteran of the sexual revolution, or, perhaps
more accurately, one of its correspondents. I collect war stories. I've
read everything there was to read about sex, in case it ever happened to
me. I have read *The Joy of Sex; More Joy; Human Sexual Response; Homosexuality in Perspective; Xaviera's Supersex; Sex in History; Sexercise; Total Sex;
Sexual Behavior in the Human Male; The Hite Report; The Redbook Report on
Female Sexuality; The Herpes Book; It's Your Body; Our Bodies, Ourselves, The
Clitoris; Whipped Waitress; Chained Cheerleaders; Jungle Fever; Office Gynecol-
ogy;* et cetera, and nowhere in those volumes was there a paragraph on
why we like the things we like, why we want the things we want, why
we do the things we do. We know how it's done in Micronesia, Polynesia, in the blue-blood streets of Boston, up in Berkeley and out in
Queens, but we don't know why. What *is* this thing called lust?

"You can't photograph desire. You can't put it on tape. You can't measure it in any way. It is a very slippery concept." That was the response of the first sex researcher I called. A month later, I was mostly willing to believe him.

I had talked with therapists, social psychologists, medical investigators, biologists, friends and lovers. I had added another shelf of books to my library. I had discovered that we are just *beginning* to look at the roots of sexual excitement, at what turns us on and why. The research is as intriguing as it is incomplete. Is desire the result of the male hormone testosterone? Is immediate, undying love an altered state of consciousness, a by-product of a kissing cousin of Dexedrine that the body releases in the brain? What are the roots of attraction? Is the desire that drives a rapist to commit his crime the same that causes the rest of us to cruise for action? Can the fascinating variety of sexual behavior be traced to fantasy, the secret garden of erotic daydreams? Perhaps it's all of the above.

Sociobiology is a theoretical discipline that tries to analyze social behavior in terms of genetic imperatives of natural selection. In the sociobiological scheme of things, I try to get into your jeans because my *genes* want to get into your genes. In lower life forms, mating behavior is automatic, the result of genetically inherited signals and responses. At first glance, it seems that the biochemical puppet strings have been severed in humans. We are the only species that deliberately separates sex from reproduction. We have to invent reasons to reproduce the reasons to have sex. Pleasure is our rationale.

It is suggestive work, this sociobiology. Its premise is that we are not far removed from our ancestors stalking the savanna, and, in fact, I've *been* to bars where some of the males have not yet descended from the trees. One sociobiologist—Richard Hagen, author of *The Bio-Sexual Factor*—cites studies that seem to suggest, for all the potential equality of the sexes, that males are far and away the more interested party. One study revealed that the average male has over 1500 orgasms before marriage, while the average female has fewer than 250. Another study suggests that the difference begins early: During adolescence, single males report 20 times as many orgasms from all sources as do single females. Single males report 131 times as many orgasms from nocturnal dreams as do single females. A nocturnal dream is not learned behavior; it is what the body discovers for itself.

"Why did we ever start the myth that women are just as orgasmic as men?" asks Hagen. "There is no evidence for it. In fact, there is all kinds of evidence against it. And from an evolutionary standpoint, there is no logical justification for it." Hagen parades an intriguing array of statistics showing that approximately half the sexual encounters that end in orgasm for a male partner do not end in orgasm for a female partner. It is not a matter of technique or timing.

Hagen believes that nature has "selected" males who are both more interested in sex and more successful at sex for two reasons: (1) the fact that, historically, males have had to be aroused in order to copulate, while females can copulate while unaroused; and (2) the fact that males must be orgasmic if they are to pass on their genes, while females may pass on their genes whether they are orgasmic or not. In other words, men are horny because they are descended from generations of fathers who were horny at least once in their lives. Hagen does some nice probability studies to show that it is to nature's advantage for males to mate with anything that moves, while it makes little difference to females. Lenny Bruce apparently understood this—he once noted that a man will fuck mud.

Sociobiologists believe that the trigger for desire is testosterone, the so-called male sex hormone. Actually, testosterone is present in both males and females. So, for that matter, is estrogen, the female hormone.

During adolescence, the surge of sex hormones ignites the development of secondary sex characteristics that separate the men from the boys, and—hallelujah!—the women from the girls. In the female, progesterone causes the hips to flare and the breasts to swell—producing the hourglass shape of the mature woman. Girls develop internal genitalia and the ability to lubricate—which is a sign of receptivity according to some and of arousal according to others. On the other side of the fence, the tide of testosterone gives the boy a beard, lowers his voice, broadens his shoulders, puts hair on his chest and starts to take it off his head, precipitates sexual fantasies, frequent erections, nocturnal emissions—the whole ball game.

Testosterone seems to be partly responsible for whatever level of desire there is in women. A man who is castrated may gradually lose interest in sex. If a woman loses her adrenal gland (the source of testosterone in females), the same thing may happen. There are also suggestions that women with high levels of testosterone experience greater levels of desire.

John Wincze, a clinical psychologist at Brown University in Rhode Island, found that if a normal male takes a shot of testosterone, he can get an erection quicker—but he'll lose it quicker, too. Big deal. Anke Ehrhardt, a psychologist who specializes in gender differences, warns against making too much of testosterone. "We like to say that testosterone is the fuel of desire," she says, "It puts gas in the tank. It adds octane. But the basic vehicle is already there."

The onset of the sex hormones in puberty is dramatic. Most of us experience our first infatuation around the age of thirteen and our first real love around seventeen. But after we reach adulthood, there doesn't seem to be a clear connection between hormones and sexuality. As long as we're not running on empty, the level of sex hormone doesn't seem to account for the variety of desire. Says Ehrhardt, "It is an open system. We know that hormones affect behavior, but behavior also affects the level of hormones. Soldiers facing battle have low levels of testosterone. Fear reduces testosterone. But after a battle, levels return to normal.

"Even in lower primates, you can castrate an adult male, but he will still be able to function with his preferred partner—at least a bit. Choice is as important as hormone level."

Two New York psychoanalysts, Donald F. Klein and Michael R. Liebowitz, believe they've found the secret of desire. They speculate that passionate love, the sudden surge or attraction we feel for another, is the result of an amphetamine like substance in the brain. When we fall in love or lust, the brain produces phenylethylamine—a molecule that is one carbon atom away from amphetamine. When we fall out of love, the brain shuts down the speed pump and we experience all the symptoms of withdrawal.

Indeed, the similarity between love-sickness and "crashing" was what suggested the theory to Klein in the first place. He was treating a group of women who were classic sensation seekers. They took more than their usual amount of cocaine and amphetamines. When they fell in love, they felt a zap that many compared to the rush from amphetamines, or the rush of adrenaline one would experience when she worked onstage. When they experienced a setback in love, they became depressed, irritable. They overslept and overate—in short, they exhibited the symptoms of someone crashing from a 30-to-40-grain-per-day amphetamine habit. They did not respond to tricyclic antidepressants, but they did seem to respond to chemicals called MAO—inhibitors that slow down the breakdown of phenylethylamine. Interestingly, the women often consumed large quantities of chocolate, a substance rich in phenylethylamine.

Klein and Liebowitz stress that their theory of chemical attraction is pure speculation, but it seems to make some sense. We have learned that the brain produces its own pharmacology—the endorphins are the body's own morphine. There appears to be a natural Valium, a natural PCP, a natural psychedelic. Given its choice, it seems logical that nature would choose the most potent substance to fuel reproduction. Klein: "If social approval and coupling are important to nature, it seems that there would be a mechanism in the body that would make social approval very rewarding.

* * *

Two researchers named Elaine Hatfield and Ellen Berscheid spent years studying attraction. "We find, says Hatfield, "that physical beauty is crucial. If you ask people what they would *like* to have, the desire for the most beautiful is never extinguished. Given a choice, we would all like to date the most beautiful partner available. But if faced with a real date, that choice is held in rein by our sense of self-esteem, what we have to offer. Sexual relations seem to be based on a marketing model. You settle for what you can get. People end up with partners who are similar in physical appearance, mental health, physical health, family background (including race, religion, parent's status, education and income) and family solidity (i.e., happiness of parents' marriage) and popularity. It's astonishing. When you see an imbalance in a couple, the discrepancy is usually accounted for by an imbalance on one of the other scales. Economic. Power. It is a bargain.

"We do seem to have an erotic type," says Hatfield. "It seems that we like people who look like us—and yet the intensity of the affair comes not from the similarities but from the perceived differences.

"I know this is going to sound illogical, but if I had to bet, from just talking to lots of people, I would say that passion is the result of these differences. What we want is someone who is mostly similar to us, so that he doesn't seem bizarre. But what people describe when they talk about intense attraction goes all the way back to Reich. We feel that we are missing something, that there is a part of us that isn't expressed or isn't fulfilled, and out there in the world is someone who is the essence of what we're missing. When we find someone who has everything we wish we had, that person tends to have a really strong impact. The research to date has measured only the similarities—that lovers tend to be alike in earlobe length, eye color, I.Q., personality. But we have yet to measure those passion-inspiring differences, the things that make us think, this person is everything I'm not."

There are tit men, ass men, eye, ear, nose and throat men, and there are the female equivalents. Why do we focus on one aspect of a person and not on the entire person? The late Ernest Becker suggested that the dynamics of normal attraction are similar to those of the fetishes. In an essay called "Everyman as Pervert," he wrote, "There is nothing per se about a large breast that has any more inherent sexual stimulation to the partner than a small one. Obviously, it is all in the eye of the beholder. But our culture teaches us to become committed in some way to the body of the opposite sex, and we are eager for cues that give us a passport to permissive excitation. When we learn such a cue, we invest it with rich significance. Each culture heightens the meaning of certain qualities of objects so that its members can easily bring into play the approved responsive behavior: lace underwear and steatopygia for sex objects, tailfins and chrome for cars."

Part of the process of falling in love is the cataloging of the "perfect" cues in our partners. We run the selective memories like erotic slide shows, to confirm, fuel, reinforce our choices. When it starts to go bad, we flip to the negatives to kill desire.

The penile transducer, or strain gauge, is a semicircular stainless-steel band, not unlike a bracelet, that encloses the shaft of the penis. Tiny elastic cords, not unlike the bungi cords used to attach luggage to a motorcycle, complete the circuit. These bands translate fluctuations in the diameter of the penis, via a bundle of tiny wires, to a needle moving on a polygraph. The strain gauge is the scientific tool by which we determine the truth of the body. It gives an objective measure of sexual arousal.

If you attach a strain gauge to a volunteer, then show him an erotic movie—or, better yet, play him a tape recording of an erotic fantasy that allows him to fill in the gaps with his own details—he will be able to tell you what turns him on—or how turned on he is at any given moment— some 90 percent of the time. The rise and fall of his self-report will agree with the rise and fall of the polygraph.

Gene Abel is a psychiatrist at the New York State Psychiatric Institute, working in a large tan-brick building up around 168th street in New York City. He uses the strain gauge to investigate sexual arousal of sex offenders—rapists and child molesters—and the idiosyncratic. He starts with the bizarre, because funding is available for the study of the bizarre. "We study people with unacceptable erotic fantasies because that's what society is interested in."

According to Abel, the stranger the turn-on, the less likely you are to have a match between the subject's self-report and the truth of the body, as measured by the strain gauge. "People can't always identify what it is that's erotic to them."

When I read about Abel and the strain gauge, I told my editor that I might volunteer to be tested, to spend an afternoon in the lab, looking at pictures and listening to tapes, in order to find out once and for all what it was I was really looking for in my sex life. He was aghast.

I replied that since I was turned on by anything alive, identifiably female and of legal age, I could stand to narrow it down a bit. With my luck, I would find that I was turned on by the machine. My editor replied by quoting Oscar Wilde: "'In this world there are only two tragedies. One is not getting what one wants and the second is getting it.'"

Faced with those alternatives, I contacted Abel and asked if he had ever shown a group of standard fantasies to a "normal" population. He said no, that sex research is not TV programming. He is more interested in the subtle components of desire. He tries to isolate the cues that accelerate arousal and to edit out the extraneous ones that decelerate it.

In one study, Abel presented two groups—rapists and nonrapists—with three scenarios. The first tape describes mutually consenting intercourse between a male and a female who initiates sex: "She really cares about you . . . she says, 'Let's make love' . . . she's unsnapping your pants . . . she spreads her legs and she's helping you get your penis into her . . . she's taking your hands and moving your hands on her tits . . . She's really getting into it . . ." Both rapist and nonrapists responded to this fantasy. So, far that matter, did I.

The second tape describes a brutal rape: "You've broken into a house, where you know a woman is . . . you get your hands out . . . put them right over her mouth so she can't scream out . . . you've got a knife. If she doesn't lie still, you're going to kill her . . . she's trying to get away. It's no use . . . you tell her, 'Come on, spread your legs or I'll kill you.' She's got nice tits. A nice ass. You're right on top of her there."

The scenario continues—indeed, it reads like a police-blotter account of rape, including constant threats, body injury and fear for her life. In one such study, the group of nonrapists literally dropped out, the strain gauge recording minimal arousal. In contrast, the rapists were very aroused, recording more than 50 percent of a full erection.

The third tape describes a pure physical assault, with no sex: "You've broken into an apartment . . . it's a girl lying there on the bed. You're going to beat the shit out of her. You take that belt and you slash her across the back. She's pleading with you to stop . . . you take your fist. You give her your first right into the back. You can see the bruises starting to form."

The nonrapists did not respond to the assualt scenario, but the rapists did. In fact, says Abel, the relationship between their arousal to aggression and their arousal to rape was "disgustingly lawful." The rapists' erection to pure violence was 40 percent of their erection to rape.

The study produced one final curiosity. Abel asked each group to listen to the scenarios and try to *inhibit* their erections. The nonrapists were able to control their response to the rape and the aggression tapes. The rapists were able to control their response to the mutual-intercourse scene and the rape scene, but when they listened to the assault, they achieved greater erection. They could not control their arousal, and the more they tried, the more they became aroused.

What if you are one of those men who aroused by such an inappropriate cue? Is there anything that can be done? Abel believes there is. He claims that each of us carries around a potent fantasy. "The thoughts we recall and use a lot become tied in or associated with orgasm and generate more arousal. Those things we don't remember fade, so we have a constantly altering and evolving arousal pattern, depending upon our idiosyncratic retrieval pattern. Our past leads us into the future, to make us try to make the world match our fantasy."

Abel treats rapists with something called the masturbatory satiation technique. He has the patient reach orgasm to a scenario of mutual intercourse, then, while the erection fades, has the patient repeat aloud, over and over, the offensive fantasy until it becomes boring. Eventually, the rape fantasy, or child-molestation fantasy or whatever, loses its power—to be replaced by something more flexible, resilient and legally available. The message is, if you want to change the quality of your sexual excitement, you have to change the quality of your sexual fantasies. Freud gave fantasy a bad name by suggesting that only neurotics played in the secret garden of erotic daydreams. Nowadays, we know that everyone has fantasies and that the normal can be pretty weird.

John Money, a sex researcher at Johns Hopkins Hospital, believes that desire is the result of a core fantasy—that we reach adulthood equipped with an erotic map that dictates the perfect love affair, the perfect lover, the perfect erotic sexual experience. "The profile of one's erotic turn-on imagery is as personally idiosyncratic as one's signature, one's face or one's fingerprints," says Money.

When we reach adolescence, the map reveals itself in our erotic fantasies. The young boy already knows if he prefers Miss May to Miss October. So he begins the hunt.

"There is a sophisticated riddle about what a boyfriend (or girlfriend) and a Rorschach inkblot have in common," says Money. "The answer is that you project an image of your own onto each."

Money believes that the erotic map is the result of a hard-fought struggle against a repressive society. It's a wonder, he says, that any of us turns out remotely normal, and in his book *Love and Love Sickness*, he points out that if you take a young monkey away from its mother and its playmates, then reintroduce them at a later age, the monkey will attempt to mate, but its moves will be ludicrous and inaccurate. A young male monkey will try to mount the female sideways. It has been suggested that the sexual isolation imposed on young girls may contribute to inorgasmia in later years. In other words, if we interrupt the natural cycle, we end up with adults who don't know enough to do it right.

According to Money, we are not born with our basic sexual imagery. We learn from our parents and peers. We acquire our sexuality the way we acquire our native language. We are not born speaking English or French, but we soon acquire the words and the grammar, enough to make ourselves understood. We are not born heterosexual, but something in the mind lies waiting for the appropriate cues. We acquire our sexual imagery in the same years we acquire our language—between the ages of two and eight. "I could call it our native imagery, our native fantasy," says Money, "but we don't have a word for it, and there's a perfectly good reason. Because we believe in the innocence and asexualism of childhood. We are constantly looking for evidence of original sin, of premature wickedness.

"Something sends the normal sexuality underground," says Money, "then we don't know what's happening to this imagery. Sometimes it gets very bizarre. The child and then the adolescent struggles with a fantasy, is aware of it, and it scares the bejesus out of him. The anxiety is so deep that he deals with it by not having sex.

"People who are apathetic about sex don't even *know* that they have no sexual desire, because they don't know what sexual desire is. If you are color-blind, you don't know what color is, so you don't know what other people see, do you?"

Money believes that males are more susceptible to "improper" cues. Most of the thirty or so paraphilias (aberrations) that are recognized by Money are male practices. "It is easy for a male to become fixed on some anomaly of the visual world," says Money. "The ease of identifying male core fantasies, permissive cues, may be the reason that homosexual behavior is so ritual. They have codes and signals for their mutual fantasy. If you wear a key on the right, it means you like to be beaten, if you wear it on the left, it means you like to beat. There is an immediate match-up of the fantasy, and the results can be incredible.

"The chances of finding a satisfactory partner in a heterosexual relationship, the perfect fit for your fantasy, are small. Women really have only two core fantasies—the masochistic, or martyr fantasy, in which they sacrifice themselves to the idiosyncratic urges of their partner. . . . The other predominant fantasy that women have—of soft objects and touch, does not really lend itself to a perfect fit with the normal array of male core fantasies. So you are likely to end up with a disastrous marriage, where finally the guy decides that it's too much work to get up an erection for someone who won't go along with his fantasy."

Since sex is the same as a native language, I asked Money if we could measure desire—the same way we measure intelligence—by how well a child learns to master the sexual vocabulary. Is there the erotic equivalent of an intelligence quotient—an E.Q.? Is there such a thing as an erotic genius?

"I don't think the erotic genius would be the person with the largest vocabulary, who was turned on to all thirty of the recognized sexual aberrations," Money said. "We seldom find a person who is turned on by more than one core fantasy.

"No, I would say that the erotic genius is the person most able to satisfy his erotic map—to find his way to the right person, the right position."

I realize that my willingness to plug myself into the strain gauge, the stainless-steel band that would reveal to me the truth of my body, was simply a means of testing the wisdom I was beginning to extract from my past sexual experience. I know some of the cues that accelerate my arousal. I'm attracted to a certain erotic type, a gracious lady/wise-ass chick. Women who are strong, independent, muscle toned, more likely to be blonde, who have the grace of someone in touch with their body, whose nerve endings are not hidden, whose eyes are intelligent. As a friend says about life in Aspen: "The only requirement is keeping up." I am more responsive to collarbones and sacral dimples than to tits and ass. Jan Smithers more than Loni Anderson. I have a favorite piece of pornography, "Chapter Eight of *Jungle Fever*, by Marcus van Heller. I discovered it when a potential lover said *her* favorite piece of pornography was something by Marcus van Heller she'd read as a kid. If we ever got together, we could be dangerous.

I probably have a favorite position, but then, I've had good teachers. I can recall afternoons tangled in satin sheets on a water bed, unsure of who was doing what to whom or, for that matter, whose genitals were whose. As long as no one left with more than one set, fine. I remember an affair in a hotel room, when sex seemed to have invited us there to deliver its own lecture. When I left, I looked at the ruins and said, *That's* what I mean. It will take me a while to refold that erotic map.

The lover who now occupies my thoughts is one who can read the movements behind the movements. Who can perceive the image when I place her arms over her head, to suggest bondage, and later have her suggest the opposite, hanging me from a chin-up bar and . . . never mind. Who is not afraid to initiate her own fantasies, be it the sudden possession in a car parked in the Los Angeles airport, revisiting teenage lust while a voice intones: This white zone is for loading and unloading only. *This* is the source of sexual excitement. Trying to find a partner who fits, or comes close.

Desire is many things to many people. As one of my contacts noted, "It's amazing what can be crammed into one erection, isn't it?"

Index